Accountancy in Transition

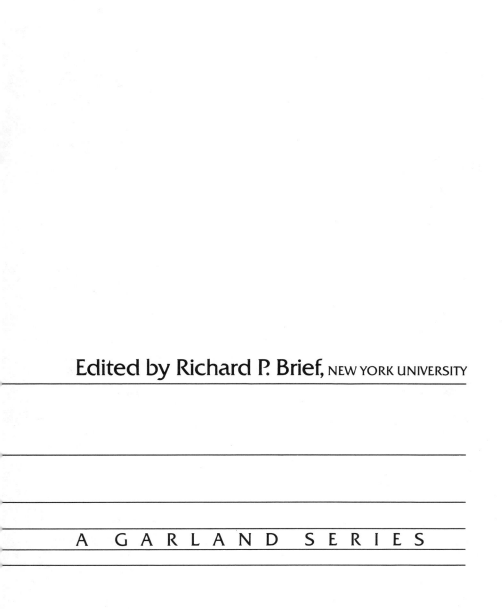

Edited by Richard P. Brief, NEW YORK UNIVERSITY

A GARLAND SERIES

Studies in Social and Private Accounting

Solomon Fabricant

Garland Publishing, Inc.
New York & London   1982

ACKNOWLEDGMENTS

"Measures of Capital Consumption, 1919–1933," "Revaluations of Fixed Assets, 1925–1934," "On the Treatment of Corporate Savings in the Measurement of National Income," and "Measuring the Nation's Consumption" are published by permission of the National Bureau of Economic Research.

"Business Costs and Business Income under Changing Price Levels," and "Inflation and Current Accounting Practice" are reprinted by permission of the American Institute of Certified Public Accountants.

"Factors in the Accumulation of Social Statistics" is reprinted by permission of the American Statistical Association.

"Prices in the National Accounts Framework," "Accounting for Business Income Under Inflation," and "Notes on the Deflation of National Accounts" are reprinted by permission of the International Association for Research in Income and Wealth.

"Inflation and the Lag in Accounting Practice" is reprinted by permission of the South-Western Publishing Co.

"Economic Calculations Under Inflation" is reprinted by permission of the Liberty Fund, Inc.

"Productivity in Asia's Developing Economies" is reprinted by permission of the Asian Productivity Organization.

Library of Congress Cataloging in Publication Data

Fabricant, Solomon, 1906–
    Studies in social and private accounting.

    (Accountancy in transition)
    "Fifteen papers, published from 1936 through 1981"—
    1. National income—Accounting—Addresses, essays,
lectures.   2. Accounting—Addresses, essays, lectures.
I. Title.   II. Series.
HC79.I5F34   1982   339.3'01   82-82488
ISBN 0-8240-5337-0

The volumes in this series are printed on acid-free, 250-year-life paper.

Printed in the United States of America

Preface

This collection of Solomon Fabricant's main writings deals principally with social and private accounting and measurement. The fifteen papers, published from 1936 through 1981, were written from the point of view of the economist interested in developing a rational set of national accounts and other aggregative measurements, and improving the comparability of private financial statements between different periods and different companies. Considerable attention is paid to the problems raised by general price inflation, especially for social and private accounting but also in other areas of economic calculation. Among other accounting problems considered are those associated with the prevailing use of an annual fiscal period in an economy characterized by business cycles well exceeding a year in length on the average, as well as by still longer-term changes. Questions arising in "productivity accounting," especially in developing economies, are considered in the final essay. This compilation includes articles and lectures by Fabricant but it does not draw upon his published books.

Contents

"Inflation and Current Accounting Practice: An Economist's View" *Journal of Accountancy*, December, New York, 1971

"Summary" in *Accounting by Business Firms for Investment in Research and Development*, New York: New York University, 1975

"Economic Calculation Under Inflation: The Problem in Perspective," in Liberty Fund, *Economic Calculation Under Inflation*, Indianapolis: Liberty Press, 1976

"Accounting for Business Income under Inflation: Current Issues and Views in the United States," *Review of Income and Wealth*, March, New Haven, 1978

"Productivity in Asia's Developing Economies: Reflections on the Design, Construction, and Analysis of Relevant Information," in *Productivity Measurement: Theory and Practice in Asia*, Tokyo: Asian Productivity Organization, 1981

National Bureau
of Economic Research

BULLETIN 60

JUNE 30, 1936

1819 *BROADWAY, NEW YORK*

A NON-PROFIT MEMBERSHIP CORPORATION FOR IMPARTIAL STUDIES IN ECONOMIC AND SOCIAL SCIENCE

Measures of Capital Consumption, 1919-1933

SOLOMON FABRICANT

THE ACCOUNTING CONCEPT OF CAPITAL CONSUMPTION

We may most conveniently clarify our notions of the meaning of capital consumption by considering what is implied by the term in business practice. Capital consumption, as the business man sees it, is chiefly represented by deductions from asset accounts (or additions to corresponding valuation accounts), and to a lesser extent by certain direct charges to operations. The relevant entries used in recording the consumption of fixed capital (to which we confine ourselves in this *Bulletin*) include those arising from the following:

1. Depreciation
2. Depletion
3. Retirement and abandonment
4. Destruction by accident
5. Loss on sale
6. Write-down
7. Repairs, renewals and maintenance
8. Capital expenditures charged directly to current operations

To obtain a national total of capital consumption mere transfers among enterprises are eliminated, as in a consolidated statement, except to the extent that they give rise to changes in book values.

Depreciation and depletion charges are estimates, admittedly and of necessity crude, made by the business man on the basis of whatever experience is available. The rate of depreciation or depletion is not the only element approximated. Even the book value to which it is applied, although more definite only if it represents original cost, is itself merely an approximation to the current value of the capital goods being depreciated or depleted. The nature of this approximation, and the bias inherent in it, will concern us later.

Entries arising out of retirements and abandonments may represent losses through depreciation, depletion and obsolescence for which inadequate allowance had been made; or they may constitute the method of currently recording capital consumption. In either case, they represent primarily a *post facto* determination of loss. This is not to imply that this determination is entirely devoid of foresight. The abandonment of workable equipment always manifests a judgment as to the future.

The value of property accidently destroyed is not equal to the deduction made for the destruction if there is any insurance reserve on the books of either the enterprise concerned or its insurance company. We may look upon such destruction as equivalent to the retirement of fully depreciated equipment, in which case part of the insurance premiums (or other charges) has already covered the loss incurred. Or we may record such destruction only when it actually occurs. The former method is the common way of handling these deductions. The latter, however, is more convenient statistically. Since insurance reserves are set up, or their absence justified for large concerns, because such destruction is fairly regular in time and therefore predictable within reasonable degrees of error, the two amounts tend to coincide. The difference between book value of destroyed property and the sum of salvage value and insurance payments chiefly indicates a change in price levels. (More is said of these price changes below.) Types of destruction not commonly taken into business calculations may only be mentioned in this *Bulletin*.

Write-downs of the values of capital goods as well as losses on their sale may, like losses on retirement or abandonment of equipment, indicate inadequate estimates of previous capital consumption. But these entries may also, perhaps more often, represent changes in prices (or even in interest rates). If use is made of original cost—or, indeed, of any estimate not as of the most recent date—price changes will become apparent upon the disposal of plant or equipment. To the extent that write-downs result in lower depreciation charges (and that is one reason given in their justification), it is necessary to include them if we are interested in measuring capital consumption in terms of dollars of original investment and if we are not to suffer an omission from our aggregates. Similar reasoning holds for

---

write-ups, which increase depreciation charges. However, since the income tax laws do not permit this kind of change to affect depreciation and depletion charges, and since we use depreciation data derived from tax returns, we have omitted from consideration, in this *Bulletin,* charges arising from write-downs.[1]

In all businesses there are minor elements, and in some industries major elements, of capital loss that are not passed through the asset accounts but are recorded when replacements are made. The entry resulting is a charge to repairs, renewals, and maintenance. The expenditures incurred in these restorations of capital are in many ways current prime costs and do not represent the consumption of capital in any ordinary sense. This is obvious when these expenditures fluctuate with output, or more definitely, with the use of capital goods (allowance being made for seasonal movements). But to the extent that they do not do so, by the amount of consequent over- or under-maintenance, we have the formation or consumption of capital. As we shall see, the total magnitude of these expenditures is quite large. A relatively small deviation from 'normal' maintenance may mean a large absolute change in capital. These expenditures, therefore, merit attention even though they fall outside the category of credits to asset accounts. 'Extraordinary' repairs and renewals that are charged to reserves for depreciation presumably represent capital formation.

As a rule capital expenditures, except occasionally those involved in acquiring intangible assets, are not charged immediately to current operations. Other exceptions occur in secret reserves and development costs in the mining industries. The latter, while including intangibles (they are, in fact, usually called by that term), also involve expenditures upon material things. We shall therefore include them, to complete our list. These also do not take the form of credits to asset accounts, except on the supposition of a simultaneous setting up and writing off of a capital asset.

The entries in the above categories are restricted to those relating to fixed capital: in this *Bulletin* we limit our attention to the type of business capital resident in fixed assets, other than land. These assets include plant, equipment, furniture and fixtures, improvements of real estate, and exhaustible resources. Land, business inventories, intangible assets, and durable goods in the possession of non-business entities—consumers and public and semi-public bodies—are not considered here, with one exception. Estimates of the consumption of capital invested in residences are presented in an appendix. Owing to lack of data it is

[1] In the National Bureau study of capital consumption of which this is an interim report, it is hoped to consider the amount of these revaluations in some detail; examination of reports made to the Securities and Exchange Commission indicates their wide prevalence.

impossible to show separately the depreciation of residential structures held by business concerns. It is combined with the depreciation of other rented residences (Appendix Table III).

In the next section we attempt to determine the quantitative importance of the items in the various categories listed above and to indicate their fluctuations during the last fifteen years. It must be remembered that full data with which to fill out our outline quantitatively are unavailable. In more instances than we would wish the information is incomplete. This follows from the very nature of the underlying phenomena, which are subtle, gradual, not susceptible of easy record, and entwined with the hopes and fears of business venture.

ACCOUNTING ESTIMATES OF CAPITAL CONSUMPTION

Available figures on the most important elements of capital consumption, supplemented by estimates of varying degree of reliability, appear in Table 1. These accounting estimates are 'institutional' estimates in the sense that they were made in accordance with current modes and habits of estimation.

The deficiencies of our data are numerous. Losses due to retirement and abandonment are given for only one industry—steam railroads. (These appear in greater detail in Appendix Table I.) Destruction by accident is estimated only for fire losses; however, these probably constitute the major part of such deductions. Losses on sale of capital assets and write-downs are not given at all. Repairs and renewals are given only for public utilities, together with major repairs and alterations of buildings. Development expenditures in mining industries constitute the only data available on capital expenditures charged directly to current operations.

One reason for the absence of data is the minor importance of some items. This appears to be the reason in the case of losses on the sale of capital assets. When reported in corporate financial statements, the amounts given are usually small. No reliable estimate may be made on the basis of figures published by the Treasury Department in *Statistics of Income.* The losses compiled by the Treasury Department are given only in combination with losses on the sale of investments (stocks and bonds). While the total of these two types of loss has been large in each of the years 1931-33, it is probable that losses incurred in disposing of investments have constituted the bulk of the total. This presumption is strengthened by the fact that companies in the financial field have reported over half the losses.

Write-downs, however, although omitted are important. A rough estimate, made in *Bulletin 55* of this series (p. 10), indicated that several billion dollars of capital assets were written off by industrial corporations alone in the

TABLE 1

ACCOUNTING MEASURES OF BUSINESS CAPITAL CONSUMPTION, 1919-1933, BY TYPE [1]

(*in millions of dollars*)

YEAR	DEPRECIATION	DEPLETION	DEPRECIATION AND DEPLETION	REPAIRS, RENEWALS AND MAINTENANCE	DEVELOPMENT EXPENSE (MINING)	FIRE LOSSES	TOTAL
1919			3,797	2,589	334	126	6,846
1920			4,154	3,305	495	176	8,130
1921			4,128	2,706	286	195	7,315
1922			4,435	2,682	312	200	7,629
1923			4,713	3,061	392	211	8,377
1924			4,825	2,762	338	216	8,141
1925	4,561	524	5,085	2,698	351	220	8,354
1926	5,109	614	5,723	2,841	373	221	9,158
1927	5,166	540	5,706	2,876	322	186	9,090
1928	5,472	555	6,027	2,735	304	183	9,249
1929	5,870	596	6,466	2,906	321	181	9,874
1930	5,940	493	6,433	2,442	260	198	9,333
1931	5,886	291	6,177	1,946	173	178	8,474
1932	5,475	263	5,738	1,365	134	158	7,395
1933	5,258	264	5,522	1,316	139	106	7,083

[1] A more detailed breakdown is given in Appendix Table I. Sources and methods of estimation appear in footnotes of that table. Properly to understand these figures requires careful attention to the methods of estimation as well as to the discussion in the text. Depreciation and depletion charges are not available separately for years prior to 1925 (see Table 5, footnote).

two years 1931 and 1932. But these revaluations need not concern us at least in so far as the general magnitude of the figures in the table is considered over long periods.

The business depreciation charges are based on those reported to the Treasury Department for use in the determination of income taxes. There is reason to believe that the basic depreciation rates are somewhat higher than would be used for determining net income for other than tax purposes. They would thus tend to include at least some allowance for that type of capital loss which ordinarily is expressed in lump sums in the form of write-offs and abandonments. The latter, of course, are not deductions recognized by the income tax laws.

Not only may the depreciation figures *accepted* by the Treasury Department be higher than those that would otherwise be charged; the figures *reported* may even be higher than those *accepted*. That this is not rare is shown by adjustments made in published financial statements increasing surplus for excess depreciation charges not allowed by the Treasury Department.[2]

The degree of overstatement may show a secular decline, especially as company estimates are reduced by governmental audit and accountants become better acquainted with what is acceptable to the tax authorities. To the extent that this occurred, the advance over the period being reviewed is understated.

[2] On the other hand, even the reported charges may appear too low to those who would make large allowances for future obsolescence. Only 'normal' obsolescence is recognized by tax authorities, except at actual retirement or other disposal of equipment.

The rise in business charges for depreciation is irregular from year to year, and is probably affected by slight changes in coverage. The only definite decline in depreciation charges began in 1931. The decline in total depreciation and depletion charges in 1927 and 1930 was due to the sharp cyclical fall in depletion charges. The excess of investments over retirements resulted in a rise in the volume of capital goods from 1926 to 1927, and from 1929 to 1930. Depreciation charges also rose, as a consequence both of this increase in the amount of depreciable assets and of the prevailing use of some form of the straight-line depreciation formula. In 1931, however, a decline set in and continued for the remainder of the period covered in our table. This decline in 1931-33 tentatively suggests an excess of business capital consumption over gross capital formation.

The rise in depreciation charges over the decade of the 'twenties was the result chiefly of an increase in capital goods and of the persistence of high price levels relative to pre-War costs. As will be shown in more detail below, even if the number and efficiency of buildings, machines and other equipment had remained constant, the price factor alone would have caused a secular rise in depreciation charges.

Depletion charges are essentially rough estimates under any conditions. The figures here presented acquire peculiar characteristics, further, from the tax law provisions regulating their computation. Depletion charges may be based on cost, on discovery value, or on gross value of mineral output, depending on the type of exhaustible resource, on the year for which they are computed, and on the election of certain alternatives offered to the taxpayer. Further, they may sometimes be limited in amount to a figure equal to or even less than the computed net income before depletion.[3] In prosperous years depletion charges computed on the basis of discovery value or gross income may exceed the amounts necessary to recover capital depletion. In years of depression, when net income before depletion is low, they may fall short of these amounts. The cyclical movements of estimates of actual depletion (and profits) will thus tend to be exaggerated. For these reasons the depletion charges shown here must be accepted with caution. The tax laws have acted, however, not only to distort the entrepreneurial estimates. Were it not for the legal requirement for such estimates, it is doubtful that any deductions would be made in many instances. The situation prevailing before the War is revealing. Although these particular estimates are rough and distorted in many respects, they constitute at least a first approximation to the depletion our natural resources have suffered.[4]

The volume of repairs, renewals and maintenance is shown to be rather large, relative to depreciation charges. This is primarily a consequence of the accounting methods prevailing among the public utilities. In this industry we find maintenance of capital taking the form chiefly of repairs and replacements. Among railroads, for example, practically no depreciation is charged on ways and structures, on the theory that they are fully maintained by current repairs and replacements. To the extent that plant and equipment are in fact not fully maintained we have under-maintenance. This may of course be followed by over-maintenance when delayed repairs are finally made.

Repairs and renewals in industries other than public utilities and real estate also reach a large total. If we may judge from the reports made to the Securities and Exchange Commission by eighty-three large industrial corporations, charges for repairs and renewals ran on the average about equal to depreciation charges in 1934.[5] Much of these charges represents current production costs. However, since their amount is probably great, even a slight deviation from normal maintenance (in the form of deferred repairs, for example) may mean an appreciable volume of capital consumption or formation.

[3] A brief statement of the various provisions and their changes in successive revenue acts is given by R. C. Epstein, *Industrial Profits in the United States* (National Bureau of Economic Research, 1934), p. 328.
[4] Such types of depletion as exhaustion of the soil are not included since no estimates whatever are made by those directly concerned. Rough estimates of soil depletion have been made by the National Resources Board; see the *Report* of December 1, 1934, pp. 15-17.
[5] Data for earlier years are not available except for a few companies, insufficient in number to provide reliable information on annual movements.

The estimates of fire losses of capital equipment are surprisingly small. There are two reasons. First, the rate of fire loss has been decreasing steadily over the last century, and the declining trend is visible even in the last fifteen years. The annual rate of premium charged per hundred dollars of insurance has fallen radically. For one company, the Manufacturers Mutual, the figures (as published in *The Factory Mutuals, 1835-1935*), are as follows:

1845	$ .84	1895	$ .162
1855	.39	1905	.112
1865	.308	1915	.066
1875	.355	1925	.033
1885	.229	1935	.028

Second, during the period covered by the present estimates no conflagration of major proportions occurred. The San Francisco fire of 1906 cost the nation about 350 million dollars: over 25,000 buildings and their contents were destroyed. Obviously, one major disaster like this can wipe out a large fraction of a year's gross increment in capital.

Perhaps more important than such spectacular occurrences, which are rare and of diminishing probability, are the losses arising from soil exhaustion and erosion, which are indirect as well as direct. Since these losses are slow in accumulating, and are not obvious in any case, it is easy to overlook them. Absence of business estimates covering them indicates as much.

A factor affecting the relative values of the several types of capital consumption presented in Table 1 is the average durability of capital goods.[6] If the average life of producers' equipment were shorter, it is improbable that depreciation charges would be affected to the same extent as fire losses.

ACCOUNTING ESTIMATES AND ECONOMIC CONCEPTS

Most broadly defined, the consumption of business capital is measured by the sum of the above entries on the books of business concerns. A somewhat narrower concept omits changes in book valuations arising from the recognition and recording of substantially new price levels, namely, a large portion of write-downs and of losses on sale.

It must be remembered, however, that these measures are aggregates of accounting data, and are based on the accounting concept of capital consumption. Are they satisfactory measures from a social standpoint?

The accountant's conceptions of cost constitute economic forces which affect the conduct of business and the laws of value and production.[6a] Therefore, regardless of the accuracy of the business estimates of capital consumption,

[6] Adequate consideration of this factor raises interesting problems involving rates of interest and prices of capital goods as well as durability. But they cannot be examined here.
[6a] J. M. Clark, *Economics of Overhead Costs* (University of Chicago, 1923), p. x.

business records may not be mere reflections of individual cognizances. Accounts, and the limitations to which they are subject, may in turn influence the sensitivity of business men and the manner of their reaction to the fact of capital decline. But while the accounting concept and the accounting estimates of capital consumption are essential objects of study in the analysis of business behavior, they do not constitute the most adequate concept and estimates of capital consumption from the broad social point of view. In an economic evaluation of national income, savings and wealth, they can be accepted only as first approximations, subject to revision.

Thus, the recognition and recording of capital consumption by business men differ from one industry to another, from one period to another and perhaps also by size of concern. In the estimation of capital consumption from the economic point of view these differences must be taken into account. It is a question whether the particular method of evaluating capital consumption current in each business is not the one to be preferred by the economist even at the expense of consistency. It appears at first sight that the method is current because it *is* the most suitable under the given conditions: who is a better judge of suitability than the entrepreneur, experienced through years of contact with the special conditions of the industry? The economist, however, would be passing by the problem rather than answering it if he were to take this position. It would mean assuming that the given process of evaluation is in fact the most suitable *now*, rather than a habit inherited from the past.

There is also the general bias of business men and accountants in the direction of 'conservatism,' and their understandable penchant for the objectivity of original cost. Further, the reluctance to admit capital consumption is revealed in the not infrequent accumulations necessitating charges to capital. The question whether credits to contingency reserves, or even business savings as such, represent rough forecasts of, and provisions for, future capital losses is not clearly answered in business records. This ambiguity is itself one phase of the difficult problem of allocation in time. Of course an asset account is eventually credited for any losses that occur. But this eventual credit cannot easily be accepted as an adequate record without further consideration. Finally, there is the occasional confusion of tangible and intangible assets. In the valuation (perhaps more frequently, the revaluation) of fixed assets there is sometimes a tendency to ascribe to them monopoly values that are ordinarily imputed to intangibles. From the private viewpoint, of course, the distinction is in some ways academic and, on account of the difficulties involved, is not pressed. But monopoly values are doubtful measures in so far as the economic system at large is concerned. These are some of the ambiguities and faults inherent

in the business concepts of capital consumption. We should not, however, expect to find satisfactory concepts being applied in business practice. Economic theory also has so far failed to provide us with satisfactory concepts of capital and capital consumption, even within the limitations theorists may impose. And for much the same reason. The difficulties involved in constructing rigorous theoretical concepts of capital consumption are identical in nature and source with many of the difficulties troubling accountants and statisticians in their attempts adequately to describe the changing status of business enterprises. Changes in relative prices, technological progress, improvements in quality of goods, the discovery and exhaustion of natural resources—all these dynamic factors continually complicate the situation with which we must deal. They subject even our unit of measurement—money—to changes that restrict its efficiency in aiding us to cope with the evolving environment. In dealing with concrete situations, further, 'noneconomic' factors must be taken into account, factors that may be set aside in theoretical considerations. But although theoretical discussions have not yet led to definitive concepts, they have resulted in several valuable guide posts to the direction modification of the business concepts may usefully take.

In the next sections will be considered two striking characteristics of business estimates of capital consumption: the omission of under-maintenance and the use of cost prices.

UNDER-MAINTENANCE

Under-maintenance is almost inevitably a consequence of the desire to avoid making investments that may be postponed and to maintain the apparent rate of profits. For this reason the available figures are few and difficult to interpret. Secret reserves and secret drafts upon capital are, by their very nature, not made public. If maintenance costs are spread over several accounting periods on a budget basis, through reserve accounts, the data are not necessarily secret. But this method of handling such costs, although recommended by accountants where the sums are appreciable, is not widely prevalent or at least is not often revealed by available statements. Indirect evidence is the only means we have of detecting the phenomena of under-maintenance.[7]

[7] If our measures of gross capital formation contain the value of output of repair parts and similar goods, obviously we must include at least that portion of maintenance costs in the measures of capital consumption. Our treatment of both measures must be consistent. Capital formation within the business enterprise, except in public utilities and certain types of construction, and except for the value of parts used in repairs and renewals, has been excluded by Dr. Kuznets from his measures, primarily because of lack of data (see *Bulletin 52*, Gross Capital Formation, 1919-1933). The figures on maintenance presented in this *Bulletin* are still more narrowly limited to public utilities, and to major repairs

TABLE 2

MAINTENANCE RATIOS, CLASS I STEAM RAILWAYS, 1919-1933

YEAR	MAINTENANCE CHARGES OTHER THAN DEPRECIATION, RETIREMENTS, AND INSURANCE, AS A PERCENTAGE OF OPERATING REVENUES	MAN-HOURS OF MAINTENANCE EMPLOYEES PER 100 CAR-MILES [1]
1919	36.20	—
1920	39.77	—
1921	33.20	—
1922	32.21	8.52
1923	32.62	8.74
1924	30.77	8.00
1925	29.90	7.46
1926	29.70	7.16
1927	29.76	6.97
1928	28.50	6.47
1929	28.31	6.39
1930	27.69	5.93
1931	26.49	5.32
1932	23.93	4.95
1933	22.94	4.67

Source: Derived from various data collected by the Interstate Commerce Commission and published in the annual issues of *Statistics of Railways*.

[1] Comparable data are not available for 1919-21.

TABLE 3

MEASURES OF MAINTENANCE, CLASS I STEAM RAILWAYS, 1919-1934

YEAR	REPLACEMENTS Rails (thousand tons)	Ties (million)	PERCENTAGE OF UNSERVICEABLE EQUIPMENT [1] Freight cars	Locomotives Passenger	Freight
1919	2,335	80.9	—	—	—
1920	2,507	86.8	7.0	24.8	24.5
1921	2,588	86.5	13.1	23.1	24.0
1922	2.619	86.6	12.8	23.5	25.5
1923	3,139	84.4	8.0	20.8	21.6
1924	3,185	83.1	7.8	18.4	18.8
1925	3,485	82.7	7.7	17.8	17.8
1926	3,818	80.7	6.5	17.0	16.4
1927	3,819	78.3	5.9	16.4	16.1
1928	3,806	77.4	6.2	16.4	16.3
1929	3,610	74.7	6.0	16.2	16.4
1930	2,674	63.4	6.2	17.0	17.5
1931	1.715	51.5	7.8	20.5	20.7
1932	797	39.2	10.6	24.9	26.6
1933	862	37.3	14.1	28.6	32.7
1934	1,165	43.3	14.6	29.3	33.8

Source: Figures collected by the Interstate Commerce Commission, some of which are published in *Statistics of Railways*.

[1] Comparable data are not available for 1919.

The most detailed—and the most adequate—figures bearing on the general question of under-maintenance in business establishments are those compiled by the Interstate Commerce Commission from the reports of steam railroads (Table 2). During the 1920's a declining trend is evidenced in the ratio of maintenance expenditures to gross operating revenue, with pronounced cyclical falls obvious in 1921 and in 1930-33. The trend is probably due to diverse price movements and to changes in technique. Further evidence is afforded by the ratio of man-hours of maintenance employees to car-miles of traffic. Use of this ratio avoids the difficulties arising from diverse price movements. The element of secular decline arising from changing technical methods remains, however, and obscures the conclusions to be drawn from the data. But even if we assume that the trend apparent in the preceding ten years continued through 1930-33, there is definite evidence of under-maintenance of some 15 per cent in 1933 relative to 1929. If deterioration goes on and maintenance be required whether or not traffic declines—and to some extent this is so—the degree of under-maintenance is considerably greater than this figure would suggest. Direct evidence of under-maintenance is provided by quantity figures on maintenance of track and equipment (Table 3). Beginning with 1930 the secular declines apparent in the replacement of rails and ties appear to have speeded up, and by 1932 and 1933 replace-

and alterations of buildings. For these and other reasons, comparisons between the figures in this *Bulletin* and those of Dr. Kuznets may not be made without sundry adjustments.

ments were only a fraction of the 1929 amounts. The decline in rails replaced from 1929 to 1932 reached the large figure of 78 per cent; replacement of ties dropped one-half from 1929 to 1933. The piling up since 1929 of equipment requiring repairs confirms the evidence already presented.

CAPITAL CONSUMPTION IN CONSTANT AND CURRENT PRICES

Until gains, or even losses, are realized by exposure and sale in the market-place, capital assets are usually valued on the books of a business enterprise in terms of their original cost. As a consequence of this method of accounting, one supported by the requirements of the tax laws, depreciation charges represent an amalgam of non-contemporaneous prices. The various items of capital equipment and buildings are of diverse average spans of life. The anticipated useful life of the capital goods produced in 1929, for example, ranged from two years to one hundred, with concentrations (indicative of the approximate character of the estimates) at 10, 15, and 20 years (see Table 4). Half of the 1929 output in value had an anticipated life of between 10 and 30 years; one-fourth exceeded 30 years. We are not wrong in supposing, therefore, that even as late as 1929 capital goods purchased at 1913 and earlier price levels were still being depreciated.

The measures in Table 1 are strictly comparable in the sense that they represent the accounting estimates of capital consumption for the year to which they refer. As such their significance in an analysis of economic behavior cannot be denied. But to the extent that the price units actually

TABLE 4

VALUE OF OUTPUT OF BUSINESS CAPITAL GOODS IN 1929, DISTRIBUTED BY LENGTH OF ANTICIPATED USEFUL LIFE [1]

LIFE [2] (years)	VALUE OF OUTPUT (percentage of total)	CUMULATED VALUE OF OUTPUT (percentage of total)	DEPRECIATION RATE (per cent)
75	0.3	100.0	1-1/3
50	5.1	99.7	2
44	1.4	94.6	2-1/4
40	7.5	93.2	2-1/2
35	4.0	85.7	2-6/7
33	3.8	81.7	3
30	4.5	77.9	3-1/3
29	2.6	73.4	3-1/2
25	5.9	70.8	4
22	1.0	64.9	4-1/2
20	9.5	63.9	5
18	2.8	54.4	5-1/2
17	1.4	51.6	6
16	1.5	50.2	6-1/4
15	11.0	48.7	6-2/3
14	2.2	37.7	7
13	0.6	35.5	7-1/2
12.5	3.0	34.9	8
12	2.7	31.9	8-1/3
11	0.5	29.2	9
10	7.6	28.7	10
9	0.4	21.1	11
8	2.8	20.7	12-1/2
7	1.6	17.9	14
6	4.2	16.3	16-2/3
5	4.3	12.1	20
4	3.9	7.8	25
3	2.0	3.9	33-1/3
2.5	1.1	1.9	40
2	0.8	0.8	50
Total	100.0		

[1] The depreciation rates are taken from *Depreciation Studies—Preliminary Report of the Bureau of Internal Revenue* (1931). They have been appropriately weighted by the value of business capital goods of each average life span produced in 1929. The weights were derived from the *Census of Manufactures* and Dr. Kuznets' estimates of construction (*Bulletin 52*).

[2] Reciprocal of depreciation rate, not allowing for scrap value.

used in the evaluations are not contemporaneous, the meaning of the measures is obscured. Such items as repairs and fire losses are already priced in current units. But charges for depreciation, depletion, and retirements are in terms of prices paid at the time of original investment. If we are to modify these charges in order to express them in the prices of some common period, rather than in the original cost prices of many periods, a step must be taken beyond Table 1.

Price changes themselves result in one form of capital consumption (and formation) as it appears in the computations of business men. (Write-downs, the major type of entries taking specific account of price changes, have been omitted from the present set of figures, however.) In reducing the measures in Table 1 to contemporaneous price units, therefore, we are ignoring the effects of some of these

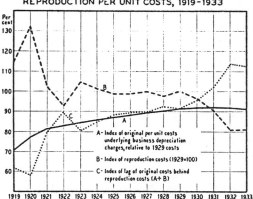

CHART I

ESTIMATES OF ORIGINAL AND OF REPRODUCTION PER UNIT COSTS, 1919-1933

A- Index of original per unit costs underlying business depreciation charges, relative to 1929 costs

B- Index of reproduction costs (1929=100)

C- Index of lag of original costs behind reproduction costs (A÷B)

changes. From a social point of view this is defensible on the ground that a general deflation of values does not in itself signify the loss of physical capacity to produce.

As a result of the great fall in the purchasing power of the dollar during the War, the prices implicit in depreciation charges were usually lower than the prices actually paid for replacements. This situation, revealed by the indexes in Chart 1, prevailed during most of the period we are observing. The index portrayed by the solid line represents the original cost prices on the basis of which depreciation charges are computed, as a percentage of the corresponding 1929 prices.[*] Thus, in 1929 the original cost prices of the equipment and buildings being depreciated averaged about 9 per cent less than reproduction costs in 1929. In 1919 the prices originally paid for capital assets in existence averaged some 29 per cent less than 1929 prices. Not until the collapse of prices in 1930 did reproduction costs fall below the amounts set aside in depreciation reserves to make possible the replacement of equipment. The extent of the lag is indicated by a line representing the ratio of this index to an index of current prices.

It is this index of the original cost prices underlying depreciation charges that we must use in reducing the charges

[*] The index is an harmonic mean of various available indexes of prices of capital goods and construction costs weighted by the estimated depreciation charge applicable to the goods produced at the given prices. The harmonic mean of prices was employed because, when used to deflate a value series, it yields a series expressed in constant prices.

The underlying price indexes, especially those of construction, are not entirely satisfactory, and the weights used are rather rough. There can be little doubt, however, that the picture as a whole is as outlined here.

The figures are given in Appendix Table II, with some further details on the method of computation.

to constant dollars. The deflating index number is, in many respects, a peculiar price level. It measures one of the factors tying together different periods and suggests the extent of the influence of previous prices upon the present economic situation. As such it represents an institutional force of some weight and indicates one lagging element through which rising prices are a stimulus to business enterprise, and declining prices are a depressant.

The depletion charges in Table 1 also are composites including prices determined in different years. The adjustment of depletion charges, although somewhat analogous to modifying depreciation charges to reflect changes in prices, presents additional difficulties. Unlike depreciation charges, which are computed chiefly as a percentage of original cost, depletion charges are based on a more heterogeneous mixture of prices. The basic values used relate to discovery values as well as to cost, and in some instances depletion charges are calculated simply as percentages of gross income. In a stationary state we might measure depletion by an amount "adequate to provide some form of man-made capital equivalent in 'value' to this wear and tear."[9] In a dynamic industrial system, however, the task is more difficult and only the roughest approximations are possible. This is recognized in the entrepreneurial estimates themselves, and in the degree of reliability ascribed to them by business men and accountants.

[9] A. C. Pigou, *Economics of Stationary States* (Macmillan, 1935) p. 22.

In this *Bulletin* we attack the problem of reducing depletion charges to constant dollars by going directly to an index of output of raw minerals and forest products. This index is taken to represent the movements of these charges had they been expressed in constant dollars. The index of depletion thus derived may be expressed in dollars by the further assumption that the actual charges in some one year are correct. We select 1929 as this base. Only slightly different results are yielded by the use of other years.

To express depletion charges in 'current' dollars is even more difficult. The use of prices of mineral products or of mines and timber tracts is either incorrect or impossible. For our purposes we might, with some reason, use an index of the general price level or of the prices of capital goods. The latter is our most readily available choice. This assumes that among other things our knowledge of mineral resources is constant, that technological changes have been relatively unimportant, and that relative price changes have been small. These are bold assumptions, of course, involving as they do the absence of change in the chief elements characteristic of a dynamic economy. However, any other reasonable treatment would affect the total but slightly since depletion charges constitute a relatively small portion of our total.

The estimates in Table 1 other than charges for depreciation, depletion and retirements, are already in terms of current prices. Their deflation by appropriate indexes to convert them into constant dollars expressed in 1929 prices

TABLE 5

MEASURES OF BUSINESS CAPITAL CONSUMPTION, 1919-1933, BY TYPE, IN TERMS OF 1929 PRICES[1]

(in millions of dollars)

YEAR	DEPRECIATION	DEPLETION	DEPRECIATION AND DEPLETION	REPAIRS, RENEWALS AND MAINTENANCE	DEVELOPMENT EXPENSE (MINING)	FIRE LOSSES	TOTAL
1919	4,662	409	5,071	2,225	292	110	7,698
1920	4,584	460	5,044	2,438	374	133	7,989
1921	4,569	363	4,932	2,638	279	190	8,039
1922	4,820	390	5,210	2,921	337	216	8,684
1923	4,952	523	5,475	2,905	374	202	8,956
1924	5,007	495	5,502	2,717	333	213	8,765
1925	5,249	511	5,760	2,753	356	223	9,092
1926	5,806	545	6,351	2,889	378	224	9,842
1927	5,789	548	6,337	2,878	323	187	9,725
1928	6,065	548	6,613	2,806	312	188	9,919
1929	6,443	596	7,039	2,906	321	181	10,447
1930	6,464	514	6,978	2,503	270	206	9,957
1931	6,391	424	6,815	2,173	192	197	9,377
1932	5,958	344	6,302	1,675	166	196	8,339
1933	5,765	372	6,137	1,646	172	131	8,086

[1] Derived by dividing the figures in Table 1 by the appropriate price indexes in Appendix Table II, except in the case of depletion charges, for which see the text.

The separation of depreciation from depletion charges, 1919-24, has been estimated with an error that is small relative to depreciation charges. The estimated breakdown is not given in Table 1 since the error in the above separation may be large, for depletion charges. As mentioned, depletion charges in constant dollars were derived by a procedure not making use of this estimate.

therefore requires no explanation. The deflators are given in Appendix Table II.

The results of the conversion of the estimates in Table 1 into fixed prices are presented in Table 5. The year 1929 has been selected as the base. The average of a broader period such as 1925-29 as the base yields much the same results as does the use of 1929. We are here measuring the declines in capital goods in terms of constant prices instead of the varying cost prices appearing on the books of business enterprises.

In Table 6 the same series are expressed in terms of the prices current year by year, that is, the estimate for 1925 is in terms of 1925 prices, and so on. Only the changes in per unit replacement costs are eliminated by expression of capital consumption in terms of either current or cost dollars: changes in values arising from obsolescence remain, and properly so. We thus make comparable our estimates of capital consumption and gross capital formation and in this way obtain a measure of net capital formation that is not ambiguous, from the economic point of view.

Expressing the estimates of depreciation in current prices implies measuring the capital consumption represented as if price changes were reflected periodically on the books of business enterprises. It enables us to distinguish between two types of capital consumption and thus aids in the analysis of the causes of capital consumption. This distinction is between the decline in value and the value of the decline of capital goods. But we need not attempt to name *the*

correct concept. For certain purposes it is convenient to use the concept of capital consumption that is confined to measures of depreciation, depletion and obsolescence. For other purposes the inclusion of value changes other than those arising from depreciation, depletion and obsolescence is more suitable. The figures in Tables 5 and 6, in constant and in current dollars, follow the first concept. Obviously it does not agree with the *business* concept.

The various measures presented in Tables 1, 5, and 6 are brought together in Chart 2, which makes graphic comparison possible.

As was suggested earlier the rising trend of business depreciation charges was partly a consequence of the change in price levels from 1913 to the post-War period. Elimination of the price changes leaves a less rapidly rising trend, but still one averaging about 3.7 per cent per annum between 1919 and 1929 (2.6 per cent per annum between 1919 and 1933). The response to the cyclical declines in business in years prior to 1931 is slight. Only in the major recession of 1929-33 was there a substantial decline in business depreciation charges expressed in constant dollars.[10]

The movements of depletion charges are naturally more responsive to the fluctuations in general business owing to the use of per unit of output charges.

The absence of trend in repairs, renewals and mainte-

[10] An important factor making for this stability is the widely prevalent use of the straight-line method of accruing depreciation charges. Charging on the basis of volume of output would change the figures rather appreciably.

TABLE 6

MEASURES OF BUSINESS CAPITAL CONSUMPTION, 1919-1933, BY TYPE, IN TERMS OF CURRENT PRICES [1]

(in millions of dollars)

YEAR	DEPRECIATION	DEPLETION	DEPRECIATION AND DEPLETION	REPAIRS, RENEWALS AND MAINTENANCE	DEVELOPMENT EXPENSE (MINING)	FIRE LOSSES	TOTAL
1919	5,338	468	5,806	2,589	334	126	8,855
1920	6,060	608	6,668	3,305	495	176	10,644
1921	4,683	372	5,055	2,706	286	195	8,242
1922	4,468	362	4,830	2,682	312	200	8,024
1923	5,185	548	5,733	3,061	392	211	9,397
1924	5,077	502	5,579	2,762	338	216	8,895
1925	5,181	504	5,685	2,698	351	220	8,954
1926	5,731	538	6,269	2,841	373	221	9,704
1927	5,766	546	6,312	2,876	322	186	9,696
1928	5,913	534	6,447	2,735	304	183	9,669
1929	6,443	596	7,039	2,906	321	181	10,447
1930	6,218	494	6,712	2,442	260	198	9,612
1931	5,771	383	6,154	1,946	173	178	8,451
1932	4,814	278	5,092	1,365	134	158	6,749
1933	4,670	301	4,971	1,316	139	106	6,532

[1] The figures on repairs, development expense and fire losses are the same as in Table 1. As stated in the text, these types of capital consumption are already expressed in terms of current prices. The data on depreciation and depletion are derived from the corresponding figures in Table 5 (in constant prices), multiplied by appropriate indexes of current (reproduction cost) prices. These price indexes are the same as those given on the third line of Appendix Table II.

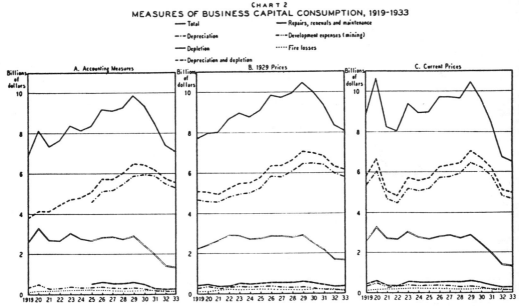

CHART 2
MEASURES OF BUSINESS CAPITAL CONSUMPTION, 1919-1933
— Total   — Repairs, renewals and maintenance
--- Depreciation   --- Development expenses (mining)
— Depletion   ..... Fire losses
--- Depreciation and depletion

nance is a consequence of the overwhelming weight of steam railroads. This industry has shown little if any growth during the post-War decade. For the same reason there was no decline in the total in 1921: the railroads were busy restoring their equipment and other property to serviceable condition. The radical decline since 1929 is indicative of the under-maintenance already discussed.

Costs of developing mines have fluctuated with the current rate of mining output. Little can be said about fire losses although the decline since 1930 attracts attention.

The figures in Table 5, from which confusing price movements have been eliminated, make possible certain conclusions with respect to the relative importance of the several types of capital consumption:

1. An increasing proportion of business capital consumption is being recorded in the form of depreciation charges rather than charges for repairs and maintenance, chiefly as a consequence of the decline in the relative importance of steam railroads.

2. Recorded depletion charges and costs of development of our national resources declined in relative importance during the fifteen years under review.

3. Despite a large increase in the nation's capital stock, losses by fire showed no appreciable upward trend.

It is interesting to observe the influence of the high post-War prices and low depression prices upon the mea-

sures of capital consumption (Table 6). Substitution of these prices for the original cost prices underlying the accounting estimates of depreciation charges raises the values assigned to the earlier years of the period 1919-33, and lowers the values of the later years. The figures given in Table 6 provide a basis for a significant comparison with current estimates of gross capital formation of similar scope, just as do the figures in Table 1.

In deriving the figures in Tables 5 and 6 we have been forced to ignore the steady improvements in quality of equipment produced. Of course changes may be foreseen and investment made or withheld accordingly. If an investment is made under these circumstances it presumably is done in the anticipation that depreciation and obsolescence charges can be raised sufficiently to take account of the future rise in quality or fall in price. This may not be as exceptional as it seems offhand. If business men have, by long experience, been inured to such relative price changes (equivalent to improvements in quality with price constant), depreciation policies may come to anticipate them in the form of allowances for 'normal' obsolescence. However, the wide prevalence of straight-line depreciation charges means that in actual practice no attempt is made to pro-rate depreciation charges so that the anticipated losses are properly allocated over the life of the equipment. The entrepreneurial estimates of depreciation in Table 1 may therefore understate the decline in value of capital goods during the first half of their useful lives and overstate the decline in the second half. In an economy in which the volume of capital is fairly constant, however, the discrepancies tend to cancel one another. If the volume of capital is growing there may be something of a continuous lag in the level of capital charges, and therefore a continuous overstatement of annual profits. Until the day of reckoning, however, no difficulties may be anticipated. But, in fact, such a day occurs whenever there is a substantial slackening in the rate of growth of capital—that is, during every major depression.[11]

The difficulties of price and quality changes confront the business man as well as the economist. One difficulty is the possibility that no replacement price may be quoted or recorded in the market. This is merely a limiting case within the broad category of 'quality' changes. Here lie some of the chief causes of difficulty in accounting for capital consumption. It is partly because of changes in the quality of the new capital equipment flowing through the market that even great changes in price levels are ignored in the records of business. Quality changes are thus not simply something to be *eliminated*. Rather, from a scientific standpoint, they are something to be *analyzed*. The difficulties of adequately measuring capital consumed, of computing costs, and of pricing, arise in large part from such changes in 'quality.' It is these difficulties which help to explain some of the recognized inadequacies of current accounting methods and current price indexes.

With reference to the direction of influence of quality changes upon the indexes in Chart 1 the following may be ventured. If improvements in capital goods may be assumed to go on at a steady rate, then in order to reflect this progressive cheapening the index of current prices (the broken line in Chart 1) would be swung about the 1929 base so that the 1919-28 figures are raised and the 1930-33 figures lowered. Similar (but not exactly the same) would be the change in the solid line. The data represented by the dotted line would be least changed. But it is these figures which reveal the lag in which we are interested.

ESTIMATES OF CAPITAL CONSUMPTION AND THE MEASUREMENT OF PROFITS AND SAVINGS

Current methods of measuring capital consumption constitute an indispensable part of the procedure of estimating business profits, national income, savings, and national

wealth. Any peculiarities characteristic of the determination by business men of their current position will thus affect not only these measures but also the influence exerted by them upon economic behavior. The computations most immediately involved are those concerned with business profits and savings. Measures of capital consumption, indeed, come into existence primarily as part of these computations. It is worth indicating the influence, upon current measures of profits and business savings, of two characteristics of business measurements—the use of original cost and of the straight-line depreciation formula in the estimation of depreciation charges.[12] The influence of the cost base is most prominent over long periods. During ordinary business cycles it is the prevailing use of some variety of the straight-line formula that appears to affect depreciation charges most prominently. Let us consider first the use of original cost as it affects depreciation estimates and measures of business savings.

Current prices may differ from original cost prices because of secular movements in the prices of capital goods or because of movements constituting parts of business cycles. But the short cyclical changes in the prices of capital goods are relatively small.[13] During recent business cycles of moderate amplitude there has been relative stability in current prices of capital goods and differences between them and the prices underlying book values have not fluctuated to any important extent. Secular movements of prices result, however, in a cumulative deviation of replacement prices from book values, which may become great. It is these larger movements that interest us in the present comparison. Even prosperity replacement costs may be on a lower secular level than original cost prices; and even depression replacement costs may be on a higher secular level than original cost prices. The magnitude of these differences in a specific historical period is indicated in Table 7.

The estimates in Table 7 of corporate savings for 1919-33 are derived, naturally, by a series of subtractions from gross income in which an estimate of depreciation in original cost prices is one of the items subtracted. If this estimate of depreciation be expressed in terms of current replacement cost, instead of in terms of original cost, we have a rather different estimate. The difference between the two (the third column) is rather large in relation to corporate savings. Modified estimates of corporate savings, in which account is taken of the differences in column

[11] In so far as there is actual shortening of life, depreciation charges may understate actual depreciation and obsolescence, account being taken of the resulting losses only on retirement and abandonment of assets. However, as we have noticed, the depreciation charges available to us tend to be estimated at higher than commonly accepted rates and indeed explicitly include an allowance for 'normal' obsolescence. To that extent obsolescence and similar declines in value are allowed for regularly.

[12] Other business practices, such as the valuation of inventories at the lower of cost or market prices, are also of interest in this connection. But here we restrict our attention to the characteristics mentioned.

[13] See Frederick C. Mills, Changes in Prices, Manufacturing Costs and Industrial Productivity, 1929-1934, *Bulletin 53* of this series.

TABLE 7

MEASURES OF DEPRECIATION AND OF CORPORATE SAVINGS, 1919-1933

ALL CORPORATIONS IN THE UNITED STATES [1]

(*in millions of dollars*)

(1) YEAR	(2) CORPORATE SAVINGS [2]	(3) DIFFERENCE BETWEEN DEPRECIATION AT COST PRICES AND AT CURRENT PRICES	(4) CORPORATE SAVINGS, MODIFIED (2) + (3)
1919	4,310	—1,000	3,310
1920	1,380	—1,390	— 10
1921	—2,670	— 570	—3,240
1922	1,660	— 290	1,370
1923	2,410	— 640	1,770
1924	1,440	— 490	950
1925	2,810	— 390	2,420
1926	2,180	— 400	1,780
1927	950	— 390	560
1928	2,330	— 290	2,040
1929	1,350	— 380	970
1930	—4,110	— 190	—4,300
1931	—6.040	80	—5,960
1932	—6,550	450	—6,100
1933	—3,060	390	—2,670
Total	—1,610	—5,500	—7,110

[1] Excluding tax-exempt and life insurance companies. The data basic to the figures in columns (2) and (3) are derived from *Statistics of Income*.

[2] Net income less cash dividends paid to individuals. For 1929-33 profits and losses derived from the sale of capital assets have been eliminated.

(3), are given in the last series of figures in the table. At the foot of the table appear algebraic totals for the entire period surveyed. Corporate savings as ordinarily computed reached a total negative figure of 1,610 million dollars, while the modified measures added up to a negative figure of 7,110 million dollars. The cumulated difference, arising out of the discrepancy between original and reproduction cost, amounted to 5,500 million dollars, also negative. The latter figure is very large, in relation to the estimated cumulated corporate savings.

The figures suggest the extent to which business savings tend to be overstated by the use of cost bases in the estimation of depreciation charges when prices are high relatively to preceding periods when investments were made. When prices are relatively low, business savings tend to be understated. We thus see that a considerable fraction of the apparent corporate savings put aside by business organizations during the early part of the 'twenties was required to restore their capital equipment at the relatively high price levels prevailing. The free funds actually available for new investment were smaller than appeared in the income accounts of business enterprises. Where dividends were sustained, at a level equal to that of computed profits, capital was in fact being depleted.[14]

Here we have reflected one factor making for the stimulation of business enterprise when the secular movement of prices is upward, and the depression of business enterprise when the secular movement of prices is downward. The reason for this phenomenon is found, in part, in the tendency of business men to look to the money counters in which business is transacted as the final criterion and purpose of their activities. When the purchasing power of money becomes the goal and measure of business enterprise, as it may in a runaway inflation, the change in business behavior is great. But inflation must go far before the rules of the game are changed.[15] In the absence of such radical changes the nominal character of money and prices is recognized only sporadically and to a small degree. This occurs, of course, when revaluations of assets are made through appraisal or other less objective estimation. To the extent that business men do in fact recognize the significance of secular changes in price levels, the figures in column (4) of Table 7 represent their estimates of savings. To the extent that they do not, their estimates are those in the second column of the table. Somewhere between these two limits, and probably closer to the figures in column (2), are the entrepreneurial measures of annual savings.

We turn now to another characteristic of business measures of depreciation, already mentioned: their remarkable steadiness. In spite of large fluctuations in gross value of product, physical volume of output, and consequently in the use made of capital equipment, depreciation costs allocated to specific years reveal relatively little change. Cyclical declines in 1921, 1924, 1927, and 1930-32 are definitely impressed even upon annual series of physical output and net income. Gross income declined in 1921 and 1930-32, and rose only fractionally in 1924 and 1927. Depreciation charges, in terms either of original cost or of current replacement cost, reveal no declines at all, except in the most recent period. The averages of the year-to-year changes in the last two series (Table 8) are minor compared with

[14] The same reasoning holds to a great extent where capital consumption is understated not because of the use of the cost base but because of failure to take obsolescence adequately into account. The situation of the street railways is already history.

It must be noted that the figures in Table 7 refer to the aggregate of all corporations in the United States. If we were to confine our attention to those industries in which depreciation charges bulk large, in comparison with business savings, the influence of price changes would be even greater than is indicated in the table.

[15] Current methods of estimating depreciation charges are but one element in the situation making for stimulus or drag when the secular movement of prices is up or down, and probably not the most important. Lagging wage rates, fixed interest charges and other costs, must be considered. Even of these other costs, however, the same fundamental reason is at the bottom, namely the tendency to rely upon money as the ultimate standard of valuation.

TABLE 8

AVERAGE ABSOLUTE ANNUAL CHANGES IN PHYSICAL OUTPUT, GROSS
AND NET INCOME, AND DEPRECIATION CHARGES, 1919-1933

ALL CORPORATIONS IN THE UNITED STATES[1]

	As a percentage of	
	1919-33 average value	1929 value
Physical volume of output	10.9	8.5
Gross income	11.8	8.8
Depreciation charges		
Expressed in original cost prices	6.8	5.4
Expressed in 1929 prices	4.9	4.0
Net income	60.0	30.7

The index of physical volume of output covers industrial production and trade. It is computed by Persons and Foster, *Review of Economic Statistics*, August 15, 1933, p. 155. The 1933 figure is estimated.

Gross income does not include tax-exempt income. The original data are from *Statistics of Income*.

The depreciation charges are also from *Statistics of Income*. They were expressed in 1929 prices by dividing by the index on the first line of Appendix Table II.

The net income is based on compiled net profits after taxes, excluding dividends received from other corporations and gains or losses on the sale of capital assets (*Statistics of Income*).

those of the other series, and are due primarily to the secular movement, rather than to the cyclical fluctuations.

Since the estimates of net income are remainders after depreciation (among other items) has been subtracted from gross income, their violent fluctuations are to be ascribed, in part at least, to the absence of large movements in depreciation charges. And this is a consequence of the widely prevalent use of the straight-line depreciation formula or other formulae not taking directly into account fluctuations in the volume of output. Here, also, the use of this particular type of formula, rather than of one that would make depreciation charges reflect the rate of production, appears to be explained chiefly by the limited visibility available to business men. The longevity of a machine or a building may be more readily and accurately predicted than the use, in terms of volume of output, that will be made of it. Another, though minor, contributing factor may be the habit in many business computations of working with rough magnitudes. This, in turn, may be a consequence of the relatively large cost inherent in fine measurements, or of the factor already mentioned—the belief that more accurate measures are impossible.

A further factor may be the continuous decay which to some extent goes on in capital goods whether they be used or not. But to the extent that the loss of value of capital goods is not simply a function of time, the straight-line method of allocating depreciation charges appears to be rigid in its lack of discrimination among time periods with varying volumes of output. Similarly, to the extent that the loss of value is directly related to the volume of output, the maintenance method used by many public utilities is too elastic, resulting in charges for maintaining capital that are of greater cyclical amplitude than is output (see Table 2).

CONCLUDING REMARKS

In this *Bulletin* we have been concerned chiefly with the available data on capital consumption, and with some of their characteristics. We have tried to indicate the reservations that must be made in using these materials, and have called attention particularly to the ambiguities resulting from changing prices. The relation of estimates of capital consumption to the measurement of profits and of corporate savings was indicated.

An attempt to learn what we can about the negative items in the nation's capital account involves more than the compilation of measures of their extent and fluctuation. The nature of the estimates themselves must be considered, for we must resort to business computations for our figures. Even if the consumption of capital is an objective fact, we become aware of it only through the minds of those who keep the records. These records are, further, influenced by efforts to control profit estimates and by other factors.

It is essential to note this fact that all measures of capital consumption are estimates. We do not know how to handle efficiently the problem of measuring capital consumption in a dynamic world. Technological and price changes 'disturb' business computations and forecasts, as well as judgments concerning the past. Reluctance to acknowledge specific instances of capital evanescence is common. The factors that make for profits make also for difficulty in the computation of profits and all related estimates. In the complex changing situation business men cannot see far enough, or clearly enough. It is partly for this reason that they tend to hold fast to the unchanging reality of cost prices, and it may be partly for this reason that waves of optimism and pessimism tend periodically to sweep over business enterprise.

FORTHCOMING PUBLICATIONS

The third *Bulletin* of the 1936 series, to be issued this summer, will be by Wesley C. Mitchell: Characteristics of the Business Cycle, 1927-1933.

Chapter III of Dr. Mitchell's second volume—*Business Cycles: Analysis of Cyclical Behavior*—has been mimeographed and is ready for distribution. Copies will be sent to all who have already purchased Chapters I and II. We still have a few copies of the first two chapters, and the three will be sent upon receipt of $1.00.

Ebb and Flow in Trade Unionism, in which Dr. Leo Wolman gives trade union membership from 1897 to date and discusses events since his volume, *The Growth of American Trade Unions, 1880-1923*, appeared, will be published next month (300 pp., 5 charts, 48 tables, price $3.00). Orders are being taken now. Some copies of the former volume are still available. As long as the supply lasts the two volumes may be purchased for $4.00.

APPENDIX TABLE I

ACCOUNTING MEASURES OF BUSINESS CAPITAL CONSUMPTION, 1919-1933, BY TYPE AND INDUSTRY [1]

(in millions of dollars)

	1919	1920	1921	1922	1923	1924	1925	1926	1927	1928	1929	1930	1931	1932	1933
Agriculture and related industries															
Depreciation							923	916	921	921	940	919	870	831	786
Depletion							23	24	22	22	25	17	12	8	10
Depreciation and depletion	1,020	1,083	957	888	878	896	946	940	943	943	965	937	882	838	796
Mining															
Depreciation							295	245	242	216	239	203	203	173	164
Depletion							297	289	242	222	254	191	113	106	115
Depreciation and depletion	508	613	542	584	705	687	592	534	484	439	492	394	316	280	279
Development expense	334	495	286	312	392	338	351	373	322	304	321	260	173	134	139
Manufacturing															
Depreciation							1,493	1,640	1,718	1,795	1,879	1,945	1,849	1,681	1,63
Depletion							156	263	244	268	277	249	126	121	114
Depreciation and depletion	1,152	1,293	1,287	1,485	1,573	1,552	1,649	1,903	1,962	2,063	2,156	2,194	1,974	1,802	1,74
Other industries (trade, construction, service, miscellaneous)															
Depreciation							741	970	848	938	1,033	1,058	1,049	1,029	92
Depletion							28	6	6	10	6	5	14	4	3
Depreciation and depletion	475	521	568	594	630	678	769	976	854	948	1,039	1,063	1,063	1,033	92
Public utilities and transportation															
Depreciation							588	720	794	898	983	1,023	1,123	1,062	99
Depletion							8	24	21	25	29	27	23	22	1
Depreciation and depletion	369	337	436	455	497	534	596	745	814	923	1,011	1,049	1,146	1,084	1,01
Repairs, renewals and maintenance	2,318	3,016	2,358	2,315	2,616	2,389	2,408	2,501	2,436	2,355	2,416	2,080	1,658	1,222	1,17
Retirements (loss on retired property and delayed income debits), steam railroads	11	10	30	52	66	49	54	59	61	50	86	90	105	63	11
Finance and real estate (non-residential)															
Depreciation							467	559	582	654	710	701	687	636	65
Depletion							12	8	5	8	6	4	3	2	
Depreciation and depletion	263	297	307	378	364	428	479	567	587	662	716	706	690	638	65
Major repairs and alterations	271	289	348	367	445	373	290	340	440	580	490	362	288	143	14
Unallocated															
Fire losses	126	176	195	200	211	216	220	221	186	183	181	198	178	158	10

[1] The data on business depreciation and depletion are based on corporate figures published in *Statistics of Income*. For farming, estimates of the Department of Agriculture were used, with several minor modifications. Non-corporate figures were estimated by stepping up the corporate figures by ratios obtained from the Censuses of Manufactures, Mines, Distribution, and Construction. Separate data for depreciation and depletion are not available for years prior to 1925.

The figures on repairs, renewals and maintenance by public utilities were collected from *Statistics of Railways*, the Census of Electrical Industries, and estimates of the Federal Employment Stabilization Board, interpolated by data published in several industrial journals and corporate reports. Retirements of equipment by steam railways are also from *Statistics of Railways*. Major repairs and alterations in the real estate field (and also of homes) are based on figures relating to permits published in the *Monthly Labor Review*, supplemented by data from the Bureau of Labor Statistics.

Development expenses in mining industries are derived from data in the Census of Mines and Quarries, *Report on Crude Petroleum and Its Liquid Refinery Products* (U. S. Tariff Commission), and *Preliminary Report on a Survey of Crude Petroleum* (Department of the Interior); with interpolations based on *Mineral Resources* (Bureau of Mines).

Total fire losses are estimated by the National Board of Fire Underwriters. To these was applied a percentage based on the ratio of value of business capital goods to the total national wealth subject to fire hazards (Federal Trade Commission estimates of national wealth, 1922).

APPENDIX TABLE II

INDEXES USED IN DEFLATING ACCOUNTING MEASURES OF BUSINESS CAPITAL CONSUMPTION, 1919-1933 [1]

(prices in 1929=100)

	1919	1920	1921	1922	1923	1924	1925	1926	1927	1928	1929	1930	1931	1932	193
Depreciation [2]	70.8	77.0	81.4	82.9	84.2	85.7	86.9	88.0	89.2	90.2	91.1	91.9	92.1	91.9	91.
Repairs, renewals and maintenance [3]	116.4	135.6	102.6	91.8	105.4	101.7	98.0	98.3	99.9	97.5	100.0	97.6	89.6	81.5	80.
Development expense [4]⎫ Fire losses ⎭	114.5	132.2	102.5	92.7	104.7	101.4	98.7	98.7	99.6	97.5	100.0	96.2	90.3	80.8	81.

[1] Depletion charges expressed in constant prices were obtained directly, without use of a price index; see explanation in the text.

[2] This is an harmonic mean of various indexes of the prices of capital equipment, weighted by the amount of depreciation charges based on each year's price. In 1929, for example, depreciation was charged on equipment and buildings purchased in 1929, 1928, 1927, and so on. The deflator for 1929 depreciation charges must therefore be a weighted average of 1929, 1928, 1927, ..., prices, the weights being the 1929 depreciation on the goods purchased in each of these years. This weighted average, relative to 1929 prices, is 91.1. To express the 1929 depreciation charges in terms of 1929 prices, it is necessary to divide the charges by this average, 91.1. The various underlying price indexes include the following: Railroad construction costs (Interstate Commerce Commission), machine tools and wood

APPENDIX TABLE III

MEASURES OF CAPITAL CONSUMPTION, RESIDENCES, AND RELATED PRICE INDEXES, 1919-1933

	1919	1920	1921	1922	1923	1924	1925	1926	1927	1928	1929	1930	1931	1932	1933
A. ACCOUNTING MEASURES OF CAPITAL CONSUMPTION (*in millions of dollars*)[1]															
RESIDENCES, RENTED															
Non-farm															
Depreciation	266	278	294	326	371	421	476	532	579	619	651	673	682	684	682
Major repairs and alterations	89	93	111	114	135	110	83	93	111	109	99	62	41	28	32
Farm															
Depreciation	28	31	23	24	24	24	24	25	25	25	25	25	22	20	20
RESIDENCES, OWNER-OCCUPIED															
Non-farm															
Depreciation	232	249	269	304	355	413	478	547	608	666	717	741	750	753	751
Major repairs and alterations	99	108	131	138	168	140	109	126	155	155	145	90	60	40	47
Farm															
Depreciation	395	428	326	333	334	333	342	344	348	344	349	342	307	284	284
UNALLOCATED															
Fire losses	63	89	98	99	105	108	111	111	94	92	91	99	89	79	53
ALL RESIDENCES															
Depreciation	921	986	912	987	1,084	1,191	1,320	1,448	1,560	1,654	1,742	1,781	1,761	1,741	1,737
Major repairs and alterations	188	201	242	252	303	250	192	219	266	264	244	152	101	68	79
Fire losses	63	89	98	99	105	108	111	111	94	92	91	99	89	79	53
Total	1,172	1,276	1,252	1,338	1,492	1,549	1,623	1,778	1,920	2,010	2,077	2,032	1,951	1,888	1,869
B. INDEXES USED IN DEFLATING ACCOUNTING MEASURES OF CAPITAL CONSUMPTION (*prices in 1929=100*)															
ALL RESIDENCES															
Depreciation [2]	43.4	45.1	47.1	49.9	53.5	57.5	61.3	64.7	67.4	69.7	71.6	72.9	73.9	74.6	75.2
Major repairs and alterations } [3]	95.9	121.4	97.5	84.3	103.4	104.1	99.9	100.5	99.6	99.9	100.0	98.0	87.6	75.8	82.2
Fire losses }															
C. MEASURES OF CAPITAL CONSUMPTION, IN TERMS OF 1929 PRICES (*in millions of dollars*)[4]															
ALL RESIDENCES															
Depreciation	2,122	2,186	1,936	1,978	2,026	2,071	2,153	2,238	2,314	2,373	2,433	2,443	2,383	2,334	2,310
Major repairs and alterations	196	166	248	299	293	240	192	218	267	264	244	155	115	90	96
Fire losses	66	73	101	117	102	104	111	110	94	92	91	101	102	104	64
Total	2,384	2,425	2,285	2,394	2,421	2,415	2,456	2,566	2,675	2,729	2,768	2,699	2,600	2,528	2,470

[1] The depreciation charges are accounting measures in the sense that they are computed in accordance with ordinary accounting practice: it is doubtful whether most owners of private residences make formal estimates of depreciation. Depreciation charges on farm homes are based on figures of the Department of Agriculture and the Census of Agriculture. Depreciation on non-farm residences are estimates derived from the value of owned homes and rentals paid in 1930 (Census of Population); new construction of residences (permits published in the *Monthly Labor Review*, contracts awarded compiled by the F. W. Dodge Corporation, and permits compiled by J. R. Riggleman); rents paid and received by corporations (*Statistics of Income*); rents paid by wage earners (*Monthly Labor Review*); ratio of depreciation charges to rentals received by realty corporations (Bureau of Internal Revenue, unpublished figures); and depreciation rates listed by the Treasury Department (*Depreciation Studies—Preliminary Report of the Bureau of Internal Revenue*, 1931).

Major repairs and alterations of homes are based on building permits published in the *Monthly Labor Review*, supplemented by unpublished data from the Bureau of Labor Statistics.

Total fire losses are estimated by the National Board of Fire Underwriters. To these was applied a percentage based on the ratio of value of residences to the total national wealth subject to fire hazards (Federal Trade Commission estimates of national wealth, 1922).

[2] Obtained by a procedure similar to that outlined in footnote 1 of Appendix Table II. The basic underlying cost index was that of the *Engineering News-Record*. In this case it was necessary to use prices of years preceding 1913.

[3] Index of building costs, *Engineering News-Record*.

[4] Derived by dividing the figures in Section A by the appropriate price indexes in Section B.

Notes to Appendix Table II continued)

working machinery (American Appraisal Company), commercial cost of cars (Brill), processed capital equipment (National Bureau of Economic Research), construction costs (American Appraisal Company, Richey, Tuttle). Owing to certain provisions in the income tax law, it is not necessary to use prices prior to 1913.

The weights were obtained from estimates of gross capital formation (*Bulletin 52*, National Bureau of Economic Research; *Census of Manufactures*, U. S., Massachusetts, and Pennsylvania, and volume of construction, Dodge Co. and Riggleman) and the depreciation rates listed by the Bureau of Internal Revenue.

[3] Weighted arithmetic average of five indexes of per unit maintenance costs: steam railroads—ways and structures (I.C.C.), steam railroads—equipment (I.C.C.), electric light and power costs (Richey), electric cars (Brill), construction (American Appraisal Company).

[4] Weighted arithmetic average of the indexes listed in footnote 2.

COOPERATIVE RESEARCH

It has been customary to give, in the June issue of the *Bulletin,* an account of our annual planning conference. This year it has been postponed because our cooperative program made so much progress after the Shawnee Conference in September (*see Bulletin 58*) that it was felt desirable to appoint an Executive Director who could devote time to its constructive planning and to following its various features. Happily Joseph H. Willits, Dean of the Wharton School of Finance and Commerce, University of Pennsylvania, a member of our Board of Directors since 1927 and its present Chairman was persuaded to undertake the task. One of his first duties, which begin in the autumn, will be to confer with representatives from the cooperating universities to report on the year's progress and to plan for improvement and expansion of a coordinated research program.

In *Retrospect and Prospect* Dr. Mitchell mentioned the establishment of the secretariat for the Price Conference, under the chairmanship of F. C. Mills, and outlined the projects suggested at the Income Conference, of which Simon Kuznets was elected chairman. We give a brief summary of developments since the publication of *Retrospect and Prospect.*

Income

In accordance with the instructions of the Income Conference the Executive Committee has set up a separate committee on concepts and terminology: Dr. Morris Copeland, chairman; Dr. Winfield Riefler and Dr. Simon Kuznets. The task of this committee is to prepare a report containing a clear exposition of the various terms, with the object of bringing about a better understanding of their significance and application and thereby helping to promote a greater uniformity of usage.

A committee was also organized to consider the possibility of a comprehensive tabulation of the individual state income tax returns for Wisconsin. Harold M. Groves was elected chairman, and Simeon Leland, Simon Kuznets and Aaron Director members. The committee met at Chicago with a group from Wisconsin, including Harry Jerome of the University of Wisconsin and Leonard Krueger of the Wisconsin State Tax Commission. A small subcommittee undertook to work out plans for the tabulation project, and submit it for consideration to the Works Progress Administration of the State of Wisconsin.

Arrangements have been made to have several problems in the field of income and wealth measurements discussed at the annual meeting of the American Economic and Statistical Associations. The Executive Committee of the Conference has arranged for the presentation of reports on the following topics: (1) Treatment of Government Income and Expenditures in Its Bearing upon the Measurement of National Income and Wealth (by Professor Gerhard Colm of the Graduate Faculty of the New School for Social Research); (2) The Concept of Income Employed in Income Taxation (by Professor Carl Shoup of Columbia University); (3) Problems in Measurement of Purchasing Power of Net Farm and Net Urban Income (by a member of the staff, not yet designated, of the Bureau of Agricultural Economics); (4) Problems in the Measurement of Labor Income (by Mr. Solomon Kuznets of the U. S. Bureau of Labor Statistics). The discussants of these reports, who have to date accepted our invitation to act in that capacity, are J. D. Black, M. R. Benedict, J. R. Blough, Mabel Newcomer, and Leo Wolman.

Prices

Further attention has been given to the possibility of cooperative research on the price problems of industry and trade. A meeting of industrial experts and economists was held at the National Bureau on February 21. The members of this group were agreed on the desirability of attaining the following objectives:

1. More accurate determination of the actual price changes among manufactured goods, account being taken of changes in quality and in design.

2. The measurement of production costs, both average and differential.

3. The measurement of changes in industrial productivity, and the determination of cost and price changes accompanying them.

4. The measurement of price-quantity relations (i.e., the determination of changes in demand associated with given changes in price).

The Price Conference also is planning for round table discussions of problems of vital concern to its field at the next meeting of the scientific societies. Meanwhile it is arranging for small committees of economists and industrial experts whose business it will be to explore the problems that would be encountered in given industries, and to frame programs of research for these industries. Such committee has been set up in the textile field, under the chairmanship of S. J. Kennedy, an economist for the Pacific Mills. It is proposed that similar committees be established for coal, boots and shoes, and automobiles. The several programs of research that will be framed by these committees will be circulated in advance of the December meetings, and will be subjected to critical review at that time. With carefully tested programs in hand, it is hoped that means will be found for prosecuting one or more of these industry studies.

The Committee is also collaborating with groups at Harvard, Pennsylvania, and Pittsburgh Universities, who are studying or planning to study prices and costs in American industries.

National Bureau
of Economic Research

BULLETIN 62

DECEMBER 7, 1936

1819 BROADWAY, NEW YORK

NON-PROFIT MEMBERSHIP CORPORATION FOR IMPARTIAL STUDIES IN ECONOMIC AND SOCIAL SCIENCE

Revaluations of Fixed Assets, 1925-1934

SOLOMON FABRICANT

SIGNIFICANCE OF REVALUATIONS

BALANCE sheet values of assets constitute essential data in estimates of wealth, capital, income and profits. Rational use of these estimates cannot be made by economists, statisticians or investors without some consideration of the manner in which assets are valued by business men and accountants.

Of particular interest at present are revaluations of fixed assets. The write-down in 1935 of the property account of the United States Steel Corporation by 270 million dollars, or 17 per cent of the net value in the account, is one spectacular instance. Business men are confronted by a dynamic situation in which price levels fluctuate, obsolescence of machines and plant becomes evident, profit-making opportunities appear and disappear, and business goodwill grows or vanishes. If their records are to reflect the changing reality about them, business men are forced to revalue their assets.

These revaluations possess considerable significance. They constitute clues to the formation and consumption of capital as it fluctuates with changes in tastes, technology and institutions. As such they are essential data in the analysis of changes in capital that is being made at the National Bureau.[1] From another point of view they reflect the discrepancies between original cost and capitalized value that arise from perpetual economic flux. Further, revaluations constitute exceptions to the usual rules of accounting. Their number and amount suggest the degree to which accounting technique has been kept in its place as a servant. For rules and procedures tend to become tyrants: they acquire the dignity and influence of custom and their origin and purpose are lost sight of.

[1] 'Gross Capital Formation, 1919-1933" (*Bulletin 52*, November , 1934) and "Measures of Capital Consumption, 1919-1933" (*Bulletin 60*, June 30, 1936).

The 'book values' found in accounting records do not represent past or present market values in any simple manner. Deductions from original cost, manifested by estimates of reserves for depreciation and depletion, and revaluations through write-ups and write-downs, give rise to book values that reflect neither original cost nor present market value. They are the product of a valuation process going on beside the market-place, not in it. Economists have envisaged an extension of value theory to this valuation process outside the market.[2] The results of our investigation are offered as a contribution towards such a supplement to the theory of market value: the theory of book value.

How important are revaluations of assets? How many concerns enter write-ups and write-downs in their books? Which particular groups of fixed assets are especially involved? Do the number and amount of revaluations vary from time to time? What reasons are usually offered in justification of revaluations? In what way may they be expected to affect computations of profits and other economic measures? These are some of the questions considered in this *Bulletin*.

THE DATA AND THEIR CHARACTERISTICS

Our analysis is based on data novel in degree of detail and comparability. They are derived from reports made by listed industrial corporations to the Securities and Exchange Commission. As sworn statements, certified by public accountants, and made in reply to a uniform and specific question, they lend themselves readily to summary.

The question asked concerning write-ups and write-downs, which appears in 'Form 10, Application for Registration Pursuant to Section 12 (b) and (c) of the Securities Exchange Act of 1934', is as follows:

[2] David Friday, "An Extension of Value Theory", *Quarterly Journal of Economics*, February 1922.

NATIONAL BUREAU OF ECONOMIC RESEARCH BULLETINS—Annual Subscription (Five Issues), $1.00
Single copies, this issue, twenty-five cents

If, since January 1, 1925, there have been any increases or decreases in *investments*, in *property, plant* and *equipment* or in *intangible assets*, resulting from substantially revaluing such assets, state:

(1) In what year or years such revaluations were made.

(2) The amounts of such write-ups or write-downs, and the accounts affected, including the contra entry or entries.

(3) If, in connection with such revaluations, any adjustments were made in related reserve accounts, state the accounts and amounts, with explanations.

The 'Instruction Book for Form 10 for Corporations', in explanation of this question, states:

These items do not refer to adjustments made in the ordinary course of business, but only to major revaluations made for the purpose of entering in the books current values, reproduction costs, or any values other than original cost.

Our study is confined to an examination of reports of 208 large industrial concerns (mining and manufacturing chiefly, with a few from trade, construction and service) covering the years 1925-34, inclusive. The companies were chosen at random from the file of S. E. C. reports of the New York Stock Exchange and therefore include only corporations listed on it. Consolidated reports, rather than the individual reports of related companies, were used wherever possible.

The data are further limited in that only solvent companies in existence in 1934 are included. Revaluations of assets made by corporations prior to consolidation or liquidation are omitted. While these revaluations may reach large amounts per company, the number of concerns involved is small. Still another qualification, related to the preceding, is that only the history of the existing legal entity is fully covered.[2] In our analysis corporations coming into existence before and after 1925 are distinguished to avoid the statistical errors that might otherwise arise.

The size of the sample may be judged by a comparison of the assets of the sample corporations with the assets of all corporations, in the comparable industrial groups, in the United States.

	ALL REPORTING CORPORATIONS 1933[1]	SAMPLE 1934	SAMPLE AS PERCENTAGE OF ALL CORPORATIONS
	(millions of dollars)		
Property, plant and equipment	34,802	6,412	18.4
Investments	12,641	1,193	9.4
Total assets	84,246	11,684	13.9

[1] SOURCE: *Statistics of Income for 1933*. The 1934 figures are not yet available. Intangible assets are not published separately by the Treasury Department.

[2] According to an amendment to the instruction book (Release No. 191, Securities Exchange Act of 1934, April 24, 1935) revaluation by predecessor companies must be included in Form 10 only if: "(1) The registrant is the successor to a predecessor and at the time of such succession continued under substantially the same ownership and control as such predecessor; and (2) the regis-

TOTAL NUMBER AND VOLUME OF REVALUATIONS

Of the 208 reports examined as many as 157 indicated some write-up or write-down during the ten years 1925-34. To the question whether there had been any substantial revaluation of investments, property, plant and equipment or intangible assets, three-fourths of the companies answered in the affirmative.

Some companies, of course, were not in existence during this entire period, and therefore had less opportunity to revalue their assets.[4] However, the difference in the proportion of companies reporting revaluations is slight when we distinguish between those incorporated before and since January 1, 1925, 76 against 75 per cent. The largest proportion reporting revaluations, 86 per cent were companies organized during the War years 1915-20 (Table 1).

TABLE 1

CORPORATIONS REPORTING REVALUATIONS OF FIXED ASSETS, 1925-1934, NUMBER

PERIOD DURING WHICH INCORPORATED	CORPORATIONS IN SAMPLE (number)	CORPORATIONS REPORTING REVALUATIONS	
		Number	Percentage of total
Before 1901	33	24	73
1901-1914	47	30	64
1915-1920	57	49	86
1921-1924	16	13	81
Before 1925	153	116	76
1925-1934	55	41	75
Total	208	157	75

Most of the revaluations, as percentages of the amount of corresponding assets,[3] were reported for intangible assets, investments being second, and property, plant and equipment last. In terms of actual amounts of revalua-

trant succeeded to: either (a) substantially all the assets of such predecessor; or (b) a substantial portion thereof and such portion was segregated on the books of such predecessor." It seems that before the date of this amendment there was no requirement that entries in the books of predecessors should be reported, and in fact they were omitted in most cases.

[4] Of the 208 companies 55 have assumed a new legal habit since 1924—a large fraction, for many are really new only in a strictly legal sense. The relative number of new corporations emphasizes the need for paying attention to changes in capital and assets in the process of reorganization, consolidation, or modification of corporate being, in any adequate historical account of the course of profits and modifications in capital structures of business enterprises.

[3] The importance of the revaluations is judged here in relation to the net book value of the corresponding assets at the end of 1934. Since some of the revaluations consisted of completely writing off an asset, the ratios derived may be very large, sometimes infinitely so. It would perhaps have been preferable to compare the amount of revaluations with the book value of the corresponding asset before revaluation. But the ratios used here are adequate for our purposes, and cost considerably less effort to obtain.

tions, however, the order is different. The amounts themselves are most significant in considering such matters as the evaluation of net worth. But in so far as the values of individual assets are concerned, the percentages are of primary interest (Table 2). Write-ups of property account were surprisingly small, the total for the decade falling well below depreciation charges for one year. For both intangibles and investments the percentages were much greater, 16 and 18 respectively.

Total write-downs exceeded write-ups of property, plant and equipment, and intangibles, and were roughly equal in investments. This preponderance of write-downs is in accord with what we know of the economic history of the period 1925-34. Write-ups during and immediately following the War probably exceeded write-downs, but that period lies outside the scope of the records analyzed here.

In percentages of the corresponding asset values in 1934, write-downs of property and equipment were apparently of minor importance, slightly exceeding 10 per cent. However, even on a per annum basis they formed an appreciable amount compared with depreciation and net income. And their significance is even greater, since it is their cumulative effect on book values that is of importance, and this is more closely measured by the total for the decade.[*]

[*] The totals are not *exact* measures of the cumulative effects because depreciation and depletion charges may eventually wipe out the book value of the asset and thus render revaluations only of passing influence on book values. For intangibles and investments and such tangible property as land, however, the situation is otherwise.

Write-downs of intangibles almost equaled their final net book value. Of course, one reason for the large relative amount of write-downs of intangibles is that the book values used are those after revaluation, not before. But that the ratio would be large in any event is to be expected from the nature of the asset. No one can accurately measure the value of goodwill, patents or trademarks; consequently, all valuations are suspect and subject to correction, and as we shall see later, influenced by the prevailing state of business hopes. It is for this reason that intangibles are so often written down, or written off, or never allowed to appear in the balance sheet. Of the 208 corporations studied here only 60 valued their intangible assets (on their books) in 1934 at more than one dollar.

If we extend our analysis to the classification by year of incorporation the distinction between corporations in existence for the entire period 1925-34 and those coming into existence during the ten years appears rather significant. The companies incorporated prior to 1925 wrote off an appreciably larger portion of their property accounts than did those in existence only part of the decade studied. This is true, also, of investments. In writing down intangibles, however, the newer companies considerably exceeded the older concerns. With respect to write-ups of intangibles and of property the relative positions are reversed.

The revaluations made by corporations in existence during the entire decade may be examined in greater detail (Table 3).[*] The most highly concentrated distributions

TABLE 2

TOTAL WRITE-UPS AND WRITE-DOWNS, 1925-1934, IN RELATION TO NET BOOK VALUES OF CORRESPONDING ASSETS IN 1934

PERIOD DURING WHICH INCORPORATED	NUMBER OF CORPORATIONS	AGGREGATE WRITE-UPS	AGGREGATE WRITE-DOWNS	NET BOOK VALUE OF ASSETS (1934)	AGGREGATE WRITE-UPS	AGGREGATE WRITE-DOWNS
		(in thousands of dollars)			(as percentages of net book value of assets)	
		PROPERTY, PLANT AND EQUIPMENT				
Before 1925	153	86,131	567,060	4,907,614	1.76	11.55
1925-1934	55	90,754	102,092	1,504,039	6.03	6.79
Total	208	176,885	669,152	6,411,653	2.76	10.44
		INTANGIBLES				
Before 1925	153	52,587	254,837	308,309	17.06	82.66
1925-1934	55	890	53,515	21,260	4.19	251.72
Total	208	53,477	308,352	329,569	16.23	93.56
		INVESTMENTS				
Before 1925	153	202,293	165,521	943,599	21.44	17.54
1925-1934	55	17,823	31,349	249,292	7.15	12.58
Total	208	220,116	196,870	1,192,891	18.45	16.50

TABLE 3

WRITE-UPS AND WRITE-DOWNS, 1925-34, AS PERCENTAGES OF THE NET BOOK VALUES OF THE CORRESPONDING ASSETS IN 1934

Frequency distribution by size of percentage

Each corporation counts as one item[1]

Percentage[2]	PROPERTY, PLANT AND EQUIPMENT			INTANGIBLE ASSETS			INVESTMENTS		
	Write-up	Write-down	Net Write-up	Write-up	Write-down	Net Write-up	Write-up	Write-down	Net Write-up
∞[3]				2		1	2		
140.0 and over	1						7		4
130.0 to 139.9									
120.0 to 129.9	1								
110.0 to 119.9	1								
100.0 to 109.9									
90.0 to 99.9							1		1
80.0 to 89.9									
70.0 to 79.9									
60.0 to 69.9	1			1					
50.0 to 59.9	1		2				1		1
40.0 to 49.9	3		2				2		
30.0 to 39.9	1		2		1		1		2
20.0 to 29.9	3		1				2		2
10.0 to 19.9							2		
0.1 to 9.9	20		7				6		
0.0	121	79	73	150	98	98	129	99	95
—0.1 to —9.9		20	17	2	2			8	6
—10.0 to —19.9		9	8	1	1			4	4
—20.0 to —29.9		5	5	1	1			2	2
—30.0 to —39.9		8	9	1				5	6
—40.0 to —49.9		2	1					3	3
—50.0 to —59.9		1	2					1	1
—60.0 to —69.9		4	2	1	1			1	1
—70.0 to —79.9		8	7					2	
—80.0 to —89.9		2	2	1	1			3	5
—90.0 to —99.9		2	2					3	
—100.0 to —109.9		1	1						
—110.0 to —119.9		1	1					1	1
—120.0 to —129.9					1	1		2	2
—130.0 to —139.9								1	1
—140.0 and under		11	9		9	9		12	11
—∞[3]					38	37		6	5
Total	153	153	153	153	153	153	153	153	153

[1] Only corporations in existence during the entire period are included.

[2] The classes '140.0 and over' and '—140.0 and under' do not include the items of infinite size.

[3] Infinite: denominator is zero.

are those for revaluations of property, plant and equipment. A definite and thick clustering about the zero point is noticeable. This means that the amount of write-up or write-down of property, plant and equipment is rather small for most companies; that, relatively speaking, there were only a few large write-ups or write-downs of this asset. Revaluations of investments were also small for

most companies but there were large amounts of write-ups and write-downs for more companies than in the case of property, plant and equipment. That is, the frequencies decrease less rapidly as the zero point is left behind. For intangibles the distribution is quite strange. Of the 55 reporting write-downs, 38 had completely written down their intangible assets.[*] It is therefore to be expected that

[†] The younger companies are omitted to avoid the possible lack of comparability that may arise from their absence during part of the period 1925-34.

[*] A qualification must be applied to the zero class in the above distributions. It will be remembered that a majority of the companies in the sample show no value of intangible assets at all.

revaluation of intangibles will tend, more than revaluations of other assets, to introduce divergencies in rates of profits, by affecting book values of net worth.

REVALUATIONS BY YEARS

The distribution of number and amount of revaluations among the years covered in our survey concerns us next (Tables 4 and 5).

Write-ups of property, plant and equipment reached a peak, in respect of number, in 1928. In 1932 and 1933 there were none. A roughly similar time pattern is found in the upward revaluations of intangible assets, though the total number involved is too small to provide much evidence. With respect to investments, write-ups fluctuated much less; consequently the turning points are less definitely established.

The effects of the most recent depression are reflected sharply in the number of write-downs of property and investments. The number of downward revaluations of tangible fixed assets fell slowly to 1928-29 and then shot up, reaching a high in 1932. Similar fluctuations are apparent for investments except that the rise to 1932 is more rapid (in percentage terms). No reliable indications of a decline between 1925 and 1928 are available. Write-

Footnote 8 concluded
Therefore a large number of companies with intangible assets valued at zero, and with no revaluations of intangibles, should be placed in a separate (indeterminate) class, since 0÷0 is mathematically indeterminate. These, however, have been placed in the zero class.

downs did not decline between 1933 and 1934, as in property, plant and equipment. The number of write-downs of intangibles did not increase appreciably between 1928 and 1932. The distribution in time is similar in some respects to that of investment write-ups. The small rise in 1932 and the relatively large number as early as 1925 lend support to the belief that intangibles are written down when business is good, to indicate caution, as frequently as they are written down when times are bad and values appear to be tottering or to have crashed.

The data on the number of revaluations may be supplemented by those on the amount. The two sets of data are of interest from different points of view, and in conjunction throw light on the changing magnitude of revaluations per company, as well as per year. From the viewpoint of economic behavior those on number are most useful, indicating more clearly the reactions of business men as reflected by changes in their accounting habits. The amount of revaluations in each year is useful in interpreting aggregate book values of assets and capital.

In the main, the material bearing on the amount of revaluations confirms the evidence gained from the number of companies involved. There are some discrepancies in high and low points: in 1926 write-downs of property account were larger than in 1928; the fewest occurred in 1930. Of the write-downs of tangible fixed assets 44 per cent were made in the one year 1932 and 18 per cent in 1931. During the four years 1931-34, 84 per cent of the aggregate write-downs of the decade occurred.

TABLE 4

CORPORATIONS REPORTING REVALUATIONS OF FIXED ASSETS, 1925-1934, NUMBER, BY YEARS

CORPORATIONS INCORPORATED BEFORE 1925	1925	1926	1927	1928	1929	1930	1931	1932	1933	1934
Write-ups										
Property, plant and equipment	4	4	7	13	7	4	3	....	....	1
Intangibles	....	....	....	2	1	1	....	....	....	....
Investments	4	4	3	2	3	2	1	3	3	7
Write-downs										
Property, plant and equipment	9	8	7	6	6	8	24	30	22	13
Intangibles	11	8	7	10	7	4	10	11	5	6
Investments	2	1	1	2	5	7	15	23	13	13
Total number of corporations	153	153	153	153	153	153	153	153	153	153
ALL CORPORATIONS IN SAMPLE										
Write-ups										
Property, plant and equipment	6	9	11	18	10	5	6	1	1	3
Intangibles	....	....	1	2	1	1	1	1	....	....
Investments	4	5	4	3	3	3	2	3	5	11
Write-downs										
Property, plant and equipment	10	9	8	7	9	11	30	41	33	19
Intangibles	13	10	11	14	12	6	11	12	9	6
Investments	3	1	3	4	8	10	20	31	18	18
Total number of corporations	159	172	181	192	199	201	202	207	208	208

TABLE 5

WRITE-UPS AND WRITE-DOWNS, 1925-1934, AMOUNT, BY YEARS

Reported by corporations in existence during the entire period[1]

(thousands of dollars)

	1925	1926	1927	1928	1929	1930	1931	1932	1933	1934
Write-ups										
Property, plant and equipment	10,254	6,614	15,980	24,086	11,426	12,315	5,343	....	....	77
Intangibles	....	....	....	16,442	25,559	10,586	....	....	....	....
Investments	17,938	33,140	7,046	6,155	24,967	3,762	49	417	1,057	8,517
Write-downs										
Property, plant and equipment	12,495	24,008	10,471	21,474	10,171	7,630	96,698	236,263	60,984	59,730
Intangibles	48,370	7,918	14,308	49,514	29,191	13,801	11,776	42,000	10,193	11,653
Investments	158	25	582	4,779	13,579	2,975	29,404	39,745	35,342	37,081
Net write-ups										
Property, plant and equipment	—2,241	—17,394	5,509	2,612	1,255	4,685	—91,355	—236,263	—60,984	—59,653
Intangibles	—48,370	—7,918	—14,308	—33,072	—3,632	—3,215	—11,776	—42,000	—10,193	—11,653
Investments	17,780	33,115	6,464	1,376	11,388	787	—29,355	—39,328	—34,285	—28,564

[1] The sum of the figures on any line does not exactly equal the corresponding aggregate in Table 2 since the latter includes some revaluations not allocated to any specific year of the period 1925-34.

The net difference between write-ups and write-downs reveals interesting features. In no year is there a net write-up of intangibles. The cyclical movements in the other two series are sharp and reflect the state of general business on the one hand and the stock market on the other.

The increase in amount of write-downs per company, of tangible fixed assets, between 1929 and 1932, is sharp. While number of write-downs rose from 6 to 30, or five-fold, the amount in dollars rose from 10 million to 236 million, or over twenty-three-fold. In investments, however, no such clear relationship and divergence is evident in the two series of number and amount.

The diverse behavior of the three classes of fixed assets reflects the factors affecting the amount and number of revaluations. To these factors we now turn.

REASONS OFFERED FOR REVALUATIONS

We have been concerned with describing the fixed assets most commonly affected by revaluations, the relative number of concerns involved and the amount of revaluations made by them, and the distribution of number and amount over the decade studied. What are the reasons offered in explanation of these various revaluations?

The type of assets involved and the relative amounts of revaluations reported for each, and their time distribution in relation to what we know of the corresponding state of business, in themselves throw light on these reasons. But there is more direct information provided in many of the original reports. Let us examine this material first.

Discrepancy between book value and some sort of 'current value' is the basis of practically all revaluations. In most of the reports that included some explanation of the entries recorded the only statement was simply to the effect

that an appraisal had been made of property, plant and equipment. Some 40 of the companies reporting write-ups and write-downs of property offer this explanation. In a sense, of course, any revaluation implies an appraisal as of a given moment. But as used here, and as understood in accounting reports, the term 'appraisal' is confined to a rather detailed inspection of physical condition together with a study of obsolescence and current reproduction costs. Not always are these appraisals reported as 'independent'— that is, made by outside experts. Some companies state that their assets were revalued simply on the basis of opinions or decisions of officers or directors.

Appraisals are usually made because a decision to revalue has already been more or less definitely formed. To this extent the opinions of officers and directors underlie every appraisal and therefore every revaluation based upon an appraisal. Necessarily these opinions and decisions also underlie every retention of existing book values.

Some companies appear to be in the habit of using expert appraisals as aids in their accounting. Thus, the F. E. Myers & Bro. Co. reports appraisals on three separate occasions, 1922, 1927 and 1933, all resulting in revaluations.

Even an independent appraisal is still subject to the superior will and responsibility of the officers and directors of a corporation. Occasionally, appraisal does not lead to immediate or ultimate revaluation, or the appraisal may be modified by decision of the directors. For example, the F. E. Myers & Bro. Co. entered one appraisal only partly at the time it was made. The balance was, however, recorded at a later date. A 1920 appraisal of the assets of Bucyrus-Erie was not written into the books until 1925. A curious appraisal of an appraisal was made when "ap praised sound values" of the property of General Cable were discounted 20 per cent and only then entered in the records.

Appraisals, of course, are not reasons for revaluations but only methods of getting at the amounts by which to revalue. They can tell us nothing in themselves of these reasons except to suggest that the fundamental factors were sufficiently strong to be sensed by the officials ordering the appraisals.

More explicit as to the kind of 'value' substituted for the superseded book value are those explanations mentioning anticipations of losses on disposal of property. These are reported by several corporations. One, George A. Fuller Company, anticipated and recorded a gain. But even this explanation tells us little as to the basic causes.

More fundamental are such factors as changes in general price levels, discovered obsolescence, and errors in earlier estimates of depreciation and depletion. Price changes are mentioned specifically by some ten corporations as the cause of the revaluations made by them. In one or two instances (e.g., Mohawk Carpet) mention is made of "current reproductive costs new" as the revised basis of book values. Changing current prices had a continuous effect on the book values of depletable assets of one subsidiary of the American Smelting and Refining Company. This company valued the "known and probable" ore in its mineral lands on the basis of the average price of metals received by it the preceding ten years. As a result, revaluations were upward in 1927, 1928 and 1929, and downward in each of the five years following. Part of these revaluations represented, of course, some allowance for depletion and made it unnecessary to compute depletion separately, since even if prices remained constant, the changing amount of ore in the mineral lands would result in a downward revaluation.

Obsolescence is mentioned specifically in only a few reports. As we shall see later, however, it is probably a major factor accounting for downward revaluations.

Revised estimates of earlier charges for depreciation and depletion are responsible for a considerable number of revaluations of property account. About a dozen reports mention this. Most of these refer to decisions of the Treasury Department in connection with the assessment of income taxes. In one or two the depreciation or depletion base also was adjusted.

Broader changes in the methods of accounting for fixed assets, as well as in the application of methods already in use, are responsible for certain revaluations. For example, development of mines and oil wells, formerly charged to income, are now often capitalized and written off periodically through depreciation charges. A change of this sort requires that the value of developments already charged to

income but still rendering service be added to fixed assets. A few instances of this sort were discovered, including the Standard Oil Company of Kansas. This change of policy was rather wide-spread after the beginning of the recent severe depression.

Other instances of changes in accounting policy occur in the case of patents (The Paraffine Cos., Inc.), improvements (South American Gold and Platinum), and lease rentals (Standard Oil of Kansas).

The idleness of certain portions of plant is given as grounds for write-down of values by ten or twelve corporations. Naturally, it is more or less permanent idleness that is anticipated. The anticipation of permanent disuse may reflect only the pessimistic mood inherent in a long and severe depression, and the concomitant conservatism it engenders. Where actually permanent this idleness is, to some extent, a consequence of obsolescence, and to some extent a result of over-investment in the preceding period of prosperity. When only temporary, write-downs arising from disuse of property may be expected to be cancelled later when fears are not realized. This is true in several instances (e.g., Gotham Silk Hose). At least one company (General Motors), however, counterbalanced restorations of the value of formerly idle property by contra entries to reserves for depreciation.

This cancelling of earlier revaluations by further revaluations is not restricted to entries arising from idle facilities. On the contrary, a considerable number, especially of write-downs during the last few years, represent cancellations of write-ups at earlier dates. Such cancellations are reported, in our sample, by as many as thirty companies. In one or two it is a revaluation by a predecessor company that is eliminated. Some of these revaluations follow one another in a rather striking manner (Byron Jackson Company, Ludlum Steel). One company (Superior Oil) reports a write-down during receivership (1931) of a former recording (1929) of an "excess appraisal value". This practice of a mutual cancelling of write-ups and write-downs is indicated by Table 6 relating to the property account. A distinct correlation is apparent although it is not high. Of the 31 companies reporting write-ups 21 (or two-thirds) reported write-downs also. But only 74 of the

TABLE 6

RELATIONSHIP OF WRITE-UPS AND WRITE-DOWNS OF PROPERTY, PLANT AND EQUIPMENT

NUMBER OF COMPANIES[1]	REPORTING WRITE-DOWNS	REPORTING NO WRITE-DOWNS	TOTAL NUMBER
Reporting write-ups	21	10	31
Reporting no write-ups	53	69	122
Total number	74	79	153

[1] Only corporations in existence during each year 1925-34 are included.

total 153 (or less than one-half) reported write-downs. If the latter ratio had applied also to the group of companies reporting write-ups, we would have expected to find only 15 reporting write-downs, instead of the 21 actually doing so.[9]

The almost universal streak of caution in business men, found side by side with receptivity to current moods, underlies many of the entries discussed above. The presence of write-downs when facilities are idle or when loss on disposal is anticipated, and the many absences of write-ups, reflect such caution. It is particularly clear, however, in the treatment of intangible fixed assets—patents, goodwill, trade-marks.

Intangible assets are reported, as already mentioned, by only 60 of the 208 companies in our sample. Many companies wrote off intangible assets as soon as they were acquired by purchase from other concerns (Borden, Devoe and Reynolds, Dupont, etc.). In other companies, when tangible fixed assets were written up, the surplus thus created was used to extinguish intangibles (Continental Can, City Ice & Fuel, Sharon Steel Hoop, Addressograph-Multigraph). When acquired for value paid, of course, adequate justification has appeared for placing intangibles upon the books.

With respect to investments, most revaluations appear to be the result of changes in market values. Differences between cost and value on the books of the issuing company also have often been eliminated in the form of a write-down. (Occasionally such differences are recorded as intangible assets.) Rather often, investments are kept on the books on a lower of cost or market basis, which may mean write-downs in a falling market, and restoration of the cost basis in a rising market. Book values of investments are also affected by the financial condition and prospects of the companies, especially subsidiaries, whose securities are being held. To some extent investments in foreign subsidiaries have been revalued as foreign exchange rates have fluctuated (National Cash Register).

So much for the explanations given in the reports; further information is provided by the figures themselves. The distribution of revaluations among the various assets, especially the proportionately large volume of write-downs of intangibles, and the response in number and amount of revaluations to the conditions prevailing during the recent severe depression further emphasize the nature of the forces making for revaluation of assets. The strange compound of conservatism and optimism, major changes in price levels, changes in accounting practice (changes that are themselves reflections of current business conditions), obso-

lescence uncovered in a severe depression—these are the factors and conditions affecting valuations on the books of business enterprises.

These bits of evidence may be supplemented by other data collected, through direct questionnaires, by the National Association of Cost Accountants.[10] Members of the association were asked, early in 1933, whether asset values should be written down. Of 117 cost accountants replying, 85 were in favor of writing down assets. Of these, 13 favored "present market value", 64 favored "net sound value" and 9 some other value. Only 13 were ready to accept "present market value", 64 advocating a net sound value which must have meant, to them, some value greater than "present" market value, probably being more in line with their estimates of future market values. The complete record is as follows:

Number of members replying to questionnaire		1?
Those against writing down assets		3?
Those in favor of writing down assets		8?
To present market value	13	
To net sound value	64	
To some other value	9	
Number of companies in which assets have not been written down		7?
Number of companies in which assets have been marked down		4?
Number of companies marking down		
Assets now or expected to be in use	35	
Assets not now or expected to be in use	33	
Assets in both groups	22	
Number of members in favor of marking down assets whose companies have not written down their assets		4?

It is difficult to determine just which factors made such a large number of the cost accountants favor the writing down of assets. "Present market value" implies, although not necessarily, that the collapse of prices was most influential. But even if we assume this, it must be remembered that 73 other accountants favored other values. It is probably not unfair to conclude that besides the fall in prices the existence of unused capacity was also a powerful force. Indeed, in the report of the St. Louis Chapter of the Association, the entire discussion of revaluation is related primarily to the existence of idle facilities. The fact that of 46 companies 33 wrote down idle plant, 11 writing down only idle plant, adds weight to the conclusion that obsolescence, unwise expansion, and the mood of depression were important elements.

We have reviewed some of the reasons offered for the revaluations made in the years covered by our survey.

[9] The significance of the difference between 15 and 21 may be demonstrated by technical statistical means.

[10] N.A.C.A. Bulletin, Section I, March 15, 1933, p. 1037; and "Idle Plant Facilities, Excess Plant Values", Report of National Association of Cost Accountants Conference (St. Louis Chapter, April 6, 1933 (mimeographed).

One of the features of the reports is the small place speci-cally accorded to such factors as faulty investment and bsolescence (assuming that these really can be distin-uished). But it is probably in the nature of the records lat they do not reveal the really fundamental factors.")ver-investment during prosperity, and changes in tastes nd technique that lead to obsolescence, find their concrete xpression in the form of idle property—unused plant—in epression. It is this concrete expression that is noted in ae records as the immediate cause of write-down.

Obsolescence appears in depression more often than in rosperity since at the latter time most capacity is in full se. The apparently temporary write-downs in severe de-ression are often really permanent write-downs, not mere-' a reflection of the moment's mood. But obsolescence is evealed also to some extent even in prosperity. It may e doubted, therefore, whether in the near future write-ups ill exceed write-downs, as a consequence of the restora-on, even if partial, of earlier (1929) price levels. It is robable that write-downs always tend to exceed write-ups, xcept possibly during or immediately after a tremendous flation, and that this excess is a reflection of the obsoles-ence not accounted for in depreciation charges.

One further question arises, namely, why so many ompanies do not revalue their assets. As we have seen Table 3), of 153 corporations, 79 did not write down eir property, plant and equipment during the decade udied, although this period included one of the severest ad longest depressions on record. Since no explanations e given, obviously only an opinion can be hazarded as to e reasons. Among these, first place must be given to the eight of accounting usage. The accounting apparatus rips most firmly those figures that are based on original st, figures that are as comfortable as old friends and as nchanging, tried as they are by the acid test of the paid ucher. Other reasons are also related to accounting actices; for example, the regulations of the Treasury De-artment which refuses to accept revaluations for tax pur-ses. The legal theory of the inviolability of corporate pital, confused though it be, may also exercise some in-uence.

It thus becomes necessary, if a conclusive statement is to be ade about the basic factors, to approach the problem from other angle by utilizing materials not given in the reports. his Bulletin presents some preliminary results derived from only e body of data.

The whole problem of revaluation is part of the broader oblem of the factors making for profits and losses. A detailed idy of the fortunes of individual industries and enterprises, ith reference to changes in demand, technology, supply prices of mpeting and joint factors of production, the state of competi-n, and legislative enactments, is required to get at a full ex-anation of the basic factors underlying revaluations.

Revaluations may not be made simply because of a re-fusal to recognize current conditions as anything but tem-porary. Such optimism (or pessimism) may persist even in the face of a fairly long period of depression or pros-perity; it is not always misplaced in so far as the ordinary business cycle is concerned.

Finally, it may be considered undesirable to revalue as-sets in order to avoid certain effects upon calculations of profits or book capital, and upon those who use these rec-ords—investors, bankers and stockholders. Or if these effects be felt desirable it may be considered unnecessary to go to the trouble of revaluation in order to attain them. This brings us to the question of the effects of revaluations, which are two-fold: they influence measures of both cap-ital and income.

EFFECTS OF REVALUATIONS

The effect on measures of fixed assets, particularly prop-erty, plant and equipment, is illustrated by certain figures collected from published reports by Arthur H. Winakor (Table 7). The individual industries given are those in

TABLE 7

CHANGES IN NET BOOK VALUE OF PROPERTY, PLANT AND EQUIP-MENT, INDUSTRIAL CORPORATIONS[1]

INDUSTRY	NET BOOK VALUE IN 1932 AS A PER-CENTAGE OF THE 1927 VALUE	
	Ignoring revalua-tions of assets	Correcting for revaluations of assets
Total	104	113
Selected industries		
Apparel	67	97
Aviation and auto accessories	101	123
Chemicals	123	142
Machinery and tools	92	100
Petroleum	104	119

[1] Arthur H. Winakor, "Maintenance of Working Capital of In-dustrial Corporations by Conversion of Fixed Assets", University of Illinois, January 23, 1934, pp. 25-6. The total number of com-panies covered is 182.

which the effect of write-ups and write-downs seemed es-pecially large. The greatest difference between book value and book value adjusted for revaluations occurs in the ap-parel industry, where it amounts to over 30 per cent of the latter figure. The property account of all industries com-bined was affected by revaluations to the extent of 8 per cent. But not only the aggregate of the assets, and the measures of total national wealth in which they are includ-ed, are subject to the influence of revaluations. Industrial comparisons and comparisons of individual companies are affected even more strongly.

Revaluations affect, also, estimates of certain current costs—depreciation and depletion—and therefore estimates of profits. They need not do so, of course. Appreciation may be written off by charging depreciation on the appreciated portion not to current income account but to surplus. There are several instances of this practice in the corporate reports examined here (e.g., Evans Products). Depreciation may continue to be charged on written-off property (that has been restored to use) and added to costs, the corresponding credit being to some surplus account (Snider Packing). Or, as one cost accountant suggested, write-down may be accomplished by setting up a reserve for property revaluation, allowing the assets to be carried at cost in the books for depreciation purposes and at present replacement value on the balance sheet.[12] Further, as already mentioned, there are the restrictions of the income tax laws which do not permit revaluations to affect the amount of depreciation charges deducted in computing taxable net income. But on the whole, the ordinary records of business depreciation and depletion are definitely affected. Indeed, actual revaluation is not necessary for this result to be accomplished. Recognition of the factors involved, leading to a change in depreciation rates, or to charging to accounts other than cost of sales the burden resulting from idle facilities, accomplishes much the same result.[13]

The effects on the computation of costs and profits are obvious. Indeed, an argument offered for writing off plant values is that it leaves the company in a "splendid competitive market position".[14] That is, its costs are lowered by the amount of depreciation on the values written off. The extent to which aggregate costs affect competitive position is, of course, a problem in itself. But in any event, the computed profits are definitely affected. With them are affected the available measures of corporate savings and of national income.

Measurement of the *rate* of profits is influenced by revaluations in two ways. The numerator, net income, is

[12] St. Louis Chapter of the N.A.C.A., *op. cit.*, p. 13.

[13] See the interesting answers to questions bearing on these points in the report of the N.A.C.A. Conference (St. Louis Chapter) already cited.

[14] Cf. W. A. Layman, *The Annalist*, August 25, 1933.

TABLE 8

TOTAL REVALUATIONS OF FIXED ASSETS, 1925-1934, AS PERCENTAGES OF THE NET BOOK VALUES OF TOTAL ASSETS IN 1934

Frequency distribution by size of percentage

Each corporation counts as one item[1]

Percentage	WRITE-UP Number	WRITE-UP Percentage	WRITE-DOWN Number	WRITE-DOWN Percentage	NET WRITE-UP Number	NET WRITE-UP Percentage
70.0 and over	1	.7				
60.0 to 69.9	2	1.3			1	.7
50.0 to 59.9	1	.7				
40.0 to 49.9	1	.7				
30.0 to 39.9	4	2.6			1	.7
20.0 to 29.9	3	2.0			3	2.0
10.0 to 19.9	6	3.9			3	2.0
0.1 to 9.9	34	22.2			7	4.6
0.0	101	66.0	42	27.5	40	26.2
−0.1 to −9.9			44	28.8	39	25.5
−10.0 to −19.9			15	9.8	13	8.5
−20.0 to −29.9			10	6.5	9	5.9
−30.0 to −39.9			10	6.5	11	7.2
−40.0 to −49.9			7	4.6	6	3.9
−50.0 to −59.9			3	2.0	2	1.3
−60.0 to −69.9			7	4.6	4	2.6
−70.0 to −79.9			1	.7	1	.7
−80.0 to −89.9			1	.7	1	.7
−90.0 to −99.9			3	2.0	2	1.3
−100.0 to −109.9					2	1.3
−110.0 to −119.9			3	2.0	1	.7
−120.0 to −129.9						
−130.0 to −139.9						
−140.0 to −149.9			3	2.0	4	2.6
−150.0 and under			4	2.6	3	2.0
Total	153	100.0	153	100.0	153	100.0

[1] Only corporations in existence during the entire period are included.

affected, and the denominator, net worth, as well. But while both change in the same direction the extent of the change is different. Some light is thrown on the possible effects of revaluations on measures of corporate net worth by the figures collected in our study. Table 8 suggests the influence of total write-ups and write-downs on total assets (which include, besides fixed assets, cash, inventories and accounts receivable). Most write-ups of fixed assets during 1925-34 were small, only 18 companies (12 per cent of the total number) reporting upward revaluations exceeding 10 per cent of total assets at the end of 1934. Write-downs exceeding 10 per cent of total assets were much more frequent. As many as 67 concerns wrote down fixed assets by more than 10 per cent, 42 writing down over 30 per cent of 1934 total assets. The net figure, write-ups less write-downs, was also large for many corporations.

About 5 per cent of the companies reported net upward revaluations exceeding 10 per cent of total assets, while almost 40 per cent reported net write-downs of more than 10 per cent of all assets. Of these, 20 companies, or over 13 per cent of the total, revealed net write-downs during the decade exceeding half of their total assets in 1934. The ratio of net worth to total assets is roughly 0.75. The effects on net worth, therefore, are understated by the figures in the table.

Because of revaluations, comparisons of profitability must be made with full recognition of the complicating features of book values. Their importance, especially to stockholders and prospective investors, is attested by the fact that our basic data originate in an attempt, by the Securities and Exchange Commission, to supply these groups with the necessary information.

ON THE TREATMENT OF CORPORATE
SAVINGS IN THE MEASUREMENT
OF NATIONAL INCOME

SOLOMON FABRICANT

I Nature of the Problem

OUR PROBLEM is part of the general problem of determining the accuracy with which the sum of personal incomes and business savings measures national income produced. More specifically, we are interested in the extent to which the concepts underlying current accounting estimates of corporate savings are congruent with the concepts of national income. The desirability of including any savings at all in the measurement of national income will not be discussed here. Since our point of view will be primarily that of national income as a measure of the productivity of an economic system, we shall be concerned only with national income produced.

One purpose of our analysis is to suggest that diverse treatment of corporate savings in the measurement of national income is desirable. The limitations of a general-purpose measure of national income, even of national income produced, must be recognized. Further, we wish to indicate the lines that such alternatives might take. Whether any particular modification of the accounting figures is desirable depends also on its relative importance and statistical practicability, concerning neither of which can much be said here. But the following discussion will, it is hoped, bring into the open the characteristics of the data with which we must

113

work, and thus the assumptions implicit in using the available figures.

Certain characteristics of the available data on net business savings or losses, which condition their interpretation, have already been mentioned by earlier writers.[1] Among these characteristics are the practice of including some profits and losses on the sale of capital assets in business savings, the estimation of depreciation charges on the basis of original cost, and the valuation of inventories at the lower of cost or market. These and other practices will concern us here.

First, we shall be concerned with the reasons for segregating corporate savings from other elements in national income. Second, we shall consider the fiscal period and the manner in which its choice is related to many of the difficulties encountered in the use of business data in the measurement of national income. Next we shall discuss in detail some of the difficulties arising from the use of an annual accounting period. These difficulties revolve about the time-allocation of revenue and cost, the fact of price changes, and the distinction between capital and revenue items. Finally, certain incidental problems of duplication and omission will be examined. Throughout, the discussion will deal with savings by private business only; no consideration will be given to the savings of public and semi-public bodies.

II Segregation of Corporate Savings

Before discussing the difficulties encountered in the utilization of business data, it is desirable to point out the characteristics that distinguish corporate savings from other business savings and make it worth while to present them apart from other savings.[2] These are first, that corporate savings are computed on the basis of a relatively sophisticated accounting technique; second, that

[1] See Simon Kuznets, 'National Income', *Encyclopedia of the Social Sciences*, XI, pp. 205–24. See also W. C. Mitchell and Simon Kuznets, 'Current Problems in Measurement of National Income', XXIIe Session de L'Institut International de Statistique, London, 1934 (La Haye, 1934).

[2] R. R. Nathan has presented the two groups of savings separately in the Department of Commerce estimates, *National Income in the United States, 1929–1935* (Washington, 1936).

they are controlled by individuals only indirectly related to the legal owners of the savings.

The form of corporate accounts, more than that of the records of other activities, is dictated. State corporation laws demand the maintenance of capital and prescribe certain records. Regulations as to liability of directors induce care in accounts. The ever-present need for arbitration among the interests of groups with diverse rights and claims to corporate income requires adequacy of records. The stock exchanges, and more recently the Securities and Exchange Commission, enforce minimum accounting requirements. With the resulting accounts may be contrasted the average records kept by small business men, professional workers, and farmers.

There is even reason for distinguishing between small concerns and large, regardless of the fact of incorporation, because of the vaguer line drawn between profits and officers' compensation in the small concerns.[3] Somewhat similar is the lack of distinction in the accounts of single proprietorships, between personal and business transactions.[4]

The point made by Simon Kuznets that net business savings or losses "can hardly be classified as a current income share of any individual member of the various (economic) groups"[5] is reason for distinguishing all business savings from other savings. The savings of a business are largely determined by the financial exigencies it encounters and by the character of its assets, rather than by any individual's personal desire to save or consume in-

[3] Even in the case of large companies, officers' salaries and other compensation possess certain entrepreneurial characteristics. It would be desirable to segregate officers' compensation in presenting data on salaries in estimates of national income.

[4] Cf. R. F. Martin, *Survey of Current Business*, January 1935. The lack of such a distinction does not mean, however, that the economist cannot or should not impose one of his own. As we shall see, even in corporate accounting, where an elaborate body of technique is well established, it is necessary to make many adjustments before the data that are the product of this technique are suitable for use in estimates of national income or wealth. These and other adjustments are also required in the case of entrepreneurial savings and income. We cannot accept, from either corporations or individual entrepreneurs, their own estimates as to their status. Not that these estimates are irrelevant to an analysis of the factors affecting economic behavior. But as measures from a national point of view, they are simply rough materials requiring adjustment.

[5] *Bulletin 59*, National Bureau of Economic Research (May 4, 1936), pp. 11–12.

come.[6] The *de facto* separation, in corporations, of the decision to save from the legal claim to the savings is reason for the further step of subdividing all business savings into corporate and other business savings. The dictated character of business savings and the separation of ownership from control are both reflected in the lack of stability of dividends during the last few years, despite the presence in many corporations of adequate balance-sheet surpluses and undivided profits.

None of these characteristics of corporate savings separates it clearly from other business savings. Thus, large partnerships may possess the attributes of corporations so far as their savings are concerned, and logically the savings of these two groups should be combined. The legal status of a group is not the prime consideration. Certain types of trust, joint-stock companies, associations and other 'quasi-corporate' bodies belong within the category of corporations, and are so regarded by the Treasury Department.[7] On the other hand, closely held corporations should, from an economic point of view, be omitted from the category with which we are dealing.

Nor is the characteristic of profit-making controlling. For example, the reserves of life insurance companies are not entirely subject to the call of individual policy holders; therefore any changes in their volume might conceivably be included with corporate savings or at least segregated from individual savings. These considerations apply especially to the annual earnings of these so-called 'associations of individuals', which are only partly credited to the individual accounts of members. All this is true of most of the tax-exempt corporations listed in the income tax law.[8]

We now pass to a discussion of the fiscal period and its relation to the available data on corporate savings. The distinction between corporate and other business savings raised above is not involved in the succeeding discussion, except that a certain level of adequacy of accounting records is taken for granted.

[6] To some extent this is true even of individual investments, the status of which affects further decisions to save. But a going concern is subject to a different order of financial pressure than any individual holder of securities.
[7] *Regulations 86, Income Tax, Revenue Act of 1934* (Washington, 1935), pp. 372–5.
[8] *Ibid.*, Section 101.

III The Fiscal Period

The first problem in the periodic determination of income is the appropriate allocation, over time, of revenues and costs. This implies the selection of a fiscal period. The difficulties and principles of allocation are dependent on the length of this period. Thus, while actual allocations are usually made forward in time, not backward, and involve some foresight, even current allocations may be made with the benefit of hindsight, to an extent limited of course by the length of the accounting period. The length of the fiscal period is intimately bound up not only with the problem of allocation, but also with the problems of price changes and of credits and charges on capital as against revenue account. Except for certain incidental problems of duplication and omission, the proper definition and measure of corporate (and other business) savings is made difficult by the use of an annual fiscal period by business men. Many of the difficulties involved in the pricing of inventories and capital goods, in the choice of a straight line depreciation formula as against a unit of production formula, and in the question of capital gains and losses, vanish when a proper accounting period is selected.[9] These problems are but detailed aspects of the general problem of the fiscal period. We therefore turn to it first.

The difficulties involved in the selection of a suitable fiscal period are illustrated by the apparent effect of crop variation upon the real national income. Is an ordinary variation in size of crops due to the usual natural elements to be considered as properly reflecting the annual efficiency of the economic system? It is arguable that a better measure of the economic machine's efficiency is the volume of crops available for consumption. A more 'natural' fiscal period than the year, one long enough to smooth out ordinary fluctuations in yield, would seem to be called for.

The same argument applies also in the case of 'purely' economic fluctuations. If business and industry are subject to sys-

[9] Many difficulties arising out of price changes may eventually be solved by the process of deflation in arriving at the 'real' national income. In measuring income in 'current' prices, however, the fiscal period must be considered. But even the deflation process implies a consideration of the fiscal period and its related problems. See the discussion in Section V below.

tematic fluctuations, movements that are cumulative connected processes persisting over periods longer than a year, the efficiency of output of the economy is most accurately measured not by ordinary annual accounts but by accounts covering a complete cycle. Once the cyclical movements of industry and business are recognized as characteristic of a modern economy, national income annually produced does not represent the fruit of that year's activities any more than does the crop reaped on a farm in a given month measure that month's income.

It is not essential that the theory of fluctuations implied be of the type in which depression leads to prosperity without any discontinuity between successive cycles. When a given cyclical process extends over a period longer than twelve months, *ordinary* annual estimates cannot be accepted as direct measures of national income. Measures related to periods shorter than the 'natural' economic fiscal period are merely raw material for the appraisal of results and the analysis of processes. We can understand the seasonal character of plant growth by monthly observations and thus construct a theory of crop growth from which we can get an inkling of the size of the final crop by monthly inspection. But the results can be accurate only to the extent of the adequacy of the theory. And they are always subject to correction when the crop matures.

Owing to irregularities in the duration and amplitude of cyclical movements, the accounting of economic processes is extremely difficult. We are never quite sure when our 'natural' fiscal period has ended! But despite the difficulties involved, this view of economic accounting as related to an organic process seems more satisfactory than any based on an arbitrary time period. A period covering a whole cycle is a more natural economic 'year'.

In much of what follows we shall usually assume the existence of a single, rhythmic type of economic fluctuation. Since our concepts of national income produced must be related to a theory of economic change, it is to be expected that they will improve as our theories gain in comprehensiveness and detail. No final definition of national income is possible in the present state of our knowledge. Or perhaps more correctly, concepts of income may be considered to be tools from which is selected the one best suited to the occasion. And like most tools, improvements in them may be expected to arise as a consequence, to some extent, of their own continued utilization.

Of course, business cycles do not describe the entire organic movement of the economy. Longer cycles and secular movements are also involved. For this reason a fiscal period based on the ordinary business cycle will not remove all our difficulties. Complications arising out of the longer movements remain when we cut across long cycles. For a thoroughgoing concept of national income we need a complete theory of economic development. Thus, in judging the ultimate efficiency of capitalism in relation, for example, to the conservation of natural resources, the business cycle period is clearly inadequate. In this case, a measuring period of secular length might prove more useful. Usually, however, treating the ordinary business cycle as the unit would probably be adequate. The longer cycles seem less relevant to most of the purposes of our records.

A way of overcoming the difficulties associated with an annual fiscal period would thus be to restrict our measures to those relating to entire business cycles. But the advantages of a shorter fiscal period cannot be denied, and need not be lost. We may break down our time unit by eliminating the cyclical fluctuations as a whole by means of some sort of a moving average, or more accurately by a correction analogous to that for seasonal movements.[10] Or we may so allocate revenues and costs as to take proper account of cyclical movements. That is the point to which we are leading. Our allocations must be based on a recognition of the fact of business fluctuations.

Even in accounting allocations of revenue and cost there is implicit some theory of business fluctuations. This inchoate theory usually takes the form of a strong doubt of stability, and manifests itself concretely in conservatism.

---

10 The annual output of an economic system may be judged not only in comparison with its average cyclical behavior, but also in terms of the annual needs of the population. After all, the distribution of national income in time has some relevance to the economic welfare derived from it. A people may starve to death, despite a total income adequate if distributed equally over the period considered. But it may be doubted that national income produced is the proper concept to be used here. Rather, national income consumed or enjoyed appears to be more relevant.

IV The Time-Allocation of Revenue and Cost

Granted that business uses annual estimates, what time-allocation of revenues and costs is common in accounting practice? [11] How satisfactory is it for the measurement of national income?

We shall not cover accounting practice in the detail it perhaps deserves. Its general characteristics are fairly well known. We shall confine our attention to certain outstanding and typical practices.

With a few exceptions, gross income is admitted only in the period when a sale is made. When the annual flow of goods and services is steady, it matters little at which point this flow is measured. But when fluctuations occur, and with them changes in selling prices, the point of measurement affects the measure.[12] It is just because fluctuations in selling prices do occur, however, that gross income is not recorded until a sale is made.

The exceptions in accounting practice occur in the case of long term operations, instalment sales and certain financial accruals. The accrual, before sale, of earnings on long term construction jobs is defended on the ground that such operations are more carefully figured. It is also recognized, however, that when possible deviations between production and sale become very large, some account must be taken of them in the interests of a fundamental accuracy even if relatively rough estimates are needed to do so.

The common treatment of instalment sales is to record revenue when cash is collected rather than when the sale is made. This would appear more conservative than the practice of recording revenue on a long job as production proceeds and before a sale is made. The largest expenditure, on cost of materials, is distributed over the period of collection in accordance with the amounts collected. In both cases, therefore, the procedure is directed to the same end—as far as possible to match revenues with the expenses to which they give rise.

[11] For discussions of the relevant accounting practices, see W. A. Paton (ed.), *Accountants' Handbook*, 2d ed., Section 20 (Ronald, 1933); and J. B. Canning, *Economics of Accountancy* (Ronald, 1929).

[12] Measures will differ only to the extent of the net profits on increments of inventory. But it is these profits with which we are dealing.

Discount on bonds purchased is recorded as revenue with the passage of time, despite the possibly long life of the bonds. It undoubtedly is so treated because of the nature of the asset and the apparent accuracy of the computations involved in the accruals. This appears to be the major exception to the recording of appreciation of capital value as revenue.

Of interest income theoretically accruing on mineral resources [13] and on durable equipment in general no cognizance is taken on the books of corporations. Appreciation of the value of land and other fixed assets also remains unrecorded, except upon realization.

It is most convenient to consider several types of costs piecemeal. In general, it is difficult to say more than that common practice attempts to match corresponding revenues and costs. This is done in the case of long term contracts and jobs by distributing revenue in accordance with the time of the major (prime) costs. The same procedure underlies the general recording of revenue at the time of sale: "the sale can be considered as the most significant event in the whole chain of operating circumstances and conditions—the climax and capstone of production and operation . . . ." [14] Since some overhead costs arise from expenditures on durable goods, however, it is necessary to distribute them over the time periods during which sales are made; that is, over time periods in which the bulk of the prime costs are incurred. But even prime costs require care in allocation.

The first cost we shall consider is that for materials and other items bulking large in inventories. The rather common practice of valuing inventories at cost or market, whichever is lower, (as well as the ordinary retail method of inventory) introduces peculiarities of some importance.[15] (Even in valuation at cost there are certain implications which are considered later.) In the downward phase of business cycles, inventories are valued at market. If physical inventories are constant and prices decline at a constant (arithmetic) rate, no difference between this valuation at market and valuation at cost will appear in the income account.

[13] Harold Hotelling, 'The Economics of Exhaustible Resources', *Journal of Political Economy*, April 1931, p. 170.
[14] *Accountants' Handbook*, p. 1079.
[15] For a more extensive discussion of this point see Simon Kuznets, Part Four.

(The balance sheet will, of course, be different from what it would otherwise be.) If physical inventories decline, however, profits for the period will be greater on the basis of inventories valued at market than they would be with inventories valued at cost. If physical inventories are constant, and prices decline at a decreasing rate, the same will be true. During the upward movement, inventories will be consistently valued at cost. At turning points, the situation is more complicated. In a year in which prices reach a maximum, assuming physical inventories to be constant, recorded profits will be lower with inventories evaluated at market than they would be if the cost basis were used. When prices reach a minimum, recorded profits will be higher.

A rough computation to indicate the possible extent of the above differences is in order.[16] We may assume that prices fall, during recession, at the rate of one per cent per month,[17] and that stocks are on the average about three months old.[18] Then, at the bottom of a depression when prices turn up (for example, in 1933), something like 360 million dollars will be written off inventories at the end of the preceding year and added to profits of the bottom year.[19] While this difference appears rather small, compared with total national income or even with corporate savings alone, it is concentrated in certain industries. In an analysis of the industrial distribution of national income these differences take on weight.

Difficulties in accounting for fixed assets also arise out of fluctuations in the flow of goods and services. If output is steady and the volume of capital used to produce it is also steady it does not matter what treatment is accorded capital equipment. Expendi-

[16] Cf. Colin Clark, *The National Income, 1924–1931* (London: Macmillan, 1932), Appendix I.

[17] The figure for wholesale prices, 1929–33, is 1.1 per cent. See F. C. Mills, *Prices in Recession and Recovery* (National Bureau of Economic Research, 1936), p. 9, footnote 3. During the recession of 1921 the decline was at the rate of 3.0 per cent per month.

[18] The inventory turnover of corporations as a whole was about 5 times in 1929 and 3.5 times in 1932; see the figures in *Statistics of Income.*

[19] Market (end of year) values will be about 3 per cent less than cost, on the assumption of a three month old inventory and a rate of price decline equal to one per cent per month. With corporate inventories equal to about 12 billion (as in 1932), this will mean about 360 million dollars difference between cost and market.

tures upon durable goods may be charged immediately to current output, or they may be capitalized. If capitalized, it does not matter whether depreciation upon them is charged to current costs or whether costs of maintenance (replacements and repairs) are so charged. If depreciated, any depreciation formula may be used with the same results. But output does vary, and the volume of capital goods in existence does not remain constant. Replacements, repairs, use made of old fixed assets, depreciation, do not occur simultaneously. As a consequence, accounting difficulties arise which are met in various ways on the books of business enterprises. Some investments (on intangibles [20] and developments in mining) are charged immediately to current costs, simultaneously with expenditures upon them. In some industries (e.g., steam railroads) the chief measure of capital consumption is the current expenditure upon repairs and replacements; in other industries it is only a supplementary measure covering minor expenditures.[21] In most industries expenditures upon durable goods are distributed among various time periods by some depreciation formula, usually the straight line formula. In some businesses depreciation charges are calculated upon a per unit of output basis; or the straight line formula may be supplemented by a segregation of depreciation on idle facilities. Depletion of forests, mines, quarries and wells are also calculated on a per unit basis.[22] The probable consequences of these diverse treatments may be

[20] Thus, a firm that advertises regularly may cut down its appropriation in a given year without immediately feeling a commensurate disadvantage in its business. Yet this disinvestment—and it is clearly a form of capital consumption—will not be indicated as such on the books. Like other types of under-maintenance, it will be hidden. (Unlike other types, however, the extent of under-maintenance will be influenced by factors external to the particular concern—by the advertising appropriations of other concerns in the same industry and of other industries.)

[21] Another supplementary item found in many industries, not discussed here in detail, is included in 'deferred charges'. This account includes small tools, dies, forms, and other similar types of capital goods. The use of deferred charges in accounts amounts to using an inventory basis for these types of goods. That is, they are not capitalized and then written off, but instead are evaluated at the end of each year and the net change in value treated as a cost if negative, or as a deduction from cost if positive. There are interesting industrial differences in the treatment of deferred charges, but these cannot be discussed here.

[22] The complications introduced by the tax law provisions governing deductions for depletion are considered in detail by Carl Shoup, Part Six, Sec. II, 3, and Appendix B.

summarized briefly: capital charges to immediate operations, and charges for repairs, replacements and maintenance may tend to fluctuate more violently than prime costs, sales or output as ordinarily measured. Depreciation charges based upon a straight line or similar formula may fluctuate less violently than output as ordinarily measured. Depreciation charges on the per unit basis, as well as depletion charges, will naturally move with output.

TABLE 1

RATIOS INDICATING RELATIVE MOVEMENTS OF OUTPUT AND
OF CERTAIN COSTS

	INTANGIBLE DEVELOPMENT COSTS AS A PERCENTAGE OF VALUE OF OIL AND GAS SALES [1]	MAN-HOURS OF MAINTENANCE EMPLOYEES PER 100 CAR-MILES, STEAM RAILROADS [2]
1929	5.0	6.4
1930	3.6	5.9
1931	2.3	5.3
1932	2.3	5.0
1933	2.2	4.7
1934	1.7	4.8

[1] Based on the annual reports of eight large oil and natural gas mining companies.
[2] Based on data compiled by the Interstate Commerce Commission; see *Bulletin 60*, National Bureau of Economic Research (June 30, 1936), Table 2.

Some of the few available figures bearing on these differences in range of fluctuation are presented in Table 1. The relative declines of capital charges to operations (intangible development costs) in the case of petroleum wells, and maintenance in the case of steam railroads, are striking. It is of course highly doubtful that these changes are typical of short recessions. The figures shown relate to a very severe recession and to only one in any case. But they do raise a question concerning the general validity of corporate accounts for our purposes. The small cyclical amplitude in depreciation charges is fairly well known and need not be illustrated here in detail. The shorter cycles between 1921 and 1929 are barely discernible, and even the 1920–21 recession made but a slight impression on these charges. Only between 1930 and 1933 was there an important decline (11 per cent).[23]

[23] 'Measures of Capital Consumption, 1919–1933', *Bulletin 60*, National Bureau of Economic Research (June 30, 1936), p. 8.

There are important implications in the various methods of handling fixed assets that bear on accounting over periods exceeding a business cycle in length. Secular movements are also involved. For example, if maintenance accounting is used instead of depreciation accounting, computed current costs will be lower in an expanding industry, and (theoretically at least) higher in a declining industry. The far-reaching influence of this fact in an industry such as steam railroads has been commented upon.[24]

What modifications in these accounting practices are suggested by theoretical considerations? One point must be mentioned before we proceed. Illogical and inconsistent accounting practices may simply be due, as suggested by J. M. Clark, to the fact that greater logic and consistency are obtainable at a price at which it does not pay to buy. This may be true also of some theoretical corrections or modifications that may be offered.

The fact that there are alternative methods of pro-rating revenues and costs suggests that there is no sure or sufficient basis in accounting technique itself for a selection among these methods, even accepting such rules of thumb as conservatism. Accounting—private accounting as well as social accounting—must derive its criteria of selection from economic concepts of income and business fluctuations and the derivative concept of a fiscal period.

The economist has the advantage in his estimation of business facts in that he need not have the scruples of the accountant. The accuracy he strives for is related to a wider vision. With the accountant he can admit, for example, that the valuation of inventory at the lower of cost or market is inconsistent. But he can do more. He can restore consistency to the accountant's figures.

Values accrue concomitantly with production in the widest sense of the word—that is, including selling. We need not wait for the moment of realization to record profits, or for the moment of loss to record losses. We can be consistent and record them as they arise, adopting either market price or cost as our measure of value. The two are not identical; whence arises the dilemma and inconsistency of the accountant, who swings from one to the other, selecting the more conservative, and thus ordinarily omitting accrued profits but retaining losses. The economist may

[24] Cf. Robert Schultz, *Depreciation and the American Railroads* (Philadelphia, 1934).

choose cost plus 'normal' profits, or market value (already including normal profits). The former would mean accruing normal
profits during the period of manufacture or display, and postponing 'speculative' profits (or losses) to the moment of realization. The latter would amount to including both normal and
speculative profits when they occur. Since even speculative profits
are only realized, rather than made, at the time of sale, it seems
more reasonable to include them in the fiscal period in which
they become apparent. Speculative profits may be considered as
arising out of the assumption of risk and the exercise of business
judgment; these productive operations are not confined to the
moment of sale. We avoid, also, the necessity of distinguishing
between 'normal' and 'speculative' profits.

If the accrual basis is the logical one to use in the economic
accounting of revenue, costs must be distributed equitably in
proportion to the concomitant revenue. But not all costs are
attached to specific units moving through the plant or shop. The
productive assistance implied by economic risk and business
judgment are related to volume of investment and time, as well
as to volume of output. A plant may depreciate merely as time
passes, regardless of the amount of use made of it. Some of the
risk mentioned attaches to the fact that the use to be made of
given equipment is itself a matter of forecast, not always characterized by measurable probabilities. The extent to which
straight line depreciation, for example, may be modified in our
measures thus hinges on the extent to which we wish to or can
distinguish between costs correlated with output (in the ordinary
sense) and costs correlated with time. The mere fact that a given
productive service is a function of time and not of output does
not, of course, mean that we must distribute the concomitant
costs evenly over time. The method of distribution depends on
what we wish to show. To that extent, the determination of net
income for periods shorter than a business cycle—the 'natural'
fiscal period—is arbitrary. Distributing fixed costs in accordance
with gross income would tend to impose, upon net income, the
cyclical pattern of gross income. It is difficult to say that the resulting measure of net income is in general less suitable than
one showing a greater cyclical amplitude. Nor need there be an

exclusive choice: depreciation may be charged on both a time and a unit basis. It is here especially that a theory of cyclical movements in business is implicit in any decision made. If it is felt, for example, that the errors of prosperity, which result in increases in capacity that prove excessive in the light of depression, are *sui generis*, to charge to that period all the costs incurred by this excessive investment may be justifiable.[25] On the other hand, if the errors of prosperity are conceived of as arising out of the entire cyclical process and as related to errors in other phases of the cycle, such allocation is less justifiable.

An equitable time distribution of costs arising from durable equipment and other assets that are prorated over long periods involves consideration of the interest discount implied in the cost of these assets. If the price of a given capital good be looked upon as the price paid for the present value of a series of future services, we must recognize the existence of the element of discount. One way of doing this would be to base the annual charges for use of equipment on the implicit annual values of the expected services at the time they are enjoyed, rather than on their values at the time purchased. Periods early in the life of the asset would be credited with interest income to be charged to later periods in the form of depreciation or interest. They would not be burdened with the full capital investment, made partly for the benefit of later periods, unless they were at the same time credited with some income derived from this investment. It is this idea that is at the basis of the annuity method of apportioning depreciation.

While straight line depreciation methods tend to undercharge the burden in the later years of use of a durable good, the error involved may be compensated, more or less, by the usually increasing burden of repairs and maintenance. Compensation of a sort may occur also in the cyclical movements of industry, when depreciation charges remain rigid, to the extent that repairs and maintenance rise and fall more than output. However, it must be remembered that the latter compensation, even if complete, is true chiefly of industry as a whole. For particular industries the

[25] Cf. the discussion by J. B. Canning, 'A Certain Erratic Tendency in Accountants' Income Procedure', *Econometrica*, January 1933.

degree of compensation is only partial, since there is some tendency to record capital consumption by the one or the other type of book entry rather than by both.

V Price Changes

One of the outstanding characteristics of business accounting is the reluctance to admit price changes to the records, especially those affecting fixed assets. Except when turnovers are made, either directly by sale of capital assets or indirectly by consolidation or reorganization, capital assets are usually valued at original cost. Depreciation and depletion charges are therefore not based on contemporary price levels. In essence this means that discrepancies between original cost and current values are, as in the case also of inventories, taken into account as part of profit or loss. Changes in the prices of assets therefore affect the amount of corporate savings.

From the viewpoint of the economy as a whole, corporate savings so measured are not quite suitable for estimates of national income. Modification is called for. We may (1) replace original cost prices by current market prices; (2) express our measures entirely in terms of constant prices; (3) in adjusting for price changes, take some account of relative movements of prices.

1 CURRENT PRICES

As accountants recognize, business records are based on what may be called hetero-temporal prices. The prices implicit in depreciation charges and in changes in inventory values do not refer to the market situation at the time depreciation is charged and changes in inventory values are added to or subtracted from cost of materials. For a sound definition of national income produced it is necessary to use contemporary market prices throughout our measures.

In the case of depreciation charges, adjustment for price changes (from original cost to current production cost) may run into a half billion dollars; and in a period of rapidly changing prices may exceed a billion. The measures for 1919-35 are presented in Table 2.

TABLE 2

DEPRECIATION CHARGES EXPRESSED IN TERMS OF ORIGINAL COST
AND REPRODUCTION COST, 1919–1935 [1]

All corporations in the United States

(millions of dollars)

YEAR	(1) DEPRECIATION CHARGE, EXPRESSED IN TERMS OF ORIGINAL COST	(2) DEPRECIATION CHARGE, EXPRESSED IN TERMS OF REPRODUCTION COST	(3) DIFFERENCE BETWEEN DEPRECIATION AT ORIGINAL COST PRICES AND AT CURRENT PRICES (1) — (2)
1919	1,620	2,620	—1,000
1920	1,940	3,330	—1,390
1921	2,200	2,770	—570
1922	2,490	2,780	—290
1923	2,620	3,260	—640
1924	2,700	3,190	—490
1925	2,860	3,250	—390
1926	3,270	3,670	—400
1927	3,350	3,740	—390
1928	3,600	3,890	—290
1929	3,870	4,250	—380
1930	3,990	4,180	—190
1931	4,000	3,920	80
1932	3,690	3,240	450
1933	3,500	3,110	390
1934	3,360	3,300	60
1935	3,420	3,410	10

[1] The figures for 1919–33 have appeared in *Bulletin 60*, National Bureau of Economic Research (June 30, 1936).

Much more important is the adjustment for inventories. For the United States we present in Table 3 Simon Kuznets' figures, discussed by him below in Part Four.

The 4,963 million dollar change in inventory values in 1931 was the net result of a decline in the physical volume of inventories (equal in value to 1,655 million dollars at 1931 average prices and to 1,940 million dollars at 1929 average prices) and a drop in prices (evaluated here at 3,308 million dollars, using the average 1931 physical volume).[26] That is, revaluation of inventories affected the computation of net income for the year to the

[26] The change in value (v), price (p) being held constant at its average amount during any short period $(t_{n+1} - t_n)$, that is at the value $\frac{1}{2}(p_{n+1} + p_n)$; plus

extent of 3,308 million dollars. The magnitudes for some other years are even greater.

2 CONSTANT PRICES

Corporate savings as a whole cannot easily be adjusted for price changes; certainly not by a simple division by a single price index. Thus, the elimination of losses arising from declines in inventory values may change corporate savings from a negative to a positive quantity. No ordinary correction of total corporate savings for price changes can yield this result.[27] The adjustment must be

the change in v, quantity (q) being held constant in a similar manner, equals the total change in v. This statement is quite general, whether p or q rise or fall with the passage of time, and whatever the manner. Thus, let p_0, q_0, v_0 be the respective values of p, q and v, at time t_0, and p_1, q_1, v_1, at time t_1. It can then easily be shown that

$$v_1 - v_0 = p_1\ q_1 - p_0\ q_0 = (q_1 - q_0)\frac{(p_1 + p_0)}{2} + (p_1 - p_0)\frac{(q_1 + q_0)}{2}.$$

The figures in the last column of Table 3 include not only the last term in this equation but also the revaluations involved in the use of the lower of cost or market price, previously discussed (see also Kuznets, Part Four).

It should be emphasized that the inventory (and depreciation) adjustments do not entail the use of a constant price during a given year. The process is not correctly described as a partial deflation. Dr. Kuznets' statement that he multiplies the physical change in stocks of goods during the year by the average weighted price prevailing during the year may be phrased in another, equivalent, fashion. That is, instead of saying that we multiply the total net change during the year by some average price, we may say that we are pricing each net change during the year at the price prevailing at the time the net change occurs. Or, if we wish to think in quasi-mathematical terms, we may say that the year is broken up into a number of sufficiently small time units (infinitesimal units at the limit) and that we simply multiply the net change during each small period by the simple arithmetic mean of the prices at the beginning and end of the period. This, in fact, is what we do in measuring other terms of the national income formula, such as wages for the year: in substance, we multiply the number of man-hours of work during a week or day by the wage-rate prevailing in *that* week or day. All this is what is implied in the phrase "properly weighted annual average price". Thus, it is clear that even the measures in terms of current market prices involve mixing together in the figures for a given year all the different price levels prevailing during the year. In order to carry through an accurate adjustment for price changes, it is necessary to unscramble this mixture by getting back to each of the original, infinitesimal or near-infinitesimal sections of the flows and the prices at which they are evaluated.

[27] There is some danger, therefore, in presenting in the same table an index of prices (cost of living or wholesale prices), and measures of components of national

TABLE 3

INVENTORY REVALUATIONS, 1919–1935

All Business Enterprises, Excluding Farms

(*millions of dollars*)

YEAR	(1) CHANGE IN INVEN- TORIES, EXPRESSED IN CONSTANT (1929) PRICES	(2) CHANGE IN INVEN- TORIES, EXPRESSED IN CURRENT PRICES	(3) CHANGE IN BOOK VALUE OF INVEN- TORIES	(4) REVALUATION INCLUDED IN YEAR'S INCOME (3) — (2)
1919	2,832	3,888	5,986	2,098
1920	3,507	5,908	1,708	—4,200
1921	522	568	—6,185	—6,753
1922	388	581	1,552	971
1923	2,802	3,001	3,219	218
1924	—218	—222	—396	—174
1925	1,068	1,075	1,469	394
1926	1,687	1,901	114	—1,787
1927	387	391	—454	—845
1928	—482	—460	—508	—48
1929	2,484	2,484	1,772	—712
1930	—978	—982	—5,313	—4,331
1931	—1,940	—1,655	—4,963	—3,308
1932	—3,614	—2,586	—4,106	—1,520
1933	—1,255	—874	1,566	2,440
1934	—994	—862	1,269	2,130
1935	—813	—630	155	785

piecemeal. An essential step in the complete adjustment of corporate savings is the substitution of current market prices for original cost prices.[28]

The use of constant prices cannot be considered a departure from the use of market values. Quantities of different goods are still combined on the basis of market value. All that is done is to substitute a constant for a fluctuating market price.

Changes in rates of interest may be handled in the same way, since they also may be looked upon as prices. Difficulties due to changes in capitalization rates may be avoided by keeping them

income produced, implying that correction of the latter by the price index will yield an adequate approximation to real income.

[28] Only in this sense can this substitution be considered a "partial deflation".

constant, at the rate in the base year, or in the given year, or some combination of the two.[29]

3 RELATIVE PRICE CHANGES

In discussing the elimination of price changes no mention was made of difficulties arising from relative price changes, of which discrepancies between reproduction cost (less accumulated depreciation) and current market values are an important group. These are best considered here in a discussion of obsolescence.

Temporary disparities of prices arise during business cycles and are characteristic features of these cycles. The problems of measurement of corporate savings to which they lead reflect the shortness of the accepted annual fiscal period and can be handled, as already suggested, by the process of adjusting for price changes or by the recognition of their essentially temporary character.[30]

Obsolescence is essentially a secular or long cycle phenomenon. Obsolescence during the business cycle has little meaning, since capital goods apparently obsolescent in the downturn and depression phases are brought back into the former sphere or level of production when business turns upward. It is relative price changes persisting over a period longer than a business cycle with which we shall be concerned in this section.

'Normal' obsolescence, obsolescence that can be foreseen even if only dimly, is written off on the books of corporations to revenue, inseparably from charges arising from physical depreciation. Unforeseen obsolescence is ignored, if the good remains in use for the length of its anticipated life. If the good is discarded earlier, a write-down is made, and charged against capital if of sufficient importance.

There are some situations in which, while the equipment or

---

29 It would seem that capitalization rate changes would be reflected in ordinary price changes, and would not require separate treatment. This is true of eternally durable goods. But in the case of goods with limited lives, it would be difficult to compare those in one period with those in another, unless they were identical in number of years of remaining life, as well as in kind.

30 Here again it is necessary to emphasize that the temporary character of these disparities, so far as business cycles are concerned, means only that they are irrelevant to the measurement of national income, and not to the factors determining the amount of national income.

structure may still be profitably used, greater profit may be obtained by substituting for it a larger or faster unit. In such a case the capital cost of the displaced asset may be added to the cost of the displacing asset, in accordance with best accounting practice. Thus, if a rentable building is torn down and replaced by an improved structure, the book value of the old structure is not a proper deduction.[31] How satisfactory are these computations for the measurement of national income?

It can be shown that anticipated obsolescence is a legitimate charge against income,[32] and if the straight line depreciation formula is used, should be expressed in terms of cost.[33]

If obsolescence is not foreseen, the question whether it is a social charge is more difficult. More or less compensating changes within the capital structure, such as those rising out of shifts in demand, may be ignored. Since increases in capital value arising out of demand changes in a part of the system will not be recorded on the books there, it seems best not to write down capital values elsewhere, but to continue to charge depreciation at book value. If the equipment is discarded, however, a write-off will be necessary. This may be charged against income (if discards are distributed fairly uniformly in time), otherwise against capital.[34]

Unforeseen obsolescence due to invention and other technological improvement would seem to be a valid social charge, as a cost underlying and offsetting the advance in technique. Since

[31] Cf., however, *Regulations 86*, Article 23 (e)-2, which seems to approve such a deduction except when a taxpayer deliberately buys real estate with a view to replacing an old building with a new one.

[32] Cf., for example, R. F. Fowler, *The Depreciation of Capital* (London: King, 1934), pp. 11–12.

[33] Strictly speaking, of course, obsolescence should be written off as it occurs. If it is, earlier years of the life of the equipment or other goods will be charged a greater amount than later years, even though straight line physical depreciation is assumed.

[34] Obsolescence may be uncovered in certain phases of the cycle (presumably depression), and may be the consequence of a progress that is pulsating—as in J. A. Schumpeter's conception. But obsolescence uncovered in depression must be confirmed in the succeeding phases of the cycle and it is therefore doubtful whether it should be associated with other than secular movements. For this reason, writedowns (which appear to be more abundant in recession and depression), represent declines in capital values accumulated in earlier periods, and should not be charged to the operations of any one phase of the cycle. This is recognized in the inclusion of write-downs among surplus (or capital) adjustments, rather than in the income account.

an increased flow of goods will result and be reflected in an increase in the gross product, it seems reasonable to charge such obsolescence as an offset. If, for the economic system as a whole, a reasonable sort of guess could be made as to its occurrence, even if it were not possible to do so for any individual part of the system, the charge would be against income, rather than against capital. That is, obsolescence unforeseen by any individual or group of entrepreneurs might be foreseen by an economist taking the broad view. Here also the short length of the fiscal period complicates the problem. For if the history of an industry be considered in its entirety, any unforeseen obsolescence is clearly a charge against its income.

The complete elimination of price changes as irrelevant to the measurement of national income, suggested above as one way out of the difficulties arising from changes in price levels, also eliminates from our figures the valid social cost involved in the investment of resources in capital goods which become obsolete. Difficulties arise, however, when we try to discriminate between different kinds of price changes. Certainly it would seem desirable to eliminate at least changes in the general price level. But the concept of a general price level has lost much of the sharpness it seemed once to possess. Perhaps the simplest procedure, in the present state of our knowledge, is to eliminate all price changes, with a realization of the assumptions this procedure involves. It must be remembered that one of our goals is to account for the entire flow of real resources into capital goods. The loss in the value of these resources should be accounted for by a deduction somewhere, whether as a current charge on revenue account, or as an extraordinary charge on capital account.

VI Capital vs. Revenue Items

Corporate savings, as available to us in accounting reports, consist of revenue items applicable to the current period, less cost items applicable to the current period, less cash dividends and income taxes. Other items and changes in position are added to or deducted from capital assets, and if not conversions of assets, are credited or charged on capital account.

These other items, which may be conveniently grouped to-gether as surplus adjustments,[35] arise out of discrepancies be-tween recorded anticipation and actuality, and out of price changes.

Discrepancies between the records and the facts are often due to the conservative nature of accounting practice with respect, for example, to intangible assets and unrealized profits. Or they may be due, as indicated above, to the mere expense of account-ing.

Discrepancies between anticipations and actuality arise out of errors. The useful life of durable goods may be incorrectly esti-mated. Or, no measurement may be made: accounts may be in-adequate, as in the case of the records of many small proprietors, farmers and professional workers. Or, finally, the probabilities of certain occurrences may be unmeasurable.

The longer the accounting period, the fewer will be the cap-ital charges (or credits), for those arising out of errors in the allocation of revenues and costs to different time intervals will decrease in number. Here again we must distinguish between the discrepancies characteristic of business cycles, which cancel out if the cycle as a whole is considered, and those persisting over periods longer than a business cycle.

Probably the major portion of surplus adjustments represent, concretely, changes in general price levels, unanticipated obso-lescence, and uninsured accidents.[36] As already suggested, mere revaluations—whether expressed in write-ups or write-downs, or profits and losses on sale of capital assets—may be ignored in the social accounts, unless they affect later charges for depletion and depreciation. An important type of upward revaluation occurs after the discovery of valuable mineral properties. Since expendi-tures for exploration and development are usually charged to current expense, whether or not the venture is successful, there are good grounds for considering these discoveries as represent-ing capital formation and part of national income. Entries for unanticipated obsolescence, already discussed, appear to be valid

[35] Most upward revaluations appear to take the form of profits on sales of capital assets (including consolidations), while most negative revaluations enter business accounts as write-downs.

[36] Cf. 'Revaluations of Fixed Assets, 1925–1934', *Bulletin 62*, National Bureau of Economic Research (December 7, 1936).

social charges, if they can be separated from corrections for general price movements. Damages due to uninsured accidents, like unforeseen obsolescence, are definitely social charges, even if only on capital account, since there can be no question of their effect on economic welfare in general, and on the status of business corporations in particular. Such losses have been discussed in recent papers where they are treated as losses on capital account.[37] Here also, if from a broad social standpoint reasonable estimates could be made—whether or not entrepreneurs take into account the possibility of their occurrence—it would be preferable to place such losses in the income account. Practically speaking, however, it is probably simplest to treat them as losses on capital account, and supplement our measures of national income by entries for charges and credits on capital account. These entries are vital in the measurement of annual changes in national wealth, but difficult to consider as affecting the measurement of the income of the specific year in which they are made.

Such surplus adjustments as charges on idle facilities are essentially applications of the per unit depreciation charge, rather than the straight line method. They can hardly be considered as proper capital charges so far as national income is concerned.

General non-specific reserves for 'contingencies' offer a knotty problem, and raise the question of the extent to which the surplus account itself is a reserve for possible future losses.[38] The creation of these reserves should ordinarily not be considered charges on capital account. Only when specific entries are made debiting these reserves and crediting capital assets does it appear reasonable to treat the items as capital charges. However, if the fact of loss is indeed clearly established, and only its exact amount is still to be determined, there would seem to be more reason to consider the entries as relevant to our measures. The distinction

[37] A. C. Pigou, 'Net Income and Capital Depletion', *The Economic Journal*, June 1935, p. 240; F. A. Hayek, 'The Maintenance of Capital', *Economica*, August 1935, p. 246.

[38] See M. C. Rorty, 'A National Money Accounting as the Basis for Studies of Income Distribution', *Journal of the American Statistical Association*, March 1921; O. W. Knauth, 'The Place of Corporate Surplus in the National Income', *Journal of the American Statistical Association*, June 1922; and W. R. Ingalls, *Wealth and Income of the American People*, 2d ed. (York: Merlin, 1923), pp. 207–14; also Dr. Knauth's discussion in *Income in the United States*, Vol. II, Ch. 25 (National Bureau of Economic Research, 1922).

is a clouded one, and superlative accuracy is not to be expected.

The whole question of anticipation is involved in these considerations. Should the economist accept, for use in his measures, whatever anticipations are offered to him, or should he correct them? And if he attempts to correct them, should he accept the average anticipation as the criterion, or the most accurate anticipation, or impose one of his own? No clear answer is possible. In an analysis of economic processes the actual distribution of anticipations constitutes vital data. But in the estimation of national income as a measure of the 'end-product' of economic processes some manipulation appears necessary. We cannot accept as measures of income, except as first approximations, what individuals believe to be their incomes. In measuring economic welfare the economist must impose and use criteria of his own. Thus the changing anticipations related to the waves of pessimism and optimism characteristic of the trade cycle may be handled as implied above in the discussion of the fiscal period.

The path of the estimator of national income is thorny in any case. He is forced to accept accounting data to which, in many cases, only a few rough corrections can be applied. Where obviously inadequate accounts are kept—those of farmers, for instance—some estimate must be supplied by him. And he must allow for capital charges and credits as a complement to his measures of national income, even though he may feel that many of these entries properly belong in the revenue account.

VII Problems of Duplication and Omission

We turn, finally, to a few questions of duplication and omission raised during the examination of the various items entering into corporate income accounts. With respect to the expense items, there is the problem raised by taxes.[39] It is easy to consider corporate taxes as a whole a legitimate expense, paid for services rendered by the state.[40] But for individual industries this way out seems less proper. Taxes paid by tobacco and liquor corporations can hardly be considered anything but transfers. For a proper

[39] Cf. Mitchell and Kuznets, *op. cit.*, p. 10.
[40] See, however, Gerhard Colm, Part Five, Sec. II and III.

industrial distribution of national income produced, it seems legitimate to deduct only those taxes paid for services rendered to the industry. This statement applies to all taxes, including income taxes, property taxes, import duties and excise taxes on such products as liquor and tobacco. The portion of taxes not required for services can be considered either as forced transfers, or as analogous to monopoly profits. In either case, it represents income produced in the industry. Probably the simplest way of handling this problem statistically is to segregate all taxes paid by corporations and other business enterprises and show the figures in conjunction with the income data by industry. The distinction between government services to business and other government expenditures would then be made in a detailed analysis of the government's budget, the portion taken to represent services to business being deducted from the total amount of taxes paid by industry. It would be difficult to attempt so to break down tax payments of individual industries. This could be done only on an arbitrary basis, such as assuming that all property taxes are for services rendered and deductible as costs, and that excise and income taxes represent income originating in the industry.

The theoretical basis for this method of treatment of taxes lies in the assumption of market price as the unit of value. A different treatment of taxes implies a deviation from this basic assumption.[41] It may be doubted whether in the present state of economic and statistical knowledge a step can be taken away from market valuations, although such a step is ultimately necessary.[42] Since the economy is characterized by change and growth, the equilibrium theory apparatus so far seems to aid us little in this eventual step. Even well established taxes vary in weight and incidence, owing to changes in total income and prices. In any case, the underlying criticism of market prices applies with equal force to the vast group of monopoly prices, and cannot be confined to the effect of taxes on prices.

An extreme instance of the importance of taxes in measures of

[41] Reduction of income to constant dollars does not rid us of market valuations, of course.

[42] An approach has been made in this direction by Professor Colm. The kind of assumptions that must be made to do so is indicated in his paper (see Part Five).

national income produced is found in the tobacco manufactures
industry (Table 4). In this group, taxes were more than twice the
amount of national income produced as measured by a method
similar to that of Messrs. Kuznets and Nathan.[43] If we include
taxes in national income produced we have figures that indicate
a degree of change between 1931 and 1933 (−12 per cent) considerably different from the figure excluding taxes (−23 per
cent). And of course the relative importance of the industry, so
far as income produced is concerned, is considerably enhanced by
including taxes.[44] For all corporations, taxes other than Federal
income taxes (property and other taxes, but not including excise
and import duties) amounted to over two billion dollars in each
of the years 1927–33. These are not only huge amounts, but also
amounts characterized by little flexibility.

TABLE 4

NATIONAL INCOME ORIGINATING IN THE TOBACCO MANUFACTURES
INDUSTRY, 1931 and 1933

(millions of dollars)

	1931	1933
National income produced, as ordinarily measured	216.3	165.6
Taxes paid		
Excise	422.0	400.8
Property, etc.	9.5	10.2
Federal income and profits (corporate)	17.1	9.0
Total taxes	448.6	420.0
National income produced, plus taxes	664.9	585.6

Sources: Wages and salaries—Census of Manufactures (1929, 1931, 1933). Salaries
for 1931 estimated on basis of wages paid. Interest—estimated interest on long
term debt, less interest received on tax-exempt investments, *Statistics of Income,*
stepped up to include non-corporate data by ratio of total value of product to
corporate value of product, Census of Manufactures, 1929. Dividends, entrepreneurial withdrawals and business savings—*Statistics of Income,* stepped up. Taxes
—excise taxes from Census of Manufactures, 1931 and 1933; other taxes from
Statistics of Income, stepped up.

[43] *National Income, 1929–1932,* 73d Cong., 2d Sess., Senate Doc. 124 (1934); *National Income in the United States, 1929–1935* (U. S. Department of Commerce,
1936).

[44] Various taxes on liquors collected by the Bureau of Internal Revenue also reach
a huge amount; 411 million dollars for the fiscal year ending June 30, 1935 (*Annual
Report of the Commissioner of Internal Revenue, Fiscal Year Ended June 30,
1935,* p. 53).

Bad debts represent a rather large item, as indicated in Table 5. Here too there is some question whether those losses incurred through credit extended to individuals should be considered as transfers or as expenses. The criterion by means of which the income derived from illegal pursuits is commonly excluded from national income is generally applied in this case. Another, perhaps more satisfactory, method is to segregate the figures. Bad debts incurred on accounts due from other corporations are not necessarily recorded as income by the defaulters.

TABLE 5

BAD DEBTS REPORTED BY CORPORATIONS, 1929–1931

(millions of dollars)

	1929	1930	1931
Total	942.0	979.5	1,182.7
Retail industries [1]	200.0	202.3	239.8

[1] Including all bad debts reported by retail trade, domestic service and amusements, and one-half of bad debts reported by corporations in the following industries: telephone and telegraph, gas, electric light, wholesale and retail, 'all other trade', professional, stock and bond brokers, real estate, loan and financing. The original data appear in National Income, 1929–1932, Appendix B, and in the annual volumes of Statistics of Income.

The same point arises in connection with losses, by corporations, on investments in other corporations. Duplication of losses occurs when the losses of a subsidiary are repeated in the loss on sale or writing-off of the stock holdings of the parent company. The elimination of duplication of corporate profits is quite easy. Profits must be reported to the Bureau of Internal Revenue for tax purposes, and income derived from dividends and gain on sale of investments are segregated in the published statistics. The elimination of duplication of losses would be just as easy if the figures were reliable. However, there is some question as to the accuracy of the reports, particularly of corporations that are dissolved or in process of dissolution. Naturally, when there is no tax to be yielded by insisting on more accurate reports, and when any losses reported will most probably not be used in the future to reduce taxable income, the Treasury Department is less likely to scrutinize with care the reports of companies in obvious difficulty and on the way out. Evidence bearing on the importance of any discrepancies that may arise in this connection is obviously lacking. It is possible that an appreciable sum of losses is omitted from our aggregates on this account.

One further possible discrepancy must be mentioned. Cash dividends declared by a corporation as of one year may be recorded as received by the stockholders in the following year. Since we obtain our figures from the payers, rather than the receivers, any resulting difficulty will arise only in the analysis of income by size.

VIII Conclusion

The definition of national income should have some relation to the economic world as we have learned to know it. The organization of modern business involves, integrally, the corporate structure and the complex of interests and controls this structure implies. It is essentially for this reason that the old division of income shares must be modified to make a place for corporate savings.

Difficulties in the definition of national income arise, as Professor Pigou has indicated, out of the fact of economic change. It is extremely difficult to compose an unambiguous definition of capital consumption—of what is meant by keeping capital intact —for an economy characterized by cyclical movements and secular trends in its every element. We cannot assume that the accounting concept of corporate savings provides us with this unambiguous definition. Accounting estimates of corporate savings cannot be accepted as more than the raw material which the statistician must shape into bricks for his structure. The characteristics of accounting practice—conservatism, inconsistency, variability from one concern to another (as in the treatment of intangibles, depreciation and maintenance), the reflection of extraneous elements (as legal requirements, division of interests within the enterprise, need for credit), mold the accounting figures into shapes not altogether fitted for our purpose.

Nor is it likely that we can make such a definition of our own *before* we commence our labor of building up a theory of economics. Economics is a continuing science. It must learn from experience, its own experience. For this reason we feel that national income must be defined with reference to what we already know of economic development and fluctuation. If we are to get back of the 'nominal' calculations and evaluations of business men and accountants, we must consider the 'law' of their speculations and valuations.

We must recognize the utility of several parallel measures of national income, supplemented by measures of capital charges and credits, and broken down in detail. When such a plurality of measures is not possible, when modifications of the available data are not practicable, we must remember the assumptions implicit in these data when we draw conclusions from them.[45]

45 Much of the above discussion has relevance also to problems in the measurement of national wealth. Thus, the remarks on the relation between a theory of cyclical movements in business and the measurement of income also apply to the measurement of wealth in connection with, for example, the question of fluctuating prices and their bearing on capital evaluation.

Measuring the Nation's Consumption

SOLOMON FABRICANT
National Bureau of Economic Research

The author is indebted to William H. Shaw for helpful comments.

I

Ordinarily national income is taken to be the net aggregate output of all sources of enjoyment except commodities produced "outside the field of economic activity proper".[1] The latter "are left to be accounted for separately".[2]

National income is, in this sense, simply one of several categories of production. This particular category has received special attention and been studied apart from the other categories. This is not reprehensible in itself. National income is a very important category of production. When total output is in question, however, an estimate based on something less than the whole has limitations.

These limitations are somewhat greater if an estimate of total consumption is the desideratum, since a smaller percentage of total consumption than of total production is likely to be covered if nonmarket activity is excluded. Further, the consumption portion of national income, while it may constitute a reasonable class of production, is not thereby a sensible category of consumption. When analyzing consumption, the distinction between food grown in the urban garden and commercially grown vegetables is not very helpful except, perhaps, with respect to such matters as vitamin content.

These limitations would not raise difficulties if we had adequate separate accounts of production in the noneconomic area. Unfortunately, such separate accounts are seldom drawn up. Because extra-economic production is not for the market, and cannot easily be measured in terms of money, there are few statistics for it. This has discouraged both comprehensive estimation of this complement to our national income measure and regular reporting of changes in it. Between confining estimates to the market economy or making up additional estimates of non-market production, the choice has usually been the former.

Perhaps the horns of the dilemma have not been properly evaluated. Estimates for the nonmarket area must be very rough, it is true (and not merely for statistical reasons), but so must estimates of some national income components. In the absence of accounts for the nonmarket area, the limitations on the exist-

[1] Simon Kuznets, *National Income and Its Composition, 1919-1938* (National Bureau of Economic Research, 1941), I, 135-6.
[2] Alfred Marshall (*Principles of Economics*, 8th ed., Macmillan, London, 1938), p. 524.

ing estimates are annoying qualifications to the conclusions we may draw from them concerning the total consumption of all or particular kinds of goods and services. This is especially true of estimates covering long periods, when even small annual changes in the proportions of market to nonmarket output may cumulate to large amounts, and to some extent also of wartime series, when the rate of change in these proportions may be high for some types of commodity. A question is thus posed: Do estimates of consumption compiled from available statistics on national income depart appreciably from the facts? Further, how suitable are the valuations commonly used and the classifications followed in national income tables for measuring national consumption and illuminating its content?

These questions are raised to remind us of problems recognized in the past. Simon Kuznets has well summarized some,[3] and analyses of international, industrial, and other differences in income levels usually refer to them. But we have not yet reached the stage where it is generally considered worth while to place even rough systematic accounts of nonmarket output and alternative valuations and classifications alongside our present income estimates.

II

Consumption of commodities and services must be measured in terms of some value unit, such as the market price of the same or similar goods in some reference base period. A nonmarket value unit is also possible and, indeed, for any rounded view of consumption the usefulness of supplementary measures based on nonmarket units cannot be overstressed. In the case of food, for example, measures in terms of calories and similar units sometimes lead to a better understanding of the nation's consumption than do deflated dollar values, and certainly all these measures combined give more knowledge than one alone.[4]

[3] *National Income and Its Composition*, Ch. 1 and 9. See also the contributions of Gerhard Colm and Clark Warburton in Volume One of *Studies in Income and Wealth*.

[4] The differences among the measures are great; e.g., between 1929 and 1939 the usual index of deflated consumers' outlay on food, which reflects various shifts in the kind and stage of preparation of the food bought, rose about 25 percent per capita, according to estimates based on Department of Commerce data. In contrast, the Department of Agriculture measures of the per capita consumption of foods, based on physical volumes multiplied by corresponding fixed base-

When the unit is some nonmarket value, such as the calorie, the same value coefficient is applied as a matter of course to all goods of the same kind prepared and used in the same way, wherever they may be consumed or whatever price is paid for them. When the value unit is price, regional or other differences in prices are usually allowed to affect the aggregates, at least when these enter national income calculations. Regional comparisons of consumption levels at a moment in time, and comparisons of total consumption over time, are thus rendered ambiguous.[5]

To illustrate: Food grown and consumed by farmers is included in national income at farm prices, which are considerably lower than food prices elsewhere. Evaluation of farm-consumed raw food at nationwide prices would not raise the total value

year retail prices, increased 1 or 2 percent; of calories, remained unchanged; of proteins, rose 1 percent; of carbohydrates, declined 5 percent; of ascorbic acid, rose 15 percent.

[5] The point may be expressed most clearly in simplified algebraic terms. Let q and p stand for the quantity and price of a given product in one economic area (industry, income level, etc.), and Q and P for the quantity and price in another area, with the usual subscripts indicating the time period; and let $P_0 = mp_0$, $P_1 = np_1$. Then the index of real consumption of the product for the two areas combined, period 1 in relation to period 0, will be

1a) $\dfrac{q_1 + nQ_1}{q_0 + mQ_0}$, if the value index $\dfrac{q_1p_1 + Q_1P_1}{q_0p_0 + Q_0P_0}$ is deflated by $\dfrac{P_1}{P_0}$; or

1b) $\dfrac{\dfrac{q_1}{n} + Q_1}{\dfrac{q_0}{m} + Q_0}$, if it is deflated by $\dfrac{P_1}{P_0}$ (both procedures are common).

The index of real consumption will be

2a) $\dfrac{q_1 + Q_1n}{q_0 + Q_0n}$, if the value index is divided by a somewhat better index

of prices, e.g., $\dfrac{q_0p_1 + Q_0np_1}{q_0p_0 + Q_0mp_0}$; or

2b) $\dfrac{q_1 + Q_1m}{q_0 + Q_0m}$, if the complementary price index with given year quantities as coefficients is used as the deflator. The index we are after is more appropriately provided by

3) $\dfrac{q_1 + Q_1}{q_0 + Q_0}$, which may be obtained in the deflation procedure only if the price index is

$$\dfrac{q_1p_1 + Q_1P_1}{q_1 + Q_1} \Bigg/ \dfrac{q_0p_0 + Q_0P_0}{q_0 + Q_0}.$$

of food consumed in any one year, if the national average price were properly computed. But it would affect the trend of the index of raw food or total food consumption—how much would depend on the rate of change in the proportion of farm to total consumption and the ratio of farm prices to national prices in the weight-base period.[6]

III

For light on national consumption everyone turns first to national income, which includes several categories that are themselves elements of national consumption or closely related to such elements. The chief category is consumers' outlay, which as a matter of fact, is frequently used to measure national consumption. The character of the accounts needed to supplement and the adjustments required to utilize existing estimates of national income, if we are to obtain a fuller view of consumption, may therefore be seen most clearly if we start with consumers' outlay.

To begin with, consumers' outlay is, as mentioned, only one of the national income categories that constitute, in some form, an element of national consumption. We find consumption items not only in consumers' outlay but also, at present, in war outlay. These are goods and services provided the armed forces. Of course, when consumers' outlay is measured in relation to the civilian population rather than to the total population, the limited scope of the former is implicitly recognized. But when it is a question of total consumption, the goods and services provided the armed forces cannot be ignored and must be covered explicitly.[7]

[6] Even for the three decades beginning in 1909, the difference between the usual index of nonmanufactured food consumption and one computed as suggested amounts to some 5 percent. For trends covering the past century, during which the rural-urban shift in population was great, the difference would be much larger, and would probably be appreciable even for a measure of total consumption.

[7] The quantities are large, since the armed forces totaled over 9 million in 1943; and in the case of food, at least, the men in the services consume more per capita than does the average civilian or even the average male civilian. Even if each serviceman is allowed only the quantity of food consumed by the average male in 1941 (worth about $200 in 1939 prices), the total for the armed forces was some $1,900 million in 1943, close to 10 percent of the 1943 value of consumers' outlay on food (also in 1939 prices).

Various estimates indicate that a considerable quantity of tobacco products is being sent abroad for the use of our armed forces stationed outside the country.

In peacetime, national income is confined to the physical boundaries of a country; i.e., the population covered excludes citizens resident abroad and includes aliens living within the country. Aliens *temporarily* domiciled within the country and citizens *temporarily* domiciled abroad are few in peacetime. During a war, however, these groups may become a fairly large percentage of the total population. For many purposes there is point to including in an estimate of national consumption the goods and services consumed by our military forces abroad, e.g., through reverse lend-lease; and excluding from it the goods and services provided the foreign soldiers stationed here.

Consumption of goods and services produced in the nonmarket area, e.g., those yielded by some or all sectors of the family, the illegal, the public and semi-public, and the eleemosynary economies, is usually omitted from consumers' outlay, because the output is omitted from national income.[8] All these belong in national consumption. Without the benefit of supplementary accounts for these areas, it is difficult to appraise estimates of national income going back to 1799 or even 1879.

Since these shipments are tax free, they are not included in the usual estimates of consumers' outlay on tobacco. The 1943 figure for the latter, about $2.5 billion (in 1939 prices), must therefore be raised one or more hundred million dollars if it is to measure total consumption.

The quantity of clothing purchased by government agencies for military use, which appears solely in war outlay, has been a very substantial portion of all clothing manufactured. This large fraction is accounted for, in part, by the enormous inventories that have been built up. But even if we take the very modest sum of $100 per year per soldier or sailor, we reach close to a billion dollars, about 10 per cent of consumers' outlay on clothing in 1943 (both values in 1939 prices). The average annual expenditure per male adult in 1934-36, for families of wage earners and clerical workers in 42 cities, was $49, according to the Bureau of Labor Statistics.

All together, including not only food, tobacco, and clothing but also all other consumer goods and services provided the armed forces, there is a substantial addition to be made to consumers' outlay if it is to reflect consumption adequately. The estimate in Kuznets' National Product, War and Prewar (National Bureau *Occasional Paper* 17, Feb. 1944)—$500 per member of the armed forces in 1942 (about $400 in 1939 prices)—is not at all too large.

8 Among the sectors of the family economy not covered in the usual indexes of consumers' outlay are nonfarm gardens which, in recent prewar years, have provided some $200 million worth of food per annum. During the war, however, the victory-garden drive has increased the yield to some 8 million tons, as estimated by the Extension Service of the War Food Administration, which may be valued at about $600 million. The increase of $400 million is an appreciable increment to the national food consumption, only slightly offset by the probable wartime decline in amateur fishing and hunting.

The most striking product of the illegal economy in recent American history

It may be objected that if personal services rendered oneself were to be included in national consumption, the rise that would otherwise appear in national consumption due to the growth of the 'service industries' would be offset and vanish. This is not strictly true since a professional shave, for example, is often worth more than one's own. But aside from this, the objection fails to note the difference between level of consumption and standard of living. The latter is a function not only of consumption but also of expenditure of time and effort.

Among the goods included in consumers' outlay are durable consumer commodities. If national consumption is to be estimated properly the outlay upon them must be taken out and the services rendered by them substituted. (This will involve a correction of both amount and timing.) Indeed, to a limited extent this is usually done even in estimating consumers' outlay and national income. Expenditures on residences owned by their occupants are treated as capital formation rather than consumers' outlay, and an imputed rent on them is included in the latter.[9] But the income from outlays on other durable consumer goods is in effect measured by total expenditure and so counted at the time the purchase is made. This treatment parallels that of the durable goods purchased by business concerns that are charged to current

Note 8 concluded:
is the illegal liquor consumed during the prohibition era. Clark Warburton's estimate for 1929 is $3,750 million, over 15 per cent of the value of all food and beverages consumed. Another large illegal item is anthracite coal mined in bootleg operations. According to the Bureau of Mines, the tonnage of this coal amounted in 1939 to some 8 per cent of the year's legal output.

Care must be taken, of course, to avoid double counting; therefore transfers of goods such as may occur in charitable transactions should be omitted except for the value added in the transaction.

I will merely mention the important discrepancy between the 'actual' value of governmental services rendered consumers and the value placed upon these services in current computations of national income. This perennial question is discussed in almost every volume of *Studies in Income and Wealth.*

[9] Curiously, the Department of Commerce includes in capital formation investment in owner-occupied houses but does not place the services rendered by them in consumers' outlay. I understand that this omission will be remedied in the next revision of the Department's series. It will probably add some $3 billion to the outlay figures for 1939, about $1.2 billion for depreciation (in 1939 prices), and $1.8 billion for net rental income.

There is, it is true, some reason for hesitating to include imputed incomes in consumers' outlay, which in its ordinary usage would cover only purchases. Perhaps imputed incomes, home-grown food consumed on the farm, etc., should constitute a new major category of national income if these items are to be kept in it at all.

operations. But such crude methods of accounting for business capital consumption are relatively unimportant. In estimating total consumption, especially when the current production of consumer durable goods is far from normal, the durability of consumer durable goods must be recognized.[10] In the case of clothing, failure to do so usually leads to no great error, because the average life of clothes is short and fluctuations in outlays have been moderate.[11] When the more durable goods are considered, the difference between outlay and consumption becomes impressive.[12] To measure consumption, some more or less arbitrary assumptions would have to be made concerning depreciation and rental rates; e.g., it would have to be decided whether rental rates should reflect differentials for the greater satisfaction derived from new goods and for their lower operating costs. But this would seem less unpalatable than to accept outlay as a measure of consumption, because of the kind of assumptions that would involve.

[10] It is so recognized by the Department of Commerce in discussing its figures on consumer expenditures; see Milton Gilbert and George Jaszi, National Income and National Product in 1942, *Survey of Current Business*, March 1943, p. 14. However, in the paper cited, depreciation charges alone are taken as a measure of consumption.

[11] The decline in consumers' outlay between 1929 and 1933 (measured in constant prices) was about 25 percent. The corresponding fall in services rendered by consumers' stocks of clothing was 15-20 percent (assuming a three-year average life).

[12] The decline in the output of such products as are covered in the usual consumer outlay category ('durable goods, other than housing', including automobiles, furniture, and similar goods), during the 1930's and since 1941, has been great compared with that in the stock of such goods held by consumers. When the imputed net rental value of this stock is also taken into account, the difference becomes even greater, as is suggested by the accompanying rough figures (in billions of 1939 dollars).

	1929	1933	1937	1941	1943
Consumers' outlay[a]	6.7	3.3	6.7	8.3	4.8
Depreciation[b]	5.8	6.0	5.8	6.2	5.6
Net rental value[c]	1.7	1.8	1.7	1.9	1.7
Depreciation plus net rental value	7.5	7.8	7.5	8.1	7.3

[a] Based on figures compiled by W. H. Shaw, Henry Shavell, Milton Gilbert, and George Jaszi, of the Department of Commerce.

[b] The depreciation estimate is that presented by Gilbert and Jaszi in their article cited in footnote 10, pushed back to 1929 and forward to 1943 in a simple calculation assuming a 10-year life for all goods covered in the category.

[c] The net rental value was taken equal to 30 per cent of the depreciation charge; i.e., a 3 percent net rent on gross assets or 6 per cent on net assets was assumed.

IV

One other difference between estimates of consumers' outlay and of consumption may be noted. From the viewpoint of most consumption problems, the subclasses of consumers' outlay are not neat categories. Outlay on foods, for example, covers many items. It measures not only food consumption but also many services purchased together with food. Yet, while the cost of preparing and serving restaurant meals appears in the outlay on food, the corresponding cost in the home is classified elsewhere.

This kind of classification sometimes leads to actual confusion, as in the recent criticisms of the Bureau of Labor Statistics cost of living index. At best it cannot be said to provide the most useful breakdown when consumption is of primary interest. A supplementary classification, in which the services are separated out by subtracting the value they add, would be useful.

If supplementary measures were attempted, many difficult decisions would have to be made, of course. The changing service element resulting from the shift of canning or dressmaking from home to factory would not be easy to determine. The restaurant performs also a food retailing function, which is difficult to separate from its other functions. But this difficulty would bother one less than the cloudiness of meaning created by the inclusion of night-club entertainment and other services in the food category.

I would not propose that this reclassification be done for every category of consumption. It is doubtful that it can be. But for such categories as food and clothing, something interesting might be worked out.[13]

V

I have argued that if a reasonably adequate notion of consumption levels is to be obtained, even rough 'separate accounts' for consumption areas not covered in present estimates of national income should be drawn up. I have noted that, naturally, a good many difficulties would be encountered and many assumptions

---

[13] The weighted index of per capita consumption of foods in the United States, prepared by Elna Anderson of the Bureau of Agricultural Economics (Consumption of Agricultural Products, March 1941), is one of the measures I have in mind.

would have to be made. To those already mentioned I should like to add another.

Services performed by housewives in adding value to the raw food, cloth, and other goods that go through further processing in the home, and in providing a large group of personal services, have been shifting almost continuously from the family to the market economy. In the case of clothing, for example, the transfer has been direct and complete; factories now cut the cloth and sew the garments together.[14] In other shifts, such as the lightening of the housewife's burden by domestic electrical appliances, the transfer has been indirect and partial. Electrical appliance manufacturers have displaced the commercial producers of the simpler home tools, but the housewife still uses the appliances. The housewife's labor has increased radically in productivity (compare lighting a gas stove with kindling a coal fire); and her hours have been shortened and her 'employment' has declined.

Consequently, it is difficult to put a dollar value on housewives' services. The usual procedure of assuming no change in such services per housewife is not very satisfactory, since it understates the shift out of the family economy. The 29 million women reported by the 1940 Census as engaged in housework constituted not only a smaller fraction of married women, as compared with earlier decades, but contributed less per person than did housewives in earlier years. The same can be said about domestic work done by children and husbands.[15]

These considerations bring us to my final comment. Specific quantitative measures are useful and their calculation should be improved. The assumptions on which they must be based may be questioned, but in some respects this is itself an advantage; for explicit assumptions are always better than the implicit ones frequently imbedded in market statistics. Beyond a certain point, however, the advantages to be expected from quantitative meas-

[14] According to estimates by William H. Shaw, 3 per cent of the flour produced was purchased by commercial bakeries in 1869; in 1919, 20 per cent. In the case of cotton goods, the corresponding percentages are 8 and 64. (Small neighborhood bakeries and seamstresses complicate the interpretation of Shaw's figures, for the present purpose, since they are not counted among commercial establishments.)

[15] It will be recalled that not so long ago house-raising was only infrequently a market product.

ures will be overcome by the doubts. The exact position of this point must be determined in each individual case. In considering trends in recreation, for example, I suspect that little value would be extracted from an attempt to estimate the quantity of 'home-made' recreation. It might be more useful simply to consider the quantity of 'commercially-produced' recreation against the background of qualitative information on all sources of recreation.

The more aspects of consumption we measure and the more qualitative information we have on each the better. This is the only way of resolving such a problem as that of distinguishing between consumer goods and goods used in the process of production, a problem which becomes more serious when, as in a great war or during the secular development of economic society, radical changes occur in occupations, family life, and place of residence or work. Current national income calculations should be supplemented by other measures, and qualitative information pursued.

VI

This discussion of the measurement of national consumption may be summarized as follows:

1) Consumers' outlay is not a completely satisfactory measure of consumption, because it fails to cover consumption items included in other national income categories, particularly war outlay.

2) Moreover, with some exceptions, consumers' outlay includes only goods and services produced in the market economy. Production in the domestic, eleemosynary, illegal, public, and semi-public economies are inadequately covered.

3) Consumers' outlay on commodities is not simultaneous with actual consumption; the difference in timing is considerable for durable goods.

4) The items included in consumers' outlay are combined in terms of the particular market prices paid for each. To measure consumption, however, all goods of a given kind could more sensibly be valued at the same price, if market prices are used; and for many purposes, non-market value units are more suitable.

5) The classifications followed in presenting information on consumers' outlay do not yield the most illuminating breakdown

of national consumption, and should be supplemented by other classifications designed to that end.

6) In general, but especially when quantitative measures are impracticable, qualitative information on aspects of consumption is desirable.

The position taken here is not that existing consumers' outlay or national income series should be revised to provide more satisfactory estimates of consumption. Rather, it is urged that when consumption is the question, supplementary estimates be calculated and presented, together with qualitative information, beside estimates of national income. These additional data are needed for international and intra-national comparisons of consumption levels as well as for the analysis of secular trends or wartime changes.

What I am really suggesting is, of course, a study of the nation's consumption. Until it is made, national income estimates, when used to indicate changes in consumption, should be carefully qualified.

Business Costs and Business Income Under Changing Price Levels

The Economist's Point of View

by Solomon Fabricant

[*Solomon Fabricant is professor of economics at New York University, a member of the research staff of the National Bureau of Economic Research, and consultant to the U. S. Bureaus of the Census and of the Budget.*]

THE NATION'S aggregate net income is the prime measure of the nation's economic activity. An important component of the national income is, of course, the net income of business enterprise. Now, that would be a good enough reason for economists to concern themselves with the measurement of business income. But there is another. Business income is not only important; it is also one of the more troublesome components of national income when it comes to putting together the figures and deciding what they mean. For these reasons economists have spent a good deal of time thinking of how to measure business income.

Economists have had to grapple with a number of problems. Some arise from changing price levels, some from fluctuations in the volume of production. There are difficulties caused by technological advances, and difficulties caused by alterations in consumers' tastes. Acts of God and the King's enemies also sometimes prove troublesome. In the course of analyzing and discussing these problems—a task that is by no means over—economists have established what may be called an economic point of view towards the measurement of business income, particularly in the computation of national income. This point of view can therefore best be presented to you by considering what kinds of figures on business income economists put into their calculations of the nation's aggregate income. On this occasion we shall want to limit ourselves to the way economists handle the problem of changing price levels. That is the big problem of today.

I said that economists have been worrying about the calculation of business income. I do not want to imply, however, that the business profit figures included in national income statistics are based entirely or even largely on the calculations of economists. On the contrary, the basic data on business income—and other income as well—come out of accountants' reports. What the economist worries about is the meaning of the accountant's figures, the coverage of these figures, and the adjustments needed to mold them to his own needs. What the economist does is to combine the figures accountants prepare for various industries, make estimates to fill in the gaps (for he wants a complete national aggregate), and introduce a relatively few—though far-reaching—adjustments to adapt the figures to his conception of the business income that is appropriate for inclusion in the national income. Even these adjustments, we shall see, are mainly applications on a larger and more consistent scale of adjustments that accountants here and there have already introduced.

The economist sometimes boasts of his advantage, over other social scientists, in possessing an objective means of measurement. The magnitude of the forces and effects with which he is concerned can be assessed with the measuring rod of money. But the economist above all is aware of the great significance of changes in the value of money. He knows that his measuring rod contracts with shrinkage in the value of money and expands with growth in its value, like the standard meter does with changes in temperature. To keep this measuring rod firm—or perhaps better expressed, to correct the observations he makes with it— the economist has developed the supplementary device of index numbers of prices. A decline in the value of money is indicated by a general price rise; a general price decline indicates a rise in the value of money. Price indexes, being essentially averages of price changes, measure these general price changes. They therefore provide an approximation to changes in the value of money. Properly used, they help to eliminate the bias that would otherwise arise were money values, such as appear in the market transactions of different times, compared as they stand.

One adjustment, then, that the economist makes of accounting figures on business income, to lessen the effect of changes in the value of money, is to multiply the dollar figures by an index of the value of money. Or—what is the same thing—he divides the dollar figures by an index of the general price level. As is commonly said, the dollar values are "deflated" or expressed in terms of "constant prices." Historically, this was the first adjustment developed by economists. Usually, also, it is still one of the most important.

All are familiar with this adjustment. Few today would dream of presenting figures on wages without a correction for the increased cost of living; and indexes of the prices and incomes farmers receive are, almost by legal fiat, accompanied by indexes of the prices they pay. "Real wages" and "parity prices" are common lingo. Economists, at least, are consistent in applying similar adjustments to business income. Since everyone is acquainted with this particular adjustment, I need say no more about it, except to comment on two points.

First, while economists are thoroughly agreed that correction for changes in the general price level is necessary, there is less agreement on just how much correction is needed, in any particular case. By that I mean, simply, that there are available a number of different indexes of prices (and of course there are many more that could be computed); that these usually reveal somewhat different rates of change in prices, between any two dates; and that opinions differ as to which is most appropriate for deflating business income. For the value of money depends on what is to be done with the money: whether it is spent on consumers' goods or capital goods; whether it is spent on rich-man's goods or poor-man's goods. And, also, indexes of the prices even of the same group of goods will vary with the compiling agency. Over relatively short periods of time, however, these differences are usually not great. The area of agreement is far greater than the area of disagreement. Economists, having learned to concentrate on important issues, accept approximate measures with which they may differ in detail. National income statistics are expressed in round billions of dollars, not in dollars and cents.

My second comment is necessary to emphasize a point that is frequently misunderstood. The deflation procedure I have been discussing, namely, correction for changes in the general price level, does not remove all the biases or difficulties that arise from changes in the value of money. This correction cannot, by itself, place the business income figures for two different periods on a par with one another and render them fully comparable. One important reason is that the various business costs set off against gross income, in the usual profit and loss statement, are based on "heterotemporal" prices. When I first used that word I was accused of indecently coupling Greek and Latin roots. Yet it expresses the idea succinctly. What I mean, of course, is that costs charged in, say 1940, involve prices paid not only in 1940 but also in earlier years. The ordinary deflation will not take care of this peculiarity of accounting figures. Other adjustments are needed to do that, and the economist has applied them to charges for cost of materials and charges for depreciation and depletion.

The first wrinkle in the accounting treatment of inventories and thus of cost of goods sold, that bothered economists was the "lower of cost or market" valuation practice. As early as 1932, Colin Clark felt it necessary to adjust the British figures, because of it, in order to attain comparability between periods of rising prices and periods of falling prices.

Soon, however, Simon Kuznets' work on capital formation at the National Bureau of Economic Research led him to take an additional and bigger step towards adjusting the accounting figures on inventories and costs of materials. He broke down changes in the reported book values of inventories into two components. For example, when both the physical volume of inventory and the market price of the goods held in inventory rose between the beginning and end of the year, he distinguished between:

(1) the value (at cost) of the increase in the number of physical units of inventory; and (2) the increase in the value of the opening physical inventory resulting from the replacement of units purchased at lower prices by units purchased at higher prices. To the economist, only the first component represents a real accretion to the country's wealth. Only the value of the physical increase in inventory is capital formation from an economic or social point of view. The second component, the increase in the value of the opening inventory, merely represents an upward revaluation of wealth already in existence, not an addition to wealth. Being such, it should not be treated as capital formation. Nor should it be considered to be part of the business income appropriate for inclusion in the national income.

Put differently, the true current cost of materials consumed is not their original cost, but their replacement value. In a period of rising prices, then, and viewing the matter from the economic or social standpoint, accounting net income is too high, because accountants charge most materials consumed at original, not replacement, cost. Accounting profits include the amount by which inventories are revalued. In a period of falling prices the reverse is true. Accounting net income is then too low, in the eyes of the economist. Business income from an economic viewpoint should be determined by subtracting from sales a cost of goods sold in which the units sold are valued at current, not original, cost prices. This explains why the series prepared by the National Bureau of Economic Research to measure the nation's income includes as a component business income adjusted to remove inventory revaluations. The Department of Commerce has taken over the notion, and its figures on national income are similarly built up.

The economist's adjustment of inventory (or cost of goods sold) strongly resembles, of course, the "last in, first out" or the LIFO method that has come into use in some business accounts, and I therefore need not take the time to develop it in detail. Nevertheless, several comments are necessary.

It should be noted, first, that this adjustment is applied by economists to *all* (or virtually all) business income. The national income figures are thus internally consistent. The data for different industries are, in this respect, fully comparable with one another. This is not true of accounting data on business income. Lifo is used by only a fraction of all business enterprises; and in the accounts of many of those using Lifo, it is not applied to all types of inventories. The adjustment made by economists was designed precisely in order to provide complete comparability between different companies or industries and between different periods of time.

The economic adjustment is different from Lifo not only in the scope of its application but also in the way it is applied. In Lifo, materials sold or consumed are charged at the cost of the most recently acquired materials. This might be the current year's price or it might be last year's price if the physical volume of inventories has been reduced from last year's level. (I am ignoring the special case of involuntary liquidation because of wartime shortages, in which the general Lifo rule is relaxed.) The economist always charges all materials sold or consumed in any year at that year's price, even when inventories are depleted during the year. The economist's method of adjustment therefore ensures that no inventory revaluation will be left in the income account to over- or under-state business income. Lifo does not. The intention, however, seems to be about the same. The purpose of Lifo, as the American Institute committee on accounting procedure states, is "to relate costs to revenues more nearly on the same price level basis than would the Fifo method." The purpose of the economist's method is to relate costs to revenues on *exactly* the same—the current—price level basis.

Though the economist tries to relate costs to revenues on the same price level basis, he cannot in fact fully attain that purpose. Accounting data constitute his raw material. To adjust them, he has to know what fraction of inventories are reported on Lifo, what portion on Fifo. Of the latter, he has to know what portion is valued at the lower of cost or market, what portion on other bases. Furthermore, he has to know how replacement prices have changed in each industry. But he does not know these things very exactly. He has to estimate them. Our national income figures, therefore, are adjusted on the basis of approximations only. But, again, the economist is glad to get closer to his objective, even if he cannot reach it fully, rather than content himself with the unadjusted figures.

The adjustment is a very considerable one, when prices are changing greatly. The Department of Commerce correction has run as high as +4 billions for 1930, —3 billions for 1933, +1 billion for 1938, —3 billions for 1941, and —6 billions for 1946. (These estimates cover not only corporations but also unincorporated enterprises, except farms.) Even if these adjustments are surrounded by considerable margins of error—and we may be sure they are—they are worth making.

If the objective is to relate costs to revenues on the same price level basis, there is no logical reason for stopping with the materials that come out of inventory. Charges for depreciation and depletion have to be treated in the same way. Capital assets consumed in the course of current production also should be charged at current prices rather than at original cost. If they are not, business income is—from the economist's point of view—overstated when prices are rising, understated when prices are falling.

The depreciation and depletion charges available to economists are, of course, the accountants' figures. These, therefore, also require adjustment. This adjustment, quite similar in principle to the adjustment made of inventories, is rather more difficult to make, however. Available depreciation and depletion data are pretty complicated. They combine figures relating to a great host of different dates;

some are in original cost, some at cost to second owners; depreciation methods and the distinction between capital charges and maintenance charges, vary among firms and even within firms; and tax-law complications, like the wartime amortization feature and the depletion methods accepted by the Treasury Department, provide stumbling blocks.

The computation of depreciation charges reminds me of a calculation reported in *Alice in Wonderland*. Because George May once told me that it is always good form to quote from that famous authority, I won't restrain myself:

"Fourteenth of March, I *think* it was," the Mad Hatter said.

"Fifteenth," said the March hare.

"Sixteenth," said the Dormouse.

"Write that down," the King said to the jury; and the jury eagerly wrote down all three dates on their slates, and then added them up, and reduced the answer to shillings and pence.

I think that is how depreciation charges are calculated — with a heavy weight given to March fifteenth, in this country. Anyway, the economist has to unscramble the data that accountants provide him. And to the components he has to apply an adjustment involving a knowledge of changes in the prices of plant and equipment when the very character of this property also is modified with time, and the prices therefore are not fully comparable from time to time.

Despite all these difficulties, however, rough approximation seems possible, in my opinion, and when price changes are great, eminently worth while. It brings us closer to the truth than if we fail to make it. Such an adjustment was put into the National Bureau's calculations of national income for the period 1919-1938. The magnitude of the adjustment may be appreciated if we glance back at those figures. Take, for example, 1919, which followed the rise in prices during World War I. Accounting measures of depreciation of business capital goods, for that year, amounted to 3.4 billion

dollars. The estimate in *current* prices, however, was 5.4 billion, a difference of 2 billions. The discrepancy for 1920 was even bigger, 2.6 billion. For 1932, of course, the current price estimate was lower than the book estimate.

By 1947, I would not be surprised, current accounting calculations may again understate the economic measure of depreciation by some billions. But the Department of Commerce, which provides the current statistics on national income, has not followed the lead of the National Bureau in this respect, and we therefore have no real estimate. It should be pointed out, however, that the Department agrees that revaluation of accounting depreciation charges is "indicated on conceptual grounds" (*Survey of Current Business, Supplement,* July, 1947, p. 11), and of course joins the National Bureau in excluding realized capital gains and losses from its measures of business income. Apparently the Department has not made an adjustment for the difference between book and current price estimates of depreciation because of the statistical difficulties involved. But whatever the reason for not making the adjustment, by not doing so the Department of Commerce overstates current business income in its presentation of the national accounts.

I might mention, also, that the Department further overstates business income because it adds back the tax-law deductions for depletion. These figures are, of course, almost meaningless from an economic standpoint, and therefore provide little information with which to start. But while the Department's attitude is quite understandable, its figures are none the less defective in this regard, too.

I come now to a question that has not received much consideration. Partly, I imagine, this is because it has seemed rather less important than the matters already mentioned, and it is less important during a period of great change in the general price level. Yet it is worth tossing into the forum because it will help us to see more clearly the meaning of the adjustments already described.

The basic idea of the inventory adjustment made by the economist is to keep out of business income, and thus out of national income, profits or losses—realized or unrealized—that arise out of mere changes in the prices at which the existing stock of the nation's wealth is assessed. For the nation *as a whole* is no better or worse off simply because the current value of a fixed number of units in its stock or goods has expanded or shrunk. (I pass over the exception created by international trade.) But is this true of the individual firm that owns a stock of goods the value of which has changed? The logic of the economist's inventory adjustment as now made—and the same goes for the adjustment of depreciation charges and for Lifo—implicitly states that it is true of the individual firm. It is assumed that, like the nation, the firm is no better or worse off because the current value of a fixed number of units in its stock of goods has changed.

It is clear, of course, that the individual firm is in fact not better or worse off if the unit value of its inventory has merely paralleled the general price level. But what if the two have diverged? Suppose, for example, that owing to the depletion of our resources, the unit value of the stock of copper held by nonferrous-metal refiners rises more rapidly than the general price level; and that, owing to technological advances, the unit value of the stock of rayon fiber held by rayon manufacturers rises less rapidly than the general price level. Can we really say that the one group has not gained, nor the other lost, by this differential price movement? Now, if the economist is interested only in the aggregate national income, he can ignore such gains and losses, for they more or less offset one another. In that case, however, he should note explicitly that the adjusted figures he presents for an *individual* industry are exclusive of its gains or losses from differential price movements. The figures measure, in a sense, what the industry puts *into* the national product, rather than what it gets *out* of the national product.

But the economist is often interested in what an industry or firm gets out of the national product. That is, the economist is then concerned with how the purchasing power resulting from business operations is distributed among industries or firms. Then it is another matter. Whether these profits or losses are or are not included does make a difference, and in the case of a particular industry or firm may sometimes make a great deal of difference. What are the pros and cons on including them?

The gain or loss arising from differential price movements may reflect differences only in the cyclical amplitudes of prices. In that case it can be argued that the profit or loss situation is only temporary, that it will soon be succeeded by the reverse situation at the next turn of the business cycle, and that this cyclical succession need not concern us. This argument is not iron-clad. But even if it is, it does not apply to the situation in which the gain or loss arises from sustained differential price movements, that is, from trend differences, rather than cyclical differences, in price movements. Here there is no cancellation. And here there seems to be little question that to the industry or firm affected the gain or loss is real.

One may grant that such gains and losses are real yet argue against including them in the economic measure of business income on the ground that they are not part of current income, but instead reflect windfall or capital gains or losses and should be treated accordingly. To this the counter-argument is, of course, that business enterprise does not take price movements to be mere disturbances of the situation in which business is done, but part and parcel thereof. Business enterprise aims at profiting, or avoiding loss, from such movements. Indeed, the exercise of foresight in this connection is a characteristic function of entrepreneurship, and active planning by business men to influence prices—whether those of goods purchased or of goods sold—rather than passively adjusting to them, is hardly unknown.

Brief mention may be made, finally, of another point. Some of the consequences of trading on a narrow equity or margin also tend to be excluded from the economic measures of business income, by the adjustments now in use. Yet the gains or losses resulting from changes in the burden of debt as price levels rise or fall influence greatly the distribution of purchasing power. For that reason these gains or losses also must find a place in a discussion of the economic measurement of business income. I will not take the time to develop these topics. Perhaps this is because I am subconsciously conforming to that professorial model of a lecture in which a third of what is said is obvious, a third is intelligible only to the brighter students, and a third is intelligible to no one. But I will admit only that I am simply trying to uncover some of the significant implications of the adjustments now used in preparing our national income figures. Only by studying these implications can we reach a real understanding of what the current economic viewpoint means, and find direction towards bettering it. In short, I am pointing to some of the unsettled problems that a study of business income must tackle.

Let me sum up the main points, on which almost all economists agree, as follows:

Accounting calculations of business income are unacceptable to economists. Current accounting reports yield figures for different companies that are not comparable with one another. Current accounting reports yield figures for a single company's operations in one year that are not comparable with figures for the same company in another year. During a period of inflation, such as we are in, these incomparabilities are serious.

To obtain comparable figures that measure business income from a consistent economic point of view, economists are therefore driven to make adjust-

ments of accounting data, or at least to attach qualifications to them. Economists follow the principle that costs should be related to revenues on the same price level basis, and that the income of one period should be compared with the income of another period on the same price level basis. In accord with this principle, economists believe that inventory revaluations should be excluded from business income, and the income estimates of the National Bureau of Economic Research and of the Department of Commerce do exclude them. Economists believe, also, that revaluations of fixed assets should be excluded from business income, and the income estimates of the National Bureau and Department of Commerce both exclude realized capital gains and losses. The estimates of the National Bureau further exclude revaluations of fixed assets arising from the charging of depreciation at original cost. The Department of Commerce also accepts the principle, but has so far implemented it only by a textual qualification of its figures. Finally, economists believe that comparisons of income over time are possible only if adjustments are made for changes in the purchasing power of money income, and all estimators of national income provide for such adjustments.

These are not small matters that we are discussing today. The accounts of business income are matters of great public concern. Cooperation among the various groups of society, so necessary to the efficient working and progressive development of our economy, is difficult to secure when there is widespread misunderstanding of how the nation's income is being distributed. To lessen—perhaps ultimately to dispel—this misunderstanding is a duty of the economists who practice social accounting. Is it not also a duty of those who practice public accounting?

The Varied Impact of Inflation on the Calculation of Business Income

By

Solomon Fabricant

A generation ago few people were interested in business accounts. I might add, also, that fewer still were able to find in the published income accounts and balance sheets the information they sought.

Much has happened since then to the role—and the rule—of business accounts in our economy. It will make a remarkable history when someone realizes the import of those events and sits down to describe them. The great economic and political changes of the past few decades have brought us to a situation in which the summary accounts of business are staked off as public domain, and the profits of business are viewed as matters of public concern. Business accounts are now being watched, analyzed and made use of not only by management and shareholders and regulatory commissions and competitors, but also by tax collectors, economists, statistical agencies, consumer organizations and trade unions. All these now seek vital information in these accounts.

When public policies and private strategies are influenced by business accounts, it is important that we understand what they have to tell us. This is especially necessary when inflation both sharpens interest in them and distorts the records they provide.

It is obvious that in a period of inflation the cost of living of wage earners goes up. It should be obvious, also, that the cost of replenishing inventories goes up, the cost of replacing worn-out equipment goes up, and the cost of living of stockholders goes up. Yet most accounting procedures fail to take any account, or adequate account, of these increases. Goods charged out of inventory are charged at their original cost, not at

17

their higher replacement cost. Depreciation is charged at the original cost of the depreciating plant and equipment, not at their higher replacement cost. As a result, inventory and plant are revalued as they are turned over. To take an example, a fixed stock of ten thousand men's shirts, worth say $20,000 in 1939, will now be valued at $40,000; and a fleet of 10 small motor trucks, worth perhaps $15,000 in 1939, will now be carried at something like $25,000, the exact amount depending on how many trucks had been replaced since 1939. Net worth will be higher by these increases in book value. Now ordinarily revaluations of assets are not allowed to get into the profit and loss account. Vigilant accountants treat them as surplus adjustments and shoo them away. But when revaluations find their way into the accounts not by deliberate reassessment of assets but by the indirect process of turnover of assets during inflation, they do get into the income account. The increase in net worth that I mentioned, the revaluation profit, will have been treated as ordinary income, indistinguishable from other income. Accountant's calculations of business profits will thus have been overstated.

Furthermore, the profits so calculated are not even corrected for changes in their purchasing power. In a nutshell, then, ordinary business accounts provide an exaggerated notion of business profits when price levels are going up.

So much, I think, is becoming recognized, though perhaps too slowly and too grudgingly. But the simple and general qualification of business accounts, to which this recognition leads, is not enough to avoid misinterpretation. We must realize, also, that the accounts of different industries and different enterprises are affected by inflation in different ways and in different degrees. Even stabilization of prices, if and when it comes, will not mean the end of inflation's effects on the calculated profits of each and every industry.

Why may the impact of inflation be greater on the business accounts of one industry than on those of another? There are a number of factors. These are: (1) variation, among industries, in the importance of physical assets in business operations; (2) variation in the rate of turnover of physical assets; (3) variation in the average age—or year of acquisition—of capital assets; (4) variation in the rate of rise in prices paid for physical assets; and (5) variation in the accounting procedures followed.

A brief comment on each of these will be sufficient to indicate its significance.

In an industry in which physical assets—plant and equipment and inventories—are of minor importance in the balance sheet, costs of materials and depreciation changes will usually be of minor importance in the income account. Even serious errors in the calculation of these costs will not appreciably distort calculated net income. When plant and equipment and inventories are important, however, and prices are rising, differences between original and replacement costs will bulk large compared with profits. Inclusion in net income of ''revaluation profits'' will seriously overstate net income.

The rate of turnover of assets also is relevant. Other things being equal, the more rapid the rate of turnover, the quicker does a rise in prices cause upward revaluations to materialize. The quicker, therefore, are calculated profits affected. Correspondingly, the slower the rate of turnover, the slower is the impact on profits. (I am, of course, discussing this factor with reference to the inflation that began only a few years ago. Should prices continue to march up indefinitely, differences in rates of turnover would eventually cease to play a significant role.) The interesting point here is that the effects of inflation on calculated business profits may appear even after—sometimes, long after—price levels have become stabilized. Thus, the public utilities, which hold long-lived assets, might be understating depreciation charges and over-stating profits for some time after the end of an inflationary movement. Indeed, they might be doing so even after deflation had begun and been reflected by downward inventory revaluations in other industries.

The effects of variation in average age of assets and in rate of price rise are obvious. Firms that were set up and in full operation in 1939 will be carrying their capital assets at values far below those of firms that sprang up or expanded greatly in recent years. Depreciation charges of the former group will understate replacement costs more seriously than depreciation charges of the latter group.

As for prices changes, variation among them is more considerable than most people suppose. It is one of the reasons why a single or general price index for putting original costs onto a replacement cost basis cannot be wholly applicable to all types of industries.

The final factor is variation in accounting procedure. Firms already using the last-in, first out, method of charging costs of materials—LIFO—are to that extent already correcting their accounts for the effects of inflation. Similarly, firms using ''accelerated'' depreciation or other devices for increasing depreciation charges above original-cost levels are recognizing and to that extent correcting for the effects of inflation. Naturally, also, when firms use maintenance rather than depreciation accounting, the impact of inflation on calculated profits is lessened. But not all firms do use these devices. Nor do those using them use them to the same extent. For this reason the accounts of different firms and industries are not comparable. Some reported profits are seriously, others are less seriously, affected by rising prices.

In principle, the net result of these several factors is measured by the sum of an inventory-revaluation adjustment and an adjustment for the difference between depreciation calculated at original cost and at replacement cost. I wish I could tell you how much these sums are, for various industries, and how their proportion to calculated profits varies from one industry to another. Unfortunately, only the inventory adjustment has been computed for each industrial group.

For all corporations, and for 1947, upward inventory revaluations accounted for 5 billion dollars of the 18 billion of corporate profits after tax, or 28 percent, according to the Department of Commerce. For wholesale trade, however, the percentage was 78, and for tobacco manufactures, 70. In contrast, for public utilities it was 15 percent and for textile mills, 12 percent, while the probable percentage for real estate and a few other like industries was too small even to be worth calculating. In the case of rubber manufactures, the inventory revaluation was downward, rather than upward as in all other industries, and as a consequence calculated profits of rubber corporations were *lower* than they would otherwise have been.

In 1948 total inventory revaluations were lower than in 1947. They amounted to 3,300 billons or 16 per cent of income after taxes, and I imagine that, unlike 1947, *downward* revaluations tended to depress calculated profits in more than one industry. The proportion of such downward revaluations may turn out to be even greater in 1949.

But revaluations that arise out of charging depreciation at original cost will continue to be positive for years to come, in most industries. The revaluations will, of course, diminish in size should levels become stabilized.

After World War I, to cite some calculations made in 1938, it took twenty years or more before the prices underlying depreciation charges caught up with current reproduction costs. In 1919 depreciation charges were about 30 percent below the amount they would have been had they been figured at the level of reproduction costs. The drop in prices after 1920 naturally reduced the gap. But since the price level in the 1920's was still well above that of 1913, the gap remained, diminishing as time went on. It was 20 percent in 1923, and still about 10 percent in 1929. Not until another drop occurred in prices, during the early 1930's, did the prices underlying depreciation charges come to equal—and then to exceed—reproduction costs. These estimates relate to business as a whole. I am sure that if we had them, the data for individual industries would show great variation in amount and timing.

I have said, enough, I think, to demonstrate that the impact of rising prices on calculations of business profits varies among industries and firms. For the sound use of business accounts we need to know what that impact is. The individual reader of an income account is in no position to make the calculation himself. I think it is up to the accountants.

REFERENCES

Simon Kuznets, "Changing Inventory Valuations and their Effect on Business Savings and on National Income Produced", in *Studies in Income and Wealth, Volume I*, National Bureau of Economic Research, 1937.

Solomon Fabricant, *Capital Consumption and Adjustment*, N. Y., National Bureau of Economic Research, 1938.

National Income Division, Department of Commerce, "National Income". Supplement to *Survey of Current Business*, July 1947.

American Institute of Accounts, *New Responsibilities of the Accounting Profession*, 1948; section on "Business Costs and Business Income under Changing Price Levels" by Solomon Fabricant, Joel M. Bowlby and Samuel J. Broad.

Reprinted from the JOURNAL OF THE AMERICAN STATISTICAL ASSOCIATION
June, 1952, Vol. 47, pp. 255-262

FACTORS IN THE ACCUMULATION OF SOCIAL STATISTICS

SOLOMON FABRICANT
New York University and *National Bureau of Economic Research*

ANALYSIS of the factors determining the stock of social statistics may be facilitated if we first formulate some general statements concerning changes in the stock itself. The appropriate viewpoint is, of course, that of the student of society. Let us, therefore, refer here to publicly available summary observations. Data reposing in private files or published only in the form of endless detail on individual economic transactions or units, like individual wholesale prices or lists of employees of state and local governments, may be processed into additions to the stock, but until this is done do not form part of it.

What has happened to the volume of social statistics in the United States during the past 160 years? The following conclusions will all seem pretty obvious to statisticians, though they are not less significant on that account.

(1) There has been a vast and fairly continuous expansion in the stock of social statistics. There are no simple measures of this stock, nor, indeed, is the way to construct them obvious. Yet even a quick thumbing through of the Bureau of the Census' *Historical Statistics of the United States, 1789–1945* (1949), should be sufficient to support our conclusion. Or one may compare the collection of time series in *Fluctuations in American Business, 1790–1860* by W. B. Smith and A. H. Cole (1935) with such a collection on the recent period as the appendix to A. F. Burns' essay on "Economic Research and the Keynesian Thinking of Our Times" (26th Annual Report of the National Bureau of Economic Research, 1946). The former shows what we have on that period better than do contemporary compendiums like Adam Seybert's *Statistical Annals* (1818), since it includes many original statistics assembled by the authors; yet it seems skimpy compared with Burns' rich and easy sampler. And the wealth of "survey" data today stands in sharp contrast to the few samples of earlier decades.

(2) Growth has occurred also in the annual accretion to the stock. More and more time series have been established to report contemporary events, and more and more historical series have been constructed from the fragmentary data of the past. The "time-period" index to *Historical Statistics* shows, approximately, the combined effect of both

developments on the number- of series available for various decades.[1] Family and other surveys have become periodic rather than sporadic.

(3) The composition of the stock of statistics has been improved with time. Surveys have come to be made of facets of social life known but not yet measured, and of facets newly developed and discovered. Some facets formerly mapped only in the large have been plotted in some detail. Thus, the bulk of the statistics relating to the opening decades of the 19th century are on population, foreign trade and shipping, wholesale prices, and the finances of the federal government. Contemporary information covers number and other characteristics of business establishments, as well as people; the volume of domestic trade and production, as well as foreign trade; farm prices, retail prices, and wage rates, as well as wholesale prices; and the finances of families, business enterprises and state and local governments, as well as federal finances. The earlier data on population tell little more than number, age, sex, and color. Today there is extensive information on birth, death, marriage, and divorce rates, family characteristics, occupation, education, and so on. And today's data are cross-classified to a greater extent than in the past. The growing number of census inquiries on each subject, summarized in C. D. Wright and W. C. Hunt's *History and Growth of the United States Census* (1900), shows how this major source of information has contributed to the increase in detail.

(4) Observations are available more frequently. The trend in the relative number of monthly and quarterly series has been upward. For evidence of this it is sufficient to refer to the collection of time series at the National Bureau of Economic Research, described briefly in A. F. Burns and W. C. Mitchell's *Measuring Business Cycles* (1946). And income and expenditure surveys, rare in the past, have become commonplace.

(5) Observations are available more promptly. Statistics are collected, tabulated and distributed more rapidly than they used to be. There is no readily available evidence on this point except for the census reports. We can be pretty sure, however, that the current lags between event and publication, some of which are given in the report on *The Statistical Agencies of the Federal Government* by F. C. Mills and C. D. Long (1949), are shorter than in the past.

(6) In other respects, too, the quality of our statistics has improved. Whatever doubts there may be about the accuracy of our current sta-

---

[1] The showing is only approximate (and biased upward) partly because the number of terminated series is not given, partly because the collection covers the earlier decades rather less adequately than the later decades, as the compilers point out.

tistics, there can be no doubt that they are on the whole more accurate and more representative of the activities they purport to cover than were statistics in the past. W. S. Holt's useful report on *The Bureau of the Census, Its History, Activities and Organization* (1929) provides summary evidence of improvement in the quality of one very important body of statistics.

Now, what factors underlie the increase in the part of the nation's capital stock with which we are concerned here? Why have these statistics been collected and published in ever-increasing quantity and ever-improving quality? Because federal, state and local governments constitute by far the chief source of social statistics, our question may be put primarily with reference to the factors accounting for growth in government's statistical output.[2]

One important reason why our statistics have grown is expansion in the nonstatistical functions of government. The sectors of social life over which government exercises its various powers have multiplied, and more aspects of the life in each sector have come under the surveillance of government. Increase in the scope of governmental activity is a phenomenon observed by all of us. Public health, factory and food inspection, charities, unemployment compensation, central banking, regulation of security issues, assistance to farmers and home owners, roads, and comprehensive river-valley development—these remind us of forms of governmental activity that have come on the scene or been greatly expanded in recent decades. The trend is one of long standing, however, as is evidenced by the formulation before the close of the nineteenth century of Adolph Wagner's "law of increasing State activities." The list of government activities has lengthened to the point where its contents, and changes in them, make substantial publications.[3] In each of its activities the government keeps records and gathers special information for use in current operations, planning, and budget preparation and justification. When released (though why they are released is a further question), these by-products pass into the stock of publicly available statistics.

The nonstatistical activities of government constitute also an important demand factor. The growing needs of administrative and regulatory agencies for information in current operations and planning led

---

[2] Of the 1,070 tables in the 1948 *Statistical Abstract* only 70 are in whole or even in part the product of private agencies.

[3] See, for example, the "Inventory of Governmental Activities in the United States" by C. H. Chatters and M. L. Hoover (1947); the several reports on the growth of city, county, and state functions, of which L. D. Upson's on Detroit ("The Growth of a City Government," 1942) is a prototype; and the useful set of "service monographs of the U. S. government" published by the Brookings Institution, one of which has already been cited.

to the expansion of statistics collected by "public-purpose collection agencies" like the Bureau of the Census and the Bureau of Labor Statistics. A fair amount of the statistics they gather is in response to demands on the part of other government agencies. For example, the basic constitutional provision underlying the work of the Bureau of the Census was intended to aid in administering another provision of the Constitution, that controlling representation, rather than to provide statistics. Further, it is in response to the demands of still other administrative agencies that some of the by-product statistics of administrative agencies are collected, even in the first instance, or if already collected are tabulated and released.

As governmental activity increased, not only absolutely, but also in relation to total activity, new sources of revenue were developed. These in turn became important sources of by-product statistics. *Statistics of Income* and the sales tax data are examples. Informational needs of the revenue agencies also helped to raise the demand for the general statistics collected by the public-purpose collection agencies, and thus contributed to the expansion of the activities of the latter. Similarly, the revenue agencies have collected statistics to meet the needs of other government agencies.

In this way, then, the volume of statistics rose with the growth of government activity. This growth led also to better balance in the composition of our statistics. The latter improvement came, however, because specific needs in the widening activities of government were met rather than because the imbalance was felt and the general needs for information about dark areas satisfied.

A special word must be said about the influence of World War I on government statistics. Even before that war the trend was toward increase in the central government's role in the regulation and administration of economic life. Exercise of that role was bound to point up the need for statistics "not only as a record of what had happened," as Professor Mitchell told the American Statistical Association right after the war, "but also as a vital factor in planning what should be done."[4] The war threw the country into a situation demanding immediate and extensive central planning and administration, and thus precipitated the need for more and better statistics. It is not an accident, therefore, that so many of our time series, especially monthly series, begin with that period.

The statistical services of government meet not only the demand of government itself but also demand on the part of the public. It is this

---

[4] *Quarterly Publications of the American Statistical Association*, March, 1919; reprinted in *The Backward Art of Spending Money and Other Essays* (1937).

demand that requires publication of statistics, for governmental needs can be, and often are, met within the confines of government without publication. What is in back of the public's demand?

Fundamental, I think, is Western civilization's tendency to become more and more "peculiarly matter-of-fact," as Thorstein Veblen put it.[5] Our attitudes and values have been shaped by the overwhelming successes of modern science and technology. We are convinced, in ever-increasing measure, that growth and diffusion of scientific—that is, matter-of-fact—knowledge is "indefeasibly right and good." As a result, we have come to value the methods of science, of which statistics is now one. We see worth in their application to all situations, including those in which they have not yet borne fruit.

Increasing public interest in and demand for social statistics rests, then, on the basic premise that the problems of society, as well as of natural science and technology, can be solved by the increase and diffusion of this especially matter-of-fact type of matter-of-fact knowledge. The whole world now seems to hold that statistics can be useful in understanding, assessing, and controlling the operations of society.

More peculiar to this country is a strong interest in ourselves, stimulated by our extraordinary growth. Growth in the population, trade, industry, and cities of the United States has always been so rapid as to command popular attention and admiration. It seems right and natural that every census should reveal expansion. Small increases surprise and appear *prima facie* questionable; the Bureau of the Census has frequently had difficulties with city fathers disappointed with the slow growth of their broods.

A society in which science and technology are transforming its industries and institutions as well as stimulating its growth, is one in which social problems crop up. These raise specific demands for information. The statistical work of the National Monetary Commission is one example of response to these needs. Once statistical explorations are made, periodic collection frequently follows: consider the history of the "Monthly Report on Labor Force." The current volume of time series and survey data being published has in this way been expanded and its composition modified.

Social changes that create problems also often lead to extensions of governmental activity to deal with them. From this, as already noted, many by-product statistics emerge, of which the great collection of Interstate Commerce Commission data is a shining example.

---

[5] "The Place of Science in Modern Civilization," *The American Journal of Sociology*, March, 1906; reprinted in *The Place of Science in Modern Civilization and Other Essays* (1919).

Concomitant change occurs also in the nature of business, thereby stimulating a demand for statistics on the part of business enterprises. Expansion of long-term investments of a type that (unlike land) is recognized as subject to obsolescence, has resulted in attempts to widen horizons. These create needs for various types of statistics not felt necessary in earlier days. Related is growing business demand for statistics on the presumption that more and better information can help prevent or ameliorate difficulties arising from short-term economic change. The great expansion of statistics by the Department of Commerce after World War I was in part founded on this presumption. The rise of advertising and national marketing is another cause of increasing business demand. And surely the expansion of trade-unionism has stimulated a demand for statistics by businessmen, as well as by the unions and government agencies concerned with industrial relations.

Development of economic and statistical science also has accompanied—been forced by—social change. These branches of learning have had a share in expanding and improving governmental statistics, as well as in swelling the demand. From its very birth the American Statistical Association has had a significant role in improving and enlarging our stock of statistics. The contribution of its members to small sample theory and practice is an example of a factor on the supply side.

Enlarged scientific experience has resulted in displacing the vague feeling that factual knowledge is good by a sharper understanding of how and in what way statistics can help. And as in other scientific work, an important consequence of statistical research and analysis has been the discovery of other, as yet uncollected, statistics that are necessary and desirable. Index numbers, national income accounts, input-output tables, and other ways of summarizing and presenting data, first developed and put to use by private investigators, have been taken over and utilized by the federal government and have thus expanded the scope of its statistical output. Realization of this fruitful interchange has provided another reason for publication of what might otherwise remain intramural governmental statistics: that is the opportunity afforded for review, assessment, and criticism, as well as use, by private agencies and scholars.

Physical science and technology appear on the supply as well as the demand side of our account. Their growth has helped to cut the costs of collecting, processing, and publishing statistics and to speed up collection and transmission. Tabulating equipment, mechanical computers, and the telephone are essential statistical tools today, without which the rapid presentation of adequate statistics would not be possible.

The spread of the pecuniary standard and improvements in records, to which government tax and regulatory requirements have contributed, has made it possible to obtain better, more uniform, and more detailed statistics from families and farmers as well as businessmen. Together with increased size of business enterprise and better instruments of communication this development has made it possible also to secure data more speedily. Appreciation of the value of statistics on the part of businessmen has also helped to lessen resistance to government questionnaires and provide the voluntary cooperation so essential to good quality.

These various factors have also swelled the flow from nongovernmental sources of statistics on "aggregates" as distinct from reports on individual economic units. As mentioned earlier, the bulk of our social statistics originate in governmental sources, one reason being that the marginal social value of statistics exceeds their marginal private value: statistics are like lighthouses and street-lamps. Another reason is the ensurance of secrecy. But nongovernmental sources like trade associations, central markets, and research institutions should not be ignored. Their summary statistics contribute to the current flow directly as well as through governmentally assembled larger aggregates. Nongovernmental statistics have increased in volume partly because their sources have grown in number, and partly because reports from them have expanded in scope. Obvious examples are provided by the trade association statistics on production used by the Federal Reserve Board; the statistics issued by the New York Stock Exchange; and the series on department stores currently compiled at Harvard University.

It appears, then, that the statistical stock of the country increased because of such factors as the widening and deepening of government activities, advances in technology, the appearance of new industries and new problems, and the growth of trade associations and similar organizations. No assessment has been attempted of shifts in the role of the several factors in the development of statistics, nor has it usually been possible to attach even a rough average weight to each. Our analysis is not much more concrete than those found in earlier discussions of this subject. One reason for this is that the various factors are not in fact independent of one another. Are they not all, indeed, characteristic features of the economic development of countries in which income rises, the main contours of industrial structure are altered in the direction expressed by the term "industrialization," people move to the cities, and so on? If we were to summarize the various factors we have considered in a few words, it might be in the proposition that the growth of our statistics is itself an aspect of our economic and social development. It has surely been greatly influenced by that development.

But we should not minimize the influence of other factors that have affected our statistical wealth directly, and perhaps also indirectly through their influence on the role of government and other factors in our development. Thus, one of the great compromises of the Constitutional Convention, that seats in the House be apportioned by population and therefore that a decennial Census be taken, must have had a special influence on the development of statistics in this country, and must help explain our high level relative to other countries. The Constitutional requirement itself is minimal, necessitating only a bare count of each of two groups of the population. But from the beginning it has been a vehicle on which more and more has been loaded. Even the first Census asked more than the minimum, and when the second was being planned, there were already requests for additional information—a demand that has grown ever since.

If we are right in our conclusion that the upward trend in the stock of statistics is largely a concomitant of economic and social growth, it follows that upward trends have characterized the statistics of all countries participating in that development. Also, if we were to take a view of the world today we would find a significant degree of correlation between volume of statistics and degree of development, whether measured by income per capita, importance of non-farming industry, or otherwise. These inferences would be confirmed by even a quick glance at Colin Clark's *Conditions of Economic Progress* and the statistical publications of the United Nations.

One implication of this for social science is that plenty of work needs to be done to extract and organize information from the meagre records of unindustrialized countries, past or present. For a necessary condition of improving our understanding of economic development is to know more about the countries and periods for which adequate social statistics are now lacking.

A final word on the question of economic development, to which we have been led. Growth of our statistics has been greatly influenced by economic development. In turn, however, statistics have helped to mold that development. For the presence of expanded statistical information affects economic behavior. It makes possible governmental activity (some would say, interference) of a kind not otherwise possible. And it influences the behavior of businessmen, who have always been sensitive to information. Like other elements in the nation's capital stock, statistics are cause as well as consequence of economic change. Statistics play their part in the cumulative process of economic development.

4

NOTES ON THE DEFLATION OF
NATIONAL ACCOUNTS

By S. Fabricant

WHEN our friend, Roy Geary, suggested that I might devote my attention at this conference to some critical comments on the ideas that members of the Association had been developing and discussing on the deflation of national accounts, I hesitated. I was not at all sure that I would disagree with anything that had been said, or know why if I did. But one can always find a few points on which it seems worthwhile to comment, and others, perhaps deserving of thought, to draw into the discussion. I proceed to do so with the warning that the word 'notes' in the title above is to be taken literally.

1. There is some danger, I suppose, that abstract discussions of the form and detail of national accounts, and of their deflation, will give as much attention to items of small or even negligible importance as to items of major importance.

Thus, in preparing a formal list of the immediate sources of increase in the total of real consumption and increment in real net worth of a nation (or other economic unit) we specialists would note that this total is greater not only when (1) real income has risen, but also when (2) increase in real net worth for reasons not associated with saving, is greater than before or (3) larger gifts have, on net balance, been received from foreigners (or other 'outsiders'). Real income, we would then go on to say, may rise because (1a) more real resources are put into production, or (1b) more real net output is obtained per unit of real resources, or – also – because (1c) prices paid for the things purchased from foreigners decline in relation to prices received in sales of output to foreigners. And real net worth may increase, apart from saving, because (2a) upward 'capital adjustments' have taken place in real assets, or downward adjustments in real liabilities, or (2b) the relative price of foreign assets has increased or the relative price of liabilities to foreigners has decreased.

In principle, if we are to know whether and by how much a nation is better or worse off in the respect considered here, and if we are to obtain some of the figures necessary (though not sufficient) to explain why, we need estimates of each of the changes mentioned.

In practice, however, some of the items in the catalogue are usually unimportant. This is very likely true of the capital adjustments (item 2b), such as those that record the uncovering of valuable mineral resources or the destruction of cities, to recall the sort of example of which Professor Pigou wrote. It is also likely that gifts to (or from) nations (item 3) are not substantial in most cases. Even the gain or loss from changes in the terms of trade (item 1c) has not usually been large in the United States, and this may well be true of some other countries as well. In 'normal' times, further, we may expect revaluations of foreign assets and liabilities to be of small importance.

On the other hand, it is well to keep such items in mind in case they become important, as they surely do on occasion, even for nations and even for periods as short as a year. The regularly published national accounts should not be cluttered up with many small items merely for the sake of formal completeness, but we need to know whether the items are small before we consolidate them with others or omit them entirely. When they are important they must be recorded in the national accounts, whether expressed in current or in constant prices, in identifiable form, if changes in income and wealth are to be properly measured and interpreted. The solution, sometimes suggested, of a full statement only at longer than annual intervals seems eminently sensible.

In describing changes in the economic well-being of groups smaller than nations, there is a higher probability that the items mentioned are important, over the short as well as the long term. I am rather doubtful, however, that the national accounts (as they are ordinarily conceived) are the place to include all the items relevant to the changing internal distribution of income. The special tables useful for this purpose need, of course, to be reconciled with the national accounts and differences clearly brought out, but there is a limit to what we should ask the national accounts to bear – especially if, as appears to be the trend, we try to broaden them to include balance sheets, interindustry tables, and flow-of-funds accounts. (See, in this connection, the report of the Goldsmith Committee, which made some far-reaching proposals with respect to the United States accounts.)

2. A question that arises in measuring 'employee input' – and other inputs as well – in constant prices, is the degree of detail with which to deal. Sometimes there is nothing to do but use the total of all man-hours worked. But more often, I am sure, different categories of labour can be distinguished. When this is possible, it is desirable to use the information and calculate a weighted man-hours series, in which a man-hour paid at a high wage or salary rate is counted as more than a man-hour paid at a low rate. The derived 'employee increment' will be correspondingly different, as will be also the whole productivity increment. The difference between the unweighted man-hours series – the simple count of man-hours – and the weighted man-hours series has in fact been of some importance in the United States even over periods of a few years, as has been demonstrated with John Kendrick's calculations in a recent National Bureau publication on *Basic Facts on Productivity Change* (Occasional Paper 63).

More is involved than inter-industry differences in hourly earnings. Labour has changed its character and composition also within industries, for example, through a general improvement in the level of education, and eventually it may be possible to take these into account. When they are not, as is presumably the usual case, the measure of 'employee increment' covers the return to increased investment in education, among other things, as well as the rise in the real wages earned in a given type of work. Presentation of such a deficient measure, even when qualified, may lead to misunderstanding and misinterpretation of the facts on the distribution of national income as well as on the 'productivity increment'.

3. Neither Geary nor Burge were able to measure capital input and thus derive a 'property increment' for the countries they dealt with, but I am glad to see a note of optimism creeping into Geary's view of the possibility.

True, the measurement of capital input is not easy. For domestic capital, the problems caused by the variety of contractual arrangements with respect to property income – fixed payments, variable payments, and mixtures of the two – can be avoided, at least at this stage of development of constant-price accounts, by dealing with capital input as a whole. But there are plenty of other difficulties. Determination of the 'physical volume' of the services of capital involves all kinds of well-known problems – concerning quality changes, depreciation and obsolescence, depletion and other items of capital consumption, and unused capacity, to mention a few – to the solution of which present answers contain arbitrary elements.

But a useful calculation can sometimes be offered, as has been done for the United States and other countries at meetings of the Association, and is done for additional countries at the present conference. Apart from short-term fluctuations, the deflated net book value of tangible assets provides a reasonably adequate approximation, I think, to an index of the 'physical volume' of services rendered by tangible capital. This measure is better, at any rate, than the depreciation charges, horsepower of equipment, fuel and other figures to which recourse has sometimes been had.

I find it more palatable, also, to use net rather than gross capital assets, even when the 'one-horse shay' may be supposed to render the same service with the same operating expenses to the day it collapses. Over a long period it makes a difference, as Kuznets' estimates for the United States have indicated. Use of gross rather than net capital assets amounts to equating the value of long-lived equipment of a given capacity to that of short-lived equipment of the same capacity. What is really involved in the proposal to use gross assets is, I think, a criticism of the straight-line depreciation formula, which is a matter handled better in other ways.

In the case of an economy in which capital invested abroad is substantial, the problem raised by contractual arrangements – the terms on which the investment is made – cannot be side-stepped if we are to measure capital input in constant prices. If the investment is 'direct', there is no reason why the quantity of input of capital abroad should not be determined in the same way as the input of domestic capital goods, using the appropriate foreign price series to deflate the value of the asset.

If the foreign assets consist of securities, there are two possibilities. In one, a problem of capital adjustment may enter. To illustrate the line of approach, it may be sufficient to say that if foreign price levels rise, or exchange rates alter, the volume of services of capital invested in foreign fixed-income securities must be assumed to decline, not because the real price of the services declines but because the quantity of capital declines as a result of downward capital adjustments. With appropriate changes, a similar procedure may be used for fixed-income debt to foreigners. On the other hand, if price increases abroad are anticipated, and interest rates are agreed upon accordingly, the appropriate treatment involves an amortization allowance, which is to be deducted from the interest payment. Instead of a periodic capital adjustment, in other words, there is a periodic (but not 'straight-line') amortization charge on current account. In either case, however, real income declines and, along with it, the volume of input of capital invested abroad.

4. Improvement in the terms of foreign trade leads to a 'trading gain', as it is called by Geary and Burge.

This gain may be viewed as consisting of two components. In the U.S. national accounts one component is swallowed up in the consumption, domestic investment, or government purchases items. The sum of these three items is larger than it would be if there were no trading gain, to the extent that improvement in the terms of trade is taken in the form of bigger imports. The other component appears in the deflated net foreign investment item – provided it is deflated directly.

But, in fact, the Department of Commerce deflates the net foreign balance by the double-deflation method, in which exports and imports of goods and services, including factor returns, are deflated separately, with the real balance derived from the difference between the two deflated series. As a result, the Department of Commerce's deflated net foreign investment item includes a component that is equal and of opposite sign to the component included in the rest of the GNP account. The application of the double-deflation method to the net foreign balance takes the trading gain out of the U.S. accounts.[1]

---

[1] Perhaps the following example will make clearer what I am trying to say. Assume an economy with a single export, the entire production of which is exported in period 0, to pay for an identical dollar value of imports. Assume, also, that the price of the export rises by 50 per cent, but that no change occurs in the price of imports. Now compare the three alternative situations in period 1: 1a, in which the entire production continues to go abroad, financing foreign investment; 1b, in which only enough production is exported to pay for a constant volume of imports, with the balance consumed domestically; and 1c, in which half of the gain is used to finance foreign investment and the other half finances higher consumption. In current prices, we have:

	0	1a	1b	1c
Production	100	150	150	150
Consumption	0	0	50	25
Exports	100	150	100	125
Imports	100	100	100	100
Foreign investment . . .	0	50	0	25

[Continued on facing page.

While I have used the export price index in the footnoted example, there is, of course, a question concerning the deflator to use in putting the net foreign balance into constant prices. I do not favour the export or the import price index, or any combination of them, whether the net foreign balance is positive or negative. The appropriate deflator seems to me to be the price of the assets acquired – the foreign price if the assets are abroad, the domestic price if they are within the country. This procedure would require breaking up the net foreign balance into its two components, capital exports and capital imports, but it would meet the test of world consolidation as well as the use of export and import prices (as would many other indexes). However, the data problem forces a simpler solution, such as the implicit GCF deflator, even though the solution does not meet the consolidation test.

Some persons may be troubled by certain of the implications of the deflation suggested. Consider the simple example of a product which can be consumed or exported to finance the acquisition of foreign property. Assume the domestic and export prices of the product are identical and that the export price rises in relation to the price of foreign property. If the product is used to acquire foreign property, deflated GNP will be larger than if the product is consumed. But this result is not peculiar to the problem under consideration. It is generally the case that shifting from dearer to cheaper commodities makes a person (or nation) better off.

5. The real income of a nation depends on the volume of resources it puts into production, the product it gets per unit of resources, and the purchasing power of the product in terms of the goods and services finally consumed and invested. In

---

In constant prices, using the export price to deflate the net foreign balance, we have:

	0	1a	1b	1c
Production	100	100	100	100
Consumption	0	0	33	17
Exports	100	100	67	83
Imports	100	100	100	100
Foreign investment:				
Direct deflation	0	33	0	17
Double deflation	0	0	−33	−17
Trading gain:				
Direct deflation	0	33	33	33
Double deflation	0	0	0	0

The direct deflation procedure yields results invariant to change in the way in which the trading gain is used.

E

the terminology of Geary and his colleagues, real income equals factor input plus productivity increment plus trading gain.

If we are to understand how real income changes, it is desirable to distinguish between the two increments or gains. We should recognize, however, that a distinction is being made between related, not independent, factors.

There is a functional relation between the productivity increment and the trading gain. Other things constant, we may expect that the bigger is the productivity increment, the smaller is the trading gain. This negative relation does in fact appear in the figures for the United States, when long-term changes in the output per unit of resources of different industries are compared with corresponding changes in relative prices. I would expect the correlation to be of some importance even for small nations, especially those concentrating heavily on the production of a few export commodities and providing a substantial fraction of the total supply entering world trade. When technological and other improvement develops a productivity increment, it tends also to develop a trading 'loss'. The effect of the improvement is the sum of the two, in the absence of other factors impinging on the terms of trade. Since there are such other factors, we do want to keep the productivity gain separate from the trading gain. But in presenting the figures, and in using them for analysis, the relation I have mentioned must be kept in mind. It is especially important to avoid the reckless charges of exploitation, to which misinterpretation of changing terms of trade has sometimes led.

In this connection, perhaps a further comment is warranted. It might be argued that the productivity increment reflects domestic or internal changes, while the trading gain reflects external changes, and the two should on that account be viewed as independent. I would question this argument. I have already indicated that the trading gain reflects internal as well as external changes. It may be said with equal truth that the productivity increment reflects external as well as internal changes. What happens to output per unit of input within a country, region, industry, or firm reflects, in part, changes in the knowledge, materials, equipment, and services that the country or other unit obtains from the outside, and the scale of markets generated by the economy of which it is a part.

6. A related point may be made in connection with the deflation of the value added by an industry.

The double-deflation method for the net foreign balance sometimes leads to a change in the sign of the balance. For examples, compare Tables I-1 and I-2 in the recent official report on *U.S. Income and Output*. This possibility is a major objection to the use of the double-deflation method in transforming the foreign balance.

As has been known for some time, such a reversal of sign is possible also in the application of the double-deflation method in calculating the constant-price net value added by an industry, that is, in getting its real net output. It will tend to occur, for example, when the price of materials rises in relation to the price of the product, and this leads to the economizing of materials by substituting for them the labour and capital used by the industry. If materials constitute a large fraction of the total input in the base period, if the rise in the relative price of the materials is great, and if total productivity – output per unit of all resources – is slow to change, it may in fact occur.

Is this an objection to the use of the double-deflation method in getting at the net output of an industry? It is, if the objective is to determine the change in the industry's purchasing power – that is, to measure the industry's output from its own point of view. If the objective is to determine the industry's contribution to the nation's output the objection does not hold. The appearance of a negative net value added will then signify a disequilibrium situation in the current period and suggest that the industry is obsolescent; or it may indicate that the weight-base price situation was abnormal.

7. The notion of disequilibrium appears also in connection with the interesting suggestion, in the UN paper on *A System of Price and Quantity Indexes for National Accounts*, that in deflating the net foreign balance it may be prudent to choose the deflator that yields the more conservative results. For 'the relative price rise for the goods comprising the export surplus of the country represents only a contingent trading gain, which may not be realized because of subsequent change in export-import price relationships . . .' Accountants have been arguing this sort of book-keeping for generations.

One may think of changes in the terms of trade as falling into three classes. One, like the seasonal, follows a more or less regular pattern which can be anticipated, and adjustment to it made – not by being conservative in the choice of deflator, but by 'deseasonalizing' the result. The second includes irregular changes, like occasional fires, the probability of which is fairly well known and for which allowance is appropriately made by setting up a reserve, credits to which are charged to current operations, and debits are viewed as capital adjustments. The third class includes all other changes.

I suspect that many, if not most of the changes in terms of trade and other items of interest in the present connection fall in the third category. Changes associated with business cycles, for example, are not regular enough to be counted in the first class, nor lend themselves to the treatment appropriate to the second. If this is true, is it not better to choose the most appropriate deflator, whether or not it is conservative? It is well to be conservative, but not to pursue the policy by what some might feel was doctoring the accounts. The 'facts' should be set forth with such notes, interpretations, and qualifications added as are desirable.

In this connection, mention may be made of the inadequacies of the straight-line or similar method of depreciating capital assets, to which Stuvel has recently drawn attention. The appropriate procedure, it seems to me, is to replace this method with one that allows for changes in the rate of wear and tear. An output method of allocating depreciation, rather than capital adjustments for abnormal or subnormal depreciation rates, is what is needed.

8. Also related to the question of disequilibrium is the matter of inter-industry shifts, as Kuznets likes to call them, or structural changes, as Geary names them in his paper.

If input is all inclusive, covering all factors of production, and each is measured by a value weighted index, such as I have suggested above, the effect of inter-industry or structural changes will vanish. For in effect, the use of such weights assumes that the unit of quantity of an input is a dollar's worth in the base period. With all inputs covered, there are no economic branches of lower or higher productivity: all are alike.

This is an assumption that cannot be fully justified, and indeed might be rejected by many who feel that agriculture, for example, is indeed an industry of low productivity.

What, in fact, might cause the average hourly earnings of labour (or rates of return on property) to differ among industries in the base period? Surely differences in the quality of labour, such as arise from differences in education, innate ability, acquired skill, age, and in some cases sex, play a very significant role. But there are other reasons, as well: difference in the cost of living; the many differences subsumed under the catch-all 'non-economic advantages and disadvantages' (including amortization of investment in education); the possibility – perhaps I should say certainty – that the economy is not in full equilibrium in the base period, so that some portion of the differentials reflect adjustments still under way to changes in demand, technology, etc.; and imperfections in the market, which are not always easy to distinguish from factors causing lags in adjustment. I rather suspect that when agricultural labour is said to be less productive, reference is being made largely to this last factor. But the wage differential can hardly be said to measure it adequately. The question deserves further empirical and theoretical investigation.

PRICES IN THE NATIONAL ACCOUNTS FRAMEWORK: A CASE FOR COST-BENEFIT ANALYSIS*

BY SOLOMON FABRICANT

New York University and National Bureau of Economic Research

There are serious questions about the social costs and benefits of extending the role of prices in the national accounts. The costs may be greater, and the benefits smaller, than is commonly supposed. Many important uses of price (and other) data do not require that these data be organized within an elaborate—or even any—framework of national accounts. Also, the basic price (and other) data are still too often very scanty and rough. Would it not be better to devote available resources to improving these data rather than trying to force them, prematurely, into an elaborated set of national accounts?

I

This is not going to be an analysis of the benefits and the costs that flow from placing prices within the framework of the national accounts, or that may be expected to flow from extending the role of prices in the national accounts. As the title of my remarks indicates, my objective is (necessarily) much more modest. I shall be content if I succeed in making a plausible case for such an analysis.

Merely to raise the question may strike some of you as more than a hint of doubt—perhaps even a show of prejudice—on my part about the value of an extension. At the risk of seeming to protest too much, I would deny the prejudice. But not the doubt. I do believe, of course—what economist does not?—in "the importance of prices, not merely as a means for deflation of current price aggregates but as a tool for understanding . . . economic processes," as Simon Goldberg put it in describing his hopes and plans for this session. And, like all of us here, I see advantages in having our price data in a well-organized form. But there are ways and ways to organize the price data. "The" system, or even "a" system, of national accounts is not the only way. And every economist knows also that "there is no such thing as a free lunch"—or a free tool or a costless elaboration of the national accounts.

We have been hearing a good deal, in the discussions here and elsewhere, about the deficiencies and limitations of the price data in the national accounts and how to remove them. Note, especially, the far-reaching proposal made in the recent U.N. report for expanding the price and quantity data in the SNA.[1] Not nearly as much has been said about the benefits that would result from these and other improvements. Nor, beyond the very little implied by suggestions on priorities and reminders about "strains on statistical resources," has anything been said about the costs of the improvements. We need to be clearer on the benefits. We need to know much more about the costs.

*Paper presented at the Eleventh General Conference of the International Association for Research in Income and Wealth, August 26, 1969, Nathanya, Israel.
[1]*A System of National Accounts*, Studies in Methods, Series F, No. 2, Rev. 3, Statistical Office of the United Nations, UN, N.Y., 1968.

It might be argued that this is not the time or place for worrying about costs or about the relation between costs and benefits. We are not in a Bureau of the Budget meeting or a meeting of a Congressional appropriations committee, to use the terminology of my country. This is a meeting, rather, of an association of technicians. Is it not proper for technicians to concentrate on ways of improving the information they supply? Granted. But even technicians may not always push aside the problem of limited resources. There is more than one way to improve the price information in (or out of) the national accounts. Which shall we choose to discuss? Which shall we choose to pursue among those we find promising? Also, some of us (particularly those from the smaller or poorer countries) have a responsibility not only for the national accounts but also for other kinds of economic and social information; and for the initial collection, as well as the organization and dissemination, of the data. We cannot ignore the competition among these tasks. We need to give some thought to how we will justify to others, and to ourselves, our requests for funds for new work—*any* new work—on the national accounts, and how we will answer questions about its cost. We have come to take the value of the national accounts framework too much for granted, and to presume—as a matter of course—that almost any elaboration of the accounts is worthwhile.

II

When we are asked, as Goldberg asked, "Where do we want to go from here?", it is not enough to reply that we want better price data, arranged within the framework of the national accounts. "Betterment" has many dimensions.

We could improve the basic price data. More and better allowances for changes in quality could be made. Our samples could be extended to cover more commodities. The reliability of the prices we cover could be improved by lengthening the list of reporters and by getting realized rather than merely list prices. The frequency with which price information is reported could be multiplied. And so on.

Besides improving the data on the prices of final and intermediate goods, we could better also the information on input prices, such as wage rates, salary rates, and rental rates. We could add more information on over-time wage rates and fringe-benefits. And we could ask for more and better information on interest rates of various kinds, including rates at time of commitment of funds as well as rates realized on portfolio holdings; and rates on second and third mortgages, as well as on first mortgages. Indeed, there is need for all the information that Goldsmith has often listed as essential if we are to understand the flow of funds through the capital and credit markets. It is obvious that there are any number of directions we can go to improve our basic price data and that these compete with one another.

Further, what price data there are can be arranged and summarized in a variety of ways. For example, suggestions are being made that we add to the implicit (Paasche) indexes now provided by the national accounts, indexes of the Laspeyres type and also of the Fisher-Ideal or Edgeworth type. We could go further in subsitituting double-deflation price (and output) indexes for the more usual single-deflation indexes available for individual industries. The various indexes could be calculated on a greater number of bases, comparing chain with direct indexes, etc. Work in these directions is also obviously competitive with improvement of the basic data.

Nor is this all. When deciding "where to go from here," we must recognize that there are other frameworks than the system of national accounts, or the particular system we call the SNA, within which to arrange the price data. Before the 1944 tripartite agreement on the standard system of national accounts,[2] price data (and other information) were nevertheless organized to a useful degree. A choice has to be made here also.

Nor are good and well-organized data wanted for their own sake. The objective, rather, is to deepen our understanding of the drift of events and of the factors that influence their course. This requires not only organized data but also resources for research on economic behavior and policy—again, a matter of competition. To illustrate, some of the time and energy spent in estimating (or maybe only pretending to estimate) double deflation indexes, might have been spent on learning more about the kind, amount, and causes of changes in technical coefficients and in relative prices.

So, the question with which we started leads to another: What are the relative benefits to be expected from the investment of another unit of resources in the various directions mentioned? It is not a simple problem of ordering priorities—first, better basic data, *then* more elaboration of the accounts. Nor should we expect equal returns from equal extensions along the competing dimensions.

III

The question of benefits is difficult partly because we are engaged in a non-profit type of activity. The returns accrue to society at large—they are indirect as well as direct—there is no market measure of their value. To complicate the problem further, a significant part of what we want to add to our work is of an R & D type that (hopefully) will break new ground. There are always uncertainties in determining the output of a research enterprise. Even when the aim is only to follow in the footsteps of others, as in the case of the less developed countries, it is necessary to adapt and adjust to different circumstances.

In addition, we have only vague notions of how to recognize and assess the extent of any improvement in the quality of our price data. It is certainly not easier than measuring improvements in the quality of the commodities to which our price data relate. There is no price differential attached to the data improvement, to which to turn; and surely we may not use the cost of the betterment. Only to a limited extent is it possible to rely on statistical criteria, such as the standard errors now provided to assess the accuracy of changes in the U.S. Consumer Price Index.

One reason why we often run into trouble when we talk about the advantages

[2]E. F. Denison, "Report on Tripartite Discussion of National Income Measurement," in Conference on Research in Income and Wealth, *Studies in Income and Wealth*, Volume Ten, NBER, 1947.

of improved statistics is that we do so without regard to the specific uses to be made of the statistics. It is impossible to decide how much, or even whether, any piece of information is deficient or better or worse than another piece of information unless the use to be made of it is specified. But even given a particular use, how can we determine—even in theory—what difference it makes in that use whether a particular item of information is off, say, by only 10 per cent instead of by as much as 20 per cent? We can hardly say that our purpose will be twice as well served by cutting the error in half. But it will be served better by just 10 per cent (the absolute reduction in the percentage error), or is the proportion something else?

All this is rather abstract, so let me cite an example suggested by the very useful Alterman-Marimont paper.[3] They mention that the Young-Harkins comparison of alternative measures of price change yielded some "rather large" differences. Between the 3rd and 4th quarters of 1965, for example, the GNP implicit deflator (essentially a Paasche index) indicated a general price change of 1.8 per cent (at an annual rate). A 1958-weighted measure (a Laspeyres index) showed an increase of 2.7 per cent—"50 per cent higher." The change in the GNP deflator is, then, off—though whether by 50 per cent or only by the difference between it and (say) the geometric mean of the Paasche and Laspeyres, or by something else, is still a question. How serious is this? How much would it be worth to incur the cost—in this particular case, obviously very slight—to compute both indexes and perhaps also a Fisher Ideal? Suppose the GNP deflator were used by the Federal Reserve Board or the Council of Economic Advisers (as I am sure it is) to judge the rate of price inflation and decide on current steps in monetary-fiscal policy. The value of the additional calculations to them would depend not only on the "rather large" difference mentioned. It would depend also on what had been happening to the index before the second half of 1965; on what other price indexes—the consumer and the wholesale price indexes, for example—were doing; and on still other available pieces of information. Were all these taken into account, the value of "correcting" the GNP deflator might be greatly diminished.

To further complicate the matter, the GNP deflator is under observation not only by the Fed and the CEA but also by many others. What difference would a better index make for their purposes? In a word, we cannot even be sure that we agree with Alterman and Marimont when they call the difference "rather large." There is no easy measure of the benefit—the social marginal product—that would be yielded by an investment in the additional calculations.

IV

Some of the difficulties in assessing and comparing the benefits of competing improvements in the price data can be overcome. I mention the difficulties precisely in order to encourage stronger efforts to deal with them. However, if a choice among possible improvements must be made now, it must be based on

[3] J. Alterman and M. L. Marimont, "Prices and Price Analysis in the Framework of the National Accounts," pp. 143–171. This issue.

an opinion formed despite the existing difficulties. To stimulate discussion, let me express my own opinion.

The resources devoted to prices seem to me to have been misallocated in the past; and I suspect that some current proposals would make for as bad or even worse an allocation. Specifically, there is some tendency to over-estimate the value of organizing price data within an elaborate system of interlocking accounts. The national accounts do have the advantages they were designed to have. They provide comprehensive, general-purpose statistics. But these advantages are inevitably accompanied by disadvantages. These can be serious.

To attain comprehensiveness and formal consistency, one must stretch and squeeze and "estimate" to the point where the accounts yield what might too often be labeled "Potemkin-village statistics." By using this term I do not mean to accuse anyone of deceit. However, it is not going too far to say that some of the information offered to the public in the U.N. Yearbook of National Accounts is more than a bit pretentious. Consider the substitutes for double-deflation used, according to McGibbon and Hill, by the OECD countries, in their efforts to measure the real net output of individual industries;[4] or what Braithwaite tells us in the paper prepared for this session (This *Review*, pp. 117–133) about the subterfuges used in Latin America to deflate some of the major components of GDP; or what is implied about the validity of the government price deflator in the U.S. national accounts, when the Bureau of Labor Statistics restricts itself to presenting national productivity indexes only for the private economy.

Nor are the comprehensiveness and consistency provided (demanded!) by national accounts always necessary. Many data need not be subjected to a cruel and costly Procrustean treatment to be effectively used in production-function analysis, or analysis of saving behavior, or even macro-models. In fact, much if not most of what we have learned in these and other important areas of analysis has been learned from the study of data that were neither comprehensive nor fully consistent—data that were not fitted, or need not have been fitted, into any system of national accounts. It may be argued that in the future it will no longer be possible to rest content with such "primitive" information; that to get at important round-about effects of changes in strategic variables, we will need to use complex models; that we had better start developing the comprehensive and consistent interlocking statistics required by these models. Maybe. We are still far from a substantial degree of consensus on the practical value of elaborate models, econometric or otherwise. These models are still very largely labeled "experimental." Until much more work has been done on them, and a clearer idea obtained of their value and of their data needs, I believe it would be premature to go further in elaborating the national accounts.

Measurement and theory cannot be expected to keep in perfect step, of course. Some anticipation of prospective needs makes sense. But what is being suggested—for example, in the U.N. report on the revised SNA[5]—goes too far to meet what is a rather uncertain need. Theorists and econometricians may

[4] A. T. P. Hill and J. McGibbon, "Growth of Sector Real Product," *Review of Income and Wealth*, March 1966.

[5] See also the paper by A. Aidenoff, "International Comparison of Price Statistics within an Integrated System of Price and Quantity Statistics," prepared for the 1969 IARIW Conference.

eventually succeed in devising practicable large-scale econometric models that prove to be worth their cost. But at this point in time, are we not being offered "a cheque drawn on the bank of an unborn Jevons," to recall Clapham's retort to Pigou?[6] One may view the elaboration of a system of national accounts as itself a worthwhile experimental exercise. But this is not the impression that most people will get when they read the U.N.'s report. If the purpose is indeed to experiment, no great expansion of price (or other) data by all countries is necessary.

I have said enough—perhaps more than enough—to arouse others here to express their opinions. Let me conclude by reminding you that to serve purposes "in general," as the national accounts try to do, is in fact to serve few purposes well. Some, maybe many, of the uses actually made of the national accounts statistics might be served as well or better or at least more cheaply, by statistics less comprehensive and more specifically tailored to the uses. I strongly suspect that we would do better to spend less on comprehensive and elaborate national accounts, and more on improving the basic price statistics. We should be following up—more vigorously than we have so far—the Stigler Committee recommendations, for example.[7] We should be developing the samples of reasonably comparable price and quantity statistics on a quarterly or monthly basis that we must have if we are to understand the short-term changes and the associated leads and lags to which current policy, public and private, must adjust.[8]

V

I have been commenting on the competition among different ways to improve the information on prices, and have thus already raised the question of costs.

There is also the competition between price information and other economic information. I believe that price information, and related information on constant-price values of output and input, have been short-changed in the past, and are in danger of being given less than they deserve in the future. According to the order of priority suggested in the discussion of the U.N.'s SNA, for example, the series of data in constant prices are classified under Priority 2, while Priority 1 covers, among other things, the consolidated accounts of the nation in current prices. Might it not be better to consider the calculation of an estimate of total real output of a higher order of priority than the completion of the accounts, even in consolidated form, in current prices?

On the important question of the cost of economic information in terms of other means of raising economic welfare, I must limit myself to just a few remarks.

---

[6]J. H. Clapham, rejoinder to A. C. Pigou, "Empty Economic Boxes: A Reply," *Economic Journal*, 1922; reprinted in G. J. Sigler and K. E. Boulding, *Readings in Price Theory*, R. D. Irwin, Inc., 1952.

[7]Price Statistics Review Committee (G. J. Stigler, Chairman), *The Price Statistics of the Federal Government*, NBER, 1961.

[8]Note the difficulties encountered, even in the United States, in getting comparable price and quantity statistics on a quarterly basis for individual industries. See T. Hultgren, *Costs, Prices, and Profits: Their Cyclical Relations*, NBER, 1965.

First, the work of providing information is done not only in government offices but also in the offices and homes of those in the private sector who fill in questionnaires and schedules. Not all the costs appear in government budgets, and we therefore tend to underestimate them.

Second, as Alterman and Marimont point out, many of the suggestions for elaborating the role of prices in the national accounts—they refer particularly to the revised SNA—would require more statistical resources than even the most developed countries can or will provide. That the costs would be high is suggested by the delay in applying the Stigler Committee recommendations and doing more on hedonic prices to deal with the problem of quality change.

Third, in the less developed countries, a smaller share of economic activity is in the market sector. As a result, the difficulties of attaining comprehensiveness and elaboration are greater than in the more developed countries. And the less developed countries can afford the associated costs even less.

Finally, we must recognize that there are absolute limits on what can be done with any amount of resources, to improve our price data and the ways we organize them. These limits are set by the very nature of the dynamic economies that we seek to understand and spur to even more rapid change. All countries, in greater or less degree, experience virtually continuous change in the qualities of goods and services, the appearance of new products and the obsolescence of old, and shifts in industrial structure that "spoil" our classifications. What this means, in terms of a cost-benefit analysis, is that costs may be expected to rise—even accelerate—in relation to benefits, as we extend our work of improving the price data. I suspect that a major value of the efforts by Stigler and Kindahl to determine the differences between realized and list prices of standardized commodities, and of Court, Griliches, Kravis and Lipsey, and others, to apply the "hedonic-price" procedure, is in the information thus provided on the difficulties and costs of correcting our basic data.[9]

We will always have to live with inadequate statistics. Important implications for economic policy flow from this fundamental fact, but these cannot be considered here.

VI

I started with one expression of doubt. Let me conclude with another. Looking to the future, I strongly suspect that no country will ever fully attain the elaboration of price and other information proposed in the new SNA. In time, if the effort should be made, it would teach us that such elaboration is very costly. I expect that experience would also teach us that the benefits can be meagre. But this knowledge will come sooner, and come at less cost, if we inquire now what the benefits and the costs have been and may be. Experts have already told us—and we should listen—that the new SNA would stretch the statistical resources of the richest countries.

[9] G. J. Stigler and J. K. Kindahl, *The Behavior of Industrial Prices*, NBER, 1970. A brief review of the recent literature on the measurement of quality changes appears in Z. Griliches, "Hedonic Price Indexes Revisited: Some Notes on the State of the Art," *Proceedings of the American Statistical Association*, 1967 *Proceedings of the Business and Economic Section*, 1968.

The difficulties of determining social benefits and costs are great. But they cannot be avoided. The difficulties make it all the more necessary not to delay in confronting the problem of costs and benefits more directly and energetically than we have in the past. No less than others we should be prepared to argue our claims on scarce resources, and use the resources we receive in the most efficient way.

In arguing the case for a cost-benefit analysis, I have been acting as the devil's advocate. If I have offended anyone, blame the devil. My own objective has been to arouse discussion.

INFLATION AND THE LAG IN ACCOUNTING PRACTICE

Solomon Fabricant*

INTRODUCTION

THE ACCOUNTING PROBLEM POSED BY INFLATION

Our era has aptly been called one of inflation. The general price level has been trending upward in the United States for almost a quarter of a century — even longer if we include the World War II period. While the rate of increase in this country has been less than in most other countries, it has not been negligible. Two or even three percent per annum may not look like much to some people, but these are compound-interest rates. Even over the few years that have elapsed since the American Institute of Certified Public Accountants [1] published its research study on *Reporting the Financial Effects of Price-Level Changes,* in 1963, the general price level has risen by 15 or 20 percent; and it is now (April, 1969) almost 60 percent above what it was in 1948 when the Institute set up its Study Group on Business Income [26].

Further, the rate of increase has been accelerating in recent years. As we all know, this has stimulated efforts now under way to stop the acceleration and then slow down the rate of inflation. The obstacles to be overcome are serious, however. No knowledgeable

*This is a revised version of the paper read at the Colloquium. Sections were added on "The Problem of Fixed Dollar Payments" and "Liberalized Depreciation Practices: An Offset?"

The paper is based on a section of a study of inflation under way at the National Bureau of Economic Research with the support of the Alfred P. Sloan Foundation. Because the paper has not gone through the Bureau's usual review procedure, it is offered on the responsibility of the author alone.

The National Income Division of the Department of Commerce kindly made available a number of unpublished series. Grateful acknowledgement is also made to Milton Friedman and Anna J. Schwartz, for access to some of their unpublished data; Chantal Dubrin, for taking charge of the calculations and for other assistance; Mildred Courtney, for valuable secretarial help; and H. Irving Forman, for the charts. For helpful comments on the first draft of the paper, I am obligated to Philip Cagan, Robert E. Lipsey, John R. Meyer, and Lee J. Seidler.

115

person expects, nor does the new Administration promise, a quick victory. But even if the current inflation should be brought to a halt within the next two or three years, it is very unlikely that there will be a return to earlier price levels. The effects of the inflation that we have already experienced will persist long after inflation is stopped. And there are some grounds for wondering whether any halt imposed on inflation will be permanent.

Surely, under these circumstances, one may ask whether it is not anachronistic, or at least incongruous, that the financial reports being issued by companies seldom breathe a word about the effects of changes in price levels on their carefully compiled and audited figures. No labor union fails to mention the consumer price index when engaged in a wage negotiation. Yet companies may report "record profits" and say nothing about the contribution of an attenuated dollar to these record highs. Only when profits decline may there be a reference to price increases, and then only to higher labor and material prices. Accounting practice has not yet been adjusted to the fact of inflation.

I hasten to add (we economists live in glass houses, just like other human beings) that the national accounts drawn up by economists are in some respects also deficient in taking account of general price changes, and I will have a word to say about this later. But these deficiencies are far less serious. Not even the most backward country today presents its estimates of Gross National Product without an accompanying set of estimates in "constant prices," if there is even the slightest basis on which to make the deflation.

THREE MAIN QUESTIONS

When the general price level is changing at a rate that may not be called negligible, to ignore its changes in the accounting reports that go to businessmen, investors, government officials, and others, can introduce significant error in their decisions and policies. Measurements of income and income distributions and the assessment of alternative investment opportunities, among other calculations, must inevitably be less accurate. And the imposition of taxes, for example, must be less equitable or otherwise fall short of attaining desired objectives. The accounts need to be adjusted in order to make more accurate the calculations on which public and private decisions and policies are based. Just how to do so is our first main question.

While I have already ventured the judgment that the miscalculations resulting from neglect of inflation are important, this judgment needs to be supported by evidence. At this point of the paper, I may claim only that the errors *can* be important. To show that the errors are in fact important, we must answer two other questions. We need to know, first, the degree of inaccuracy of various comparisons of profits and other accounting estimates over time, and also over space — for example, comparisons between industries and firms. Second, we need to know to what extent users of inaccurate accounts are in fact misled by the errors.

Economists have been worrying about these matters for a long time. One reason is their concern with the quality of the numerical data at their disposal. Another is their interest in economic behavior — in the present case, under the impact of inflation. Accountants also have been talking for decades about the problem of adjusting accounting records to changes in general price levels. But accountants seem to have done little more than talk, at any rate in the United States, where corporate reports generally neglect the problem, as I have already complained. Undoubtedly, among the factors that have given pause to accountants (and their clients) is the belief that the benefits to be derived from reporting on price-level changes would fall short of the costs. Maybe they are right. The information submitted below should help to resolve the question.

I shall add little that is new to what has already been said on the first question; i.e., how to adjust the accounts when price levels change significantly. But what has been said over the years has not been altogether consistent. There continue to be rather wide differences of opinion among accountants, and to a lesser extent also among economists, on the issues involved. Presentation, and hopefully clarification, of a consistent position and of the grounds on which it rests, may therefore be worthwhile. On the second question, the difference it would make in the figures, some added light is thrown by calculations recently made by economists working on the national income and on rates of return on business investment. The third question, whether and to what degree any or many people are misled by the unadjusted accounts, is in some respects the most interesting of the questions. It is certainly the most difficult, and one to which an answer can as yet be little more than speculative. But more work is needed on all three questions — work by accountants, by economists, and by both together. The discussion in this Colloquium will, I hope, serve to move us another step forward.

ADJUSTMENTS FOR CHANGES IN THE GENERAL PRICE LEVEL

CONVERSION TO A "STABLE DOLLAR"

To answer the question of how to adjust accounting data for changes in the general price level, we must be quite clear on what we are after. We want to make valid and useful comparisons of incomes, capital, and rates of return between different accounting periods and between different companies.

Valid comparisons require, first of all, a stable monetary unit — money adjusted not only for coin clipping, to hark back to olden times, but for any depreciation (or appreciation) of its value. The money unit would be stable, and the comparison valid for some purposes, if adjustments were made merely for changes in the value of the money in terms of gold, or silver, or any other generally acceptable single commodity. This was the adjustment of medieval times when currencies not fixed in terms of gold or silver were related to an "imaginary" or "ghost" money that was so fixed.[1] They were imaginary or ghostly, it hardly needs to be said, because no currency was able to survive the rigors of life in those days and remain stable in terms of gold or silver — any more than have the currencies of our own times. The conversion could, of course, be to another — an existent — currency that is stable, or relatively stable, in terms of gold. This is the kind of adjustment made now when calculations involving unstable currencies are converted to dollars.

An improvement over these simple methods of stabilizing the monetary unit is an adjustment that fixes the monetary unit in terms of its purchasing power over a wide range of goods and services, not just one of these. This idea came with the "tabular standard" of value suggested well over a century ago — one of a number of "rules for the guidance of mankind," as an early proponent put it — and later was made practical by the development of index numbers of prices. For most purposes the more useful, as well as stable, monetary unit is one that can purchase a fixed quantity — a "basket" — of the combination of all the goods and services (or a representative sample of all the goods and services) that are bought with money income, not a fixed quantity of just one or some of the goods and services. The value of the dollar, then, is to be fixed by correcting it for changes in the *general* price level.[2]

There are three price indexes, among those available currently, that may be regarded as indexes of the general price level — the GNP Implicit Price Index (IPI), the Consumer Price Index (CPI), and the Wholesale Price Index (WPI). The one that covers the full range of goods and services on which the national income is spent is the IPI. It is by no means perfect, as we shall see, but for our purpose it is the best there is, and it is good enough.

---

[1]Accountants were reminded of the purpose of "imaginary money," a few years ago, by Maurice Moonitz [21, pp. 19-20].

[2]John Maynard Keynes [19, Book II] provided what is still one of the best discussions of the problem of defining and measuring "the value of money."

Different groups buy somewhat different baskets of goods and services and make their purchases in different places. The purchasing power of a dollar of income received in different sectors of the economy therefore may (and to some degree does) rise more or less than the national average. This has been bothering economists, and they have asked whether it would not be appropriate, at any rate in principle, to use special indexes of prices tailored to the particular groups concerned — one index for Industry or Region or Income Class A, another for B, and so on. To this question, their answer has usually been "yes." When real incomes and changes in real incomes in Alaska in the early 1900's are to be compared with corresponding incomes and changes in incomes on the West Coast, a somewhat different price deflator for Alaska than for the State of Washington is required, and allowances must be made also for regional differences in price levels. The example is extreme, but it illustrates the general fact that anyone choosing between two places in which to live and work has to take two different price levels into account.

Our purpose, however, is to construct a stable dollar that is free of the effects of *general* price inflation or deflation. We do not want to be in the position of saying that inflation is raising the price level in Region A and deflation is reducing the price level in Region B, when the national price level is steady. The differential in the price movements between Region A and Region B is largely a reflection of relative price change, which we will discuss below, not of the inflation or deflation that is measured by changes in the general price level of the nation as a whole. It is the latter that is our present concern.

Apart from this consideration, there is another and compelling one. We need an adjusted dollar that can be used to make generally valid comparisons between many different times and places within the country. No single adjusted dollar will quite do for all of these comparisons, because of regional and other differences in price levels within the country. But it is far more convenient than a collection of many different specially adjusted dollars. The problem is, of course, the same problem, though less serious, that confronts economists when they make comparisons of the real incomes or purchasing powers of the currencies of many different countries. They have generally settled for a limited number of adjusted currencies.[3] When interest is primarily in adjusting the accounts of widely-held companies, doing a national business, adjustment of the dollar by means of a national general price index will suffice.[4]

---

[3]A recent example is provided by Braithwaite [2].

[4]We do not escape all dilemmas even for this purpose, however. When making a comparison between two dates in the same country, one must choose between the Paache and the Laspeyres price indexes, or use some rather arbitrary combination of the two. The quantitative difference between the two is usually, but not always, small.

CORRECTION FOR PRICE LEVEL "HETERO-TEMPORALITY"

To deflate accounting profits, as these are ordinarily calculated, by an index of the general price level would go a long way towards establishing comparability between the profits of different periods. But it would not go quite far enough. The reason is that the calculations in any accounting period are not entirely in terms of the current price level. They are partly in terms of the price levels of earlier periods as well, because some of the currently-charged costs (depreciation charges, for example) were incurred or contracted for in earlier periods and therefore at price levels different from the current price level. An adjustment is needed to express all costs charged during a period in terms of the price level of that period [7, 8]. Once this is done, the adjusted series of current-price incomes in successive periods can then be further adjusted to express them in terms of the price level of some single base period. This may be the most recent period, or an earlier one. It matters little which base is used, as long as it is the same for all the periods being compared. If the first step is omitted, however, the second step will not bring us quite to our goal.

This may be seen perhaps more clearly, if we imagine a situation in which the general price level and the level of prices of capital goods are moving up together and at a constant rate, and the stock of capital assets is stable in volume and composition. In this case, depreciation charges calculated at historical cost will always be less than depreciation at current replacement cost by an amount that depends on the rate of increase in the price level and the average difference between the year of acquisition of capital assets and the current year. Under the assumptions made, this difference will be equal to one-half the average length of life. Profits in each period, expressed in terms of the period's own current prices, will then be overstated by a constant fraction. The adjustment for hetero-temporality is intended to correct this overstatement. In addition, of course, the profits reported in successive periods will not be comparable to one another because they are expressed in dollars of different purchasing powers. The rates of change of profits between consecutive periods will be overstated by a constant amount, equal to the rate of change of the general price level. The adjustment for hetero-temporality corrects the *level* of reported profits. The conversion to constant prices corrects the *rate of change* (or slope) of reported profits.

An adjustment for hetero-temporality is also needed to make comparisons of rates of return, such as profits as a percentage of net worth, more valid than they would otherwise be. Were the numerators of these ratios, as given in income accounts, influenced by changes in the general price level to the same degree as the denominators given in reported balance sheets, there would be no need to adjust the ratios. But the timing of the effects on the two changes in the general price level is different. In any particular year, the prices implicit in the income account will, we may expect, reflect current prices more closely than will the balance sheet. The numerator of the rate of return ratio will therefore be subject to less correction, as a rule, than the denominator, and the rate of return will be overstated during inflation and understated during deflation. The degree of distortion in successive time periods will be similar, and therefore errors in making comparisons over time will be small, only if the rate of change of the general price level is approximately constant.

In addition to making comparisons between periods, we want to make valid and useful comparisons of income and rates of return of different firms or other economic entities in a given accounting period. The adjustment for heterogeneity of price levels within a period is necessary for this purpose also. Were the mix of price levels the same in all companies, the figures of all would be biased in the same direction and degree. In proportion to one another, then, the figures would be comparable. But the mix does vary from one company to another, because of variation in the composition and rate of turnover of assets, in the average age or year of acquisition of assets, and so on [17, 9]. This implies that the adjustments need to be tailored to the particular situation of each of the companies involved in a close comparison.

THE TREATMENT OF RELATIVE PRICE CHANGES

When material consumption and depreciation charges are calculated in terms of replacement costs, one of the two adjustments we want is thereby made. But one that we do not want is also thereby made.

To be more specific, replacement cost accounting in effect involves, first, the adjustment for hetero-temporality that we have just been discussing. The accounts of each period are expressed in terms of the period's own (homogeneous) general price level, a desirable step in adjusting the accounts for changes in the general price level. Second, however, replacement cost accounting involves also an adjustment that we do not want. This is an adjustment for changes in relative prices. Third, replacement cost accounting also fails to express the accounts of different periods in terms of the same general price level —an essential step in dealing with general price-level changes. The last is the most important failing, but it needs no discussion beyond what we have already given it. The treatment of relative price changes does require a further word. This is rather surprising because the distinction between adjustments for changes in the general price level and adjustments for changes in relative prices was made quite clear in *Accounting Research Study No. 6* [1, pp. 29–31]. However, there continues to be some confusion on the validity and significance of the distinction.

Changes in the general price level and changes in relative prices are not entirely unrelated, it is true. Some changes in relative prices take place for the same reason as changes in the general price level. Not all elements of the price system respond with equal promptitude or in equal degree to changes in money supply, for example. But most changes in relative prices occur apart from changes in the general price level. The two are influenced by largely separate and independent forces and can and should be dealt with separately.

Adjustment of accounting calculations of income for inflation or deflation — that is, for changes in the general price level — is not intended to eliminate the effects of change in relative prices. Indeed, the latter effects should not be eliminated if income is to be reported correctly, either in constant or in current prices.

To sharpen the distinction between the general price level and individual prices, consider a situation in which the general price level is stable. This does not mean that individual price levels, the average of which we call the general price level, are also stable. Changes in the weather, technological changes, depletion of subsoil assets, pressure of population on available land, and shifts in demand — all these make for increases in some prices and decreases in others. Few individual prices actually remain stable over any length of time. As was recognized in the price "guideposts" of the Kennedy and Johnson administrations, a policy designed to maintain a constant general price level must allow for changes in relative prices because productivity in different industries moves up at different rates [11, Chapter XI]. When the general price level is stable, it is because rising individual prices are being balanced by declining individual prices.

These differential price movements tend to produce gains that businessmen seek to make or losses they seek to avoid. The gains or losses resulting from differential price movements are part and parcel of the profits of business activity. While these gains or losses need to be expressed in dollars of constant purchasing power, if comparisons over time or space are to be valid, they do not need to be, nor should they be, eliminated when we adjust the accounts for changes in general price levels.[5]

---

[5]That differential price movements make for "real" profits or losses can hardly be gainsaid. The questions, rather, are: (1) whether to treat the effects of differential price movements

The point is quite general. It applies to the income of a worker, a company, an industry, or a nation. Thus, the real income of a nation may be said to depend on three things: the volume of resources it puts into production, the product it gets per unit of resources, and the purchasing power of the product in terms of the goods and services finally consumed and invested [5, p. 51]. Of these three sources of income, the last mentioned reflects the difference between the prices of the goods the nation produces (including exports) and the prices of the goods the nation consumes (the domestic production it keeps for its own consumption, plus the imports it gets for its exports) — that is, it includes gains or losses from change in the nation's foreign "terms of trade."[6]

Relative price changes in the present context mean, of course, changes in individual prices relative to the general price level. It follows that the gains or losses from the differential price changes that accrue to individual sectors of an economy must largely offset one another. For a country as a whole, then, the treatment of relative price changes will be of little moment.[7] This is hardly ground, however, for believing that it is equally unimportant for individual sectors of the economy, or for individual companies.

Let me make sure that what I am saying is not read to mean something I do not want to say. I am *not* saying that current replacement costs should be ignored, and attention focused only on original cost (adjusted or unadjusted for changes in the general price level), when businessmen or others make decisions on pricing, or production, or material purchases, or renewal of leases, or investment in additional plant and equipment. No economist taught the meaning of Jevons' "bygones are bygones" would say this. Current — and prospective — replacement prices *must* be taken into account in deciding what to do. But when calculating realized profits, the gains

as gains or losses "on capital account" — that is, to include them among the capital gains or losses restricted to the surplus account — or as items in the current income accounts; and (2) whether to show the effects in the accounts when they are recognized, even though not actually "realized," or only when they are realized. To inform all interested parties, it is necessary to show these effects when they are recognized, rather than wait until they are realized, even though this would require rough estimation; and to treat them as current income account items. However, I would propose putting this information, along with the information on the effects of changes in the general price level, in a supplement to the usual reports — in this case, also preferably a supplement that would cover an accounting period much longer than the usual 12-month period.

[6]I should add that the method of deflating exports and imports used by the Department of Commerce eliminates from national product and income these gains or losses from changes in the country's foreign terms of trade [10, pp. 446-7]. For a small country heavily engaged in foreign trade, this procedure could introduce a serious error into the estimates.

[7]Provided foreign trade and change in the foreign terms of trade are small. I am skirting, here, a controversial point — mentioned in the preceding footnote — in the theory of national accounts: I am assuming that national income is defined to include gains or losses from changes in the foreign terms of trade and that the general price level is defined as the IPI for national income so defined.

or losses from differential price movements may not be ignored.[8]   If a numerical example is necessary, then consider the case of merchandise purchased by a retailer for $1,000 in period one and sold in period two for $1,500.   In the ordinary accounting calculation, the profit (ignoring other costs) would be recorded as $500.   Suppose the general price level had risen between period one and period two by 10 percent, and the unit price of the merchandise had risen by 20 percent. The calculation of material cost at replacement prices (current prices) would yield a profit of $300 ($1,500 − $1,200).   Properly calculated for general price-level changes only, profit in terms of the period two price level would be $400 ($1,500 − $1,100).   This $400 equals the $300 plus a profit of $100 owing to a relative price change. (In terms of period one price levels, the profit would be $364 = $1,364 − $1,000. The $400 is 10 percent more than the $364 because the period two price level is 10 percent above the period one price level.) Conversion to replacement cost prices excludes what should not be excluded: the effects of relative price changes.

This criticism is applicable, with some qualifications, to LIFO as it is ordinarily used in accounting for withdrawals from inventory. LIFO substitutes current-period prices for prior-period prices and thus adjusts for hetero-temporality, but it also "adjusts out" the profits or losses sustained on inventories when relative prices change. Inventories are priced at "first-in" prices, which may be much below current prices or even actual cost during a period of inflation. Should the physical volume of inventories be reduced, however, profits reported under LIFO would not be free of price-level hetero-temporality. Indeed, in effect, all the previous adjustments would be canceled, and the full difference between book prices and current prices, which reflects the cumulative rise in the general price level (plus or minus change in relative prices) would be included in the calculated profits.

A similar, though less sharp, criticism may be made of the Inventory Valuation Adjustment, used by the Office of Business Economics of the Department of Commerce in its calculations of the national accounts [28].   This procedure is as follows: the difference between the change in the book value of inventories and the value of the change in the physical volume of inventories (valued at the current prices of the goods held in inventory) is the amount taken to be the Inventory Valuation Adjustment (IVA). This amount is subtracted from profits to reach an adjusted profits figure. In this way the IVA removes the change in book values due

---

[8]Perhaps one of the objectives of those who advocate replacement cost accounting is "conservatism." To state profits conservatively, in this way, is almost by definition, also to state profits inaccurately.

I doubt that anyone would advocate eliminating the effects of relative price movements if the relevant absolute price movements were downward.

to change in relative prices as well as to change in the general price level. It is easy to see that if the physical volume of inventories were to remain unchanged, the IVA would equal the full change in the book value of inventories, including any change in relative prices. The IVA thus eliminates from profits an item of profit that should not be eliminated.[9]

Interpretation of the charging of depreciation at replacement costs is considerably more complicated. It still remains largely a subject for discussion rather than an accounting practice. Even in the national accounts, few countries follow this procedure. However, something needs to be said about it.[10]

If it is assumed, as it generally is, that the quantity of capital consumed can be determined by means of a fairly simple depreciation formula that is independent of price change —straight-line, or declining-balance, for example — then this is the quantity to be multiplied by the replacement cost of the capital goods to get the depreciation charge in current prices. In effect, capital assets would be treated as inventories are in the national accounts: the current value of net capital formation would be taken equal to the net change in physical assets multiplied by the current replacement cost of such assets.[11] The contribution of relative price changes to profits would be eliminated, and depreciation charges at replacement cost would be subject to the same criticism as the IVA or LIFO.

The analogy between inventories and capital assets is imperfect, however. One may also — and I would argue more correctly — consider the proper depreciation (and obsolescence) charge to be the actual (necessarily estimated) decline, or anticipated decline, in the current value of the relevant capital asset.[12] This decline would

---

[9]The procedure followed by the OBE is quite correct for estimating the National Product, as I have said elsewhere [10, pp. 444–6]. I am not questioning the IVA for that purpose.

[10]In the United States, the historical estimates of national income and product provided by the NBER make use of replacement cost accounting for depreciation [20]. This is not true, however, of the currently available official national accounts published by the Department of Commerce (except for depreciation on farm plant and equipment, the estimates for which are provided by the Department of Agriculture). Although the Department of Commerce has not yet put replacement-cost depreciation charges into its official accounts, it has made valuable estimates of these depreciation charges in its Capital Stock Study [16, 31 and 32]. These are utilized below.

[11]Gross capital formation, which is already at current prices, less capital consumption at current prices, equals net capital formation at current prices.

[12]Cp. Hotelling [18]. The relevant current value is the cost, delivered and installed, to a normal buyer, not what the owner of the asset would get for it if he disposed of it in the second hand market.

The usual question arises concerning the accounting treatment of differences between the decline in value that is anticipated and the decline in value that actually occurs. As I have already implied, I would go along with treating the differences as surplus account items in the annual statements, but would favor treating them as income account items in statements covering a longer fiscal period, say 5 or 10 years. Long fiscal period statements, it goes without saying, would have to be expressed in dollars of fixed general purchasing power if the figures were to make sense. I am puzzled by the lack of interest of accountants in such long-period accounts.

reflect changes in the replacement cost of the capital asset, if it were still being produced (which is not always the case), as well as wear and tear. It would also reflect obsolescence of the capital asset due to technological improvements in later vintages of the capital asset or in substitute capital goods, changes in maintenance and operating costs due to changes in relative prices of labor and materials, as well as wear and tear, changes in the demand for the product turned out with the help of the capital asset, and changes in interest rates. In short, the decline in current value would reflect (1) the current value of the depreciation and obsolescence that has occurred (or is estimated to have occurred) plus (2) the change in the value of the asset due to change in the general price level. The first item, the "correct" charge at current prices, would not exclude changes in relative prices. If the usual procedure, described in the preceding paragraph, were to be viewed as a rough approximation to the second procedure, depreciation at replacement cost would not be subject to the criticism that it excludes relative price changes. But this view could hardly be held of depreciation based on the straight-line depreciation formula.

THE PROBLEM OF FIXED DOLLAR PAYMENTS

When inflation is expected over the term of a loan, an escalator clause — or other arrangement that reserves equity rights — may be inserted in what would otherwise be a fixed-payment contract. Alternatively, adjustment to inflation may take the form of a higher interest rate — higher, of course, by the expected rate of increase in the general price level. This arrangement may pose an accounting problem, and a source of error in the use of the usual accounting reports, that is not met by the adjustments already proposed.

Consider the case of a firm that borrows on a long-term loan at a fixed interest rate, for example, in order to finance its operations during a period of inflation. Suppose, also, that the firm's selling prices and the prices it pays for materials, etc., move up with the general price level. The firm's costs of operation — including interest charges — relative to gross income would then tend to be higher in the earlier years and lower in the later years of the term covered by the loan than over the term as a whole. Correspondingly, the firm's net income, as ordinarily calculated, would be lower during the earlier years and higher during the later years than its average net income during the period of the loan. Deflation of the reported annual net income by an index of the general price level could only partially correct the reported income. Part of the reported costs in the earlier years, even after correction for changes in the price level, would in fact simply be an advance payment that should properly be charged to the operations of later years. In addition to a price-level adjustment, then, what would be required is an annual series of accounting entries to redistribute costs and profits over the term of the loan in such a way as to equalize the expected annual rates of return.

Obviously, the accounts of creditors as well as debtors would be affected. While the problem would appear most prominently in dealing with debt arrangements, essentially the same problem would be encountered in dealing with other fixed-dollar-payment arrangements, such as rentals, long-term price contracts, and wage and salary contracts. (In these, however, recourse to escalator clauses will be more frequent.) Convertible debentures, convertible preferred stocks, and lease-back arrangements raise additional accounting problems which can only be mentioned here.

The problem described in the present section will be of minimal importance to firms that borrow on a short term basis (relative to the length of their fiscal periods), or finance their operations through a more or less continuous series of long-term contracts. The problem will be much more important for firms that borrow heavily on a long-term basis at infrequent intervals. In a period of inflation, their reported profits will require the adjustment mentioned if these profits are to be comparable with the profits of earlier or later years, or with the profits of other companies.

CLUES TO THE MAGNITUDE OF THE ADJUSTMENTS

CHANGES IN INDEXES OF THE GENERAL PRICE LEVEL

The several steps required to adapt the accounts to changing general price levels are of different degrees of importance. One or two of the adjustments may, in fact, strike the reader as picayune, and not worth a second thought. This can certainly turn out to be the case. It seemed desirable, however, to state what adjustments were required in principle, and leave the question whether any or all of them were worthwhile, in any particular case, to this section of our discussion.

Whether an adjustment is important or not depends not only on what difference it would make in the figures, but also on the standards of precision at which the user of the figures aims — which depends, in turn, on his purpose. Let us concentrate here on the first point, the quantitative difference that the adjustments would make in reported profits and rates of return.

Clearly, the importance of any of the adjustments depends, first of all, on the rate of change in the general price level.[13]

I have already noted a few summary facts on the rate of increase in the general price level and expressed the opinion that the increase has been far from negligible in the United States in recent decades. The figures in Chart 1[14] give the full picture for 1913-68 as revealed by the three currently available indexes often used to measure changes in general price level. Certainly, as far as the period since 1913 is concerned, the contours traced by these three price indexes bear a distinct resemblance to one another. All three show the sharp price rise and then decline associated with World War I and its aftermath, the slight rise and decline during the rest of the 1920's, the decline during the Great Contraction, the swing up to 1937 and then decline to 1939, the rise during World War II and then in the late 1940's when price ceilings were lifted, the Korean flare-up, the slow rate of increase after the middle 1950's and the recent acceleration. Chart 2 gives the annual percentage changes in the IPI, together with changes over the somewhat longer periods defined by business-cycle phases. During the 40-year period beginning with 1929, the GNP IPI rose at an average rate of 2.3 percent per annum, the CPI at 1.8 percent, and the WPI at 1.9 percent. But though the main outlines of the three indexes are much the same, there are differences. Especially interesting between 1958 and 1964 is the negligible change in the WPI while the other two continued to march upward. And there are some differences, also, between the IPI and the CPI [14]. Which of the three indexes is best for measuring the general price level?

The CPI covers the consumption goods and services purchased only by urban wage earners and lower salaried workers [29]. Although this is a large fraction of what is consumed by the nation, it is not the whole of it and it fails to cover business investment goods and government expenditure. The IPI does cover the full range of goods and services on which the national income is spent, and is superior to the CPI on that account. It is, in fact, essentially a weighted average of the CPI (with upward adjustments in the weights of the consumption goods bought by the higher-income groups) and indexes of the prices of investment goods and of government purchases with the CPI given the preponderant weight that it deserves [28]. The WPI, although often referred to as a measure of inflation,

---

[13]This needs a small qualification: one of our adjustments is the "correction" of the accounts for the exclusion — by replacement cost accounting — of the effect on income of relative price changes. These relative price changes will be much more important than general price changes when the latter are small. However — this is why the qualification is minor — replacement cost accounting would hardly ever be used, or the question even discussed, were changes in the general price level small.

[14]Sources of figures in the charts are given in Appendix 2.

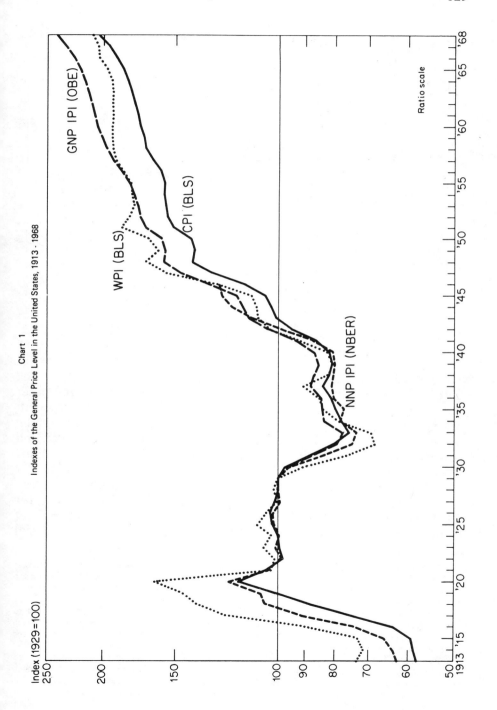

Chart 1

Indexes of the General Price Level in the United States, 1913 - 1968

Index (1929=100)

GNP IPI (OBE)

WPI (BLS)

CPI (BLS)

NNP IPI (NBER)

Ratio scale

Chart 2
Rates of Change in the General Price Level (IPI), 1929 - 1968

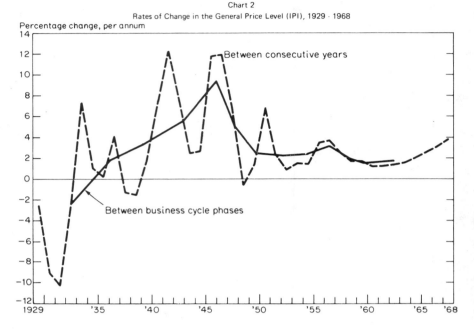

especially by businessmen, is clearly inferior to either the IPI or the CPI for our purpose. The WPI omits services, construction, and other important categories of goods and services on which incomes are spent; prices the tangible goods it covers at the wholesale stage, which precedes the stage at which most final expenditures are made; and combines the prices of the goods covered with inappropriate weights [29].[15]

None of the indexes is perfect, by any means, and one indication of this is the difference between the two IPI's shown in the chart for 1929-46. One of these is the currently available Department of Commerce's implicit price deflator for GNP. The other is an historical

---

[15]In this connection see the report by the Price Statistics Review Committee of the NBER [23] (the "Stigler report"); also Gainsbrugh and Backman [14]. One thoughtful businessman expressed a preference for the WPI over the CPI and IPI in the following words: "Give me five years of stable wholesale prices, and I think I can assure you of a healthy non-inflationary economic environment and a reasonably good bond market in spite of the upcreep in both of the other two indices." This can be interpreted as saying that when the WPI is stable, inflation cannot be a very serious problem — which is surely correct, for there are limits on the degree of divergence between the WPI and the other two indexes. But it is not obvious that the WPI would or could long remain stable if there were a continuous upcreep in the CPI and the IPI. Nor is it correct to say that a stable WPI means no inflation. If the WPI remains stable when the other two are going up, this must be because productivity in the pre-retail stages of tangible commodity production is rising more rapidly than productivity in the economy at large. In the absence of inflation the WPI would decline in these circumstances, not remain stable.

series, not currently published, prepared at the NBER by Simon Kuznets [20] and extended through the World War II period by Milton Friedman and Anna Schwartz [13]. The Department of Commerce index differs from the NBER index partly because the latter related to NNP rather than GNP. More important, the NBER index includes a rough allowance for wartime black market prices, not made in the Department of Commerce index.

There are, in fact, a considerable number of questions about the IPI, as there are about the CPI and WPI, which are better reserved for another occasion.[16] Some of these deficiencies appear to be quite minor, and some may tend to offset one another. The resulting total error is probably not as serious as a longish list of deficiencies might suggest.

The fact that the price indexes are imperfect is not a good objection to their use, however. Nor has it prevented them from being put to practical use. Despite their many deficiencies, the CPI and WPI appear in the escalator provisions of thousands of wage and purchase contracts. And the IPI, with all its imperfections, directly or indirectly affects national judgments and discussions of a most momentous sort.[17]

---

[16]Briefly, questions arise about: (1) the appropriate concept of a general price level, particularly whether or for what purposes it should cover — as did Carl Snyder's famous index — transactions in property such as real estate and stocks and bonds, services of labor at all stages of production, etc., as well as the goods and services that enter GNP; (2) the choice among various concepts of GNP, which may differ from the Department of Commerce concept in the treatment of government (particularly with regard to the treatment of government property and government services to business), education, R & D, etc.; (3) the choice between a GNP and NNP IPI; (4) whether and how to allow for the increase in productivity in government, construction, and the service industries, which current calculations of GNP in the United States largely ignore; (5) whether and how to correct for improvements in the quality of these and other goods and services — improvements not taken into account by present methods of defining and measuring price changes; and (6) the accuracy of the basic price data — particularly, to what extent the list prices of sellers correctly reflect the prices actually paid by buyers. Research on these questions is proceeding at the NBER and elsewhere.

[17]When biases in the price statistics, particularly the failure to cover quality improvements adequately, are being discussed, it is important to remember, first, that not all quality improvements are over-looked. The methods used by the BLS (especially in computing the CPI) do pick up some of the quality improvements and adjust the price statistics accordingly. Second, as has already been pointed out, the quality bias that may exist in the CPI or IPI may be unimportant. Third, it may also be irrelevant for some purposes. For example, to low-income groups that are forced to uptrade — that is, to buy better qualities of medical services, or other goods or services, than they want or can afford — the higher price is truly a price rise [24]. Fourth, to the same degree that the IPI is biased upward, because of quality improvement, the real GNP index is biased downward. To correct the rate of increase of the general price level must entail a corresponding correction in the opposite direction, in real GNP — and therefore also in national output per manhour. Consider, for example, a money-wage guidepost which combines an improvement factor and an escalator clause, such as made the headlines in 1948 when the GM-UAW contract was signed. (Such a guidepost is more like the guidepost of the Cabinet Committee on Price Stability, reported at the turn of the year, than like the original 1962 guideposts of the Council of Economic Advisers.) If the escalator factor (which is based on the price index) is corrected downward, the improvement factor (which is based on the index of output per manhour) must be corrected upward, and by an equal proportion.

The crucial question is not whether changes in the general price level can be measured with great accuracy, but rather whether a dollar adjusted for change in its purchasing power even roughly is not a more useful monetary unit than an unadjusted dollar. When the price level is changing very slowly, the answer may well be in the negative, and indeed the question would not be asked when that is the case. When the price level is changing at a Brazilian rate, or even a Japanese rate, the answer must surely be in the affirmative. When it is rising at the rate shown in the chart, the answer is less clear. Opinions will differ. But as I have said, even two percent more per annum mounts up — in ten years, to a rise of 22 percent, in twenty years, to a rise of almost 50 percent. It is doubtful that correction for the improvements in quality that are now ignored, for example, and other desirable corrections of the price indexes, would shrink the increases to negligible amounts.

Accepting the IPI as a measure of change in the purchasing power of the dollar, it is easy enough to convert existing figures on profits — which are expressed in dollars of changing (and rather mixed — hetero-temporal) purchasing power — into figures expressed in dollars of reasonably constant purchasing power. The level of the adjusted profits will depend, of course, on the base chosen. If the adjusted profits were to be expressed in terms of 1958 prices, say, rather than 1929 prices, the line tracing the adjusted profits would be raised in the proportion that the 1958 price level bears to the level of 1929. But the percentage rates of change of the adjusted profits would be largely unaffected.[18] Whichever base were chosen, the slope of the trend of the adjusted figures would be considerably less steep than the slope of the trend of book profits.

This simple adjustment would, as I have said, take us a long way along the path to a fully adjusted income figure in most cases. But it does not take care of the problem of hetero-temporality, to which we now turn.

THE INVENTORY VALUATION ADJUSTMENT

The available estimates relate entirely to calculations of re-placement cost. We first consider the effects of replacement cost

---

[18]I say "largely" because the rate of change of a price index is influenced by its weight-base. If the IPI used to obtain 1958 purchasing-power figures were a Laspeyres or other index calculated on the 1958 base year, or on that plus the given year (as in the Edgeworth), it would differ from the corresponding index used to obtain the 1929 purchasing power figures and therefore calculated on the 1929 base year. However, calculations by the Department of Commerce and others generally reveal only small differences between differently based indexes over the period since 1929. For alternative calculations covering the period 1965-68, see [33]. The Department of Commerce IPI is essentially a chain of several links, each of which is largely a Paasche index.

accounting for materials consumed, as indicated by the Department of Commerce estimates of its Inventory Valuation Adjustment.

As has already been mentioned, the IVA is designed to adjust not for changes in the general price level, but rather for the price changes that result from the turnover of inventory — that is, for changes in the prices of the goods handled on an inventory basis. Further, the intention of the IVA is not to express the consumption of goods taken out of inventory in terms of constant prices but rather in terms of current or replacement prices. In short, the IVA shifts material consumption from historical cost prices to replacement cost prices — which means an adjustment for heterotemporality of general price levels *plus* an adjustment for changes in relative prices.

The behavior of the IVA (Chart 3) indicates, as might be expected — the kinds of goods treated on an inventory basis being

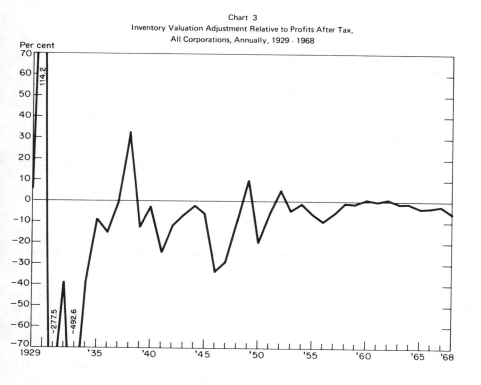

Chart 3
Inventory Valuation Adjustment Relative to Profits After Tax,
All Corporations, Annually, 1929 - 1968

what they are — that cyclical changes in these relative prices are rather prominent. Were the IVA limited to adjusting inventories for the hetero-temporality of the general price level, the series would be smoother, and there would be fewer than the nine positive adjustments shown. Nevertheless, the other 30 of the 39 annual adjustments for 1929–68 are negative. On the average, then, reported profits are shown to be too high.

A more explicit estimate (by the OBE) of the lag of book values of goods in inventory behind their replacement costs for a shorter period is given in Chart 4. During 1947–68, when the price trend was upward, the lag resulted in replacement costs being generally higher than original costs.

Chart 4

Indexes of Prices Underlying Book Values and Replacement
Costs Per Unit, Nonfarm Business Inventories,
1947 - 1968 (1958 Prices = 100)

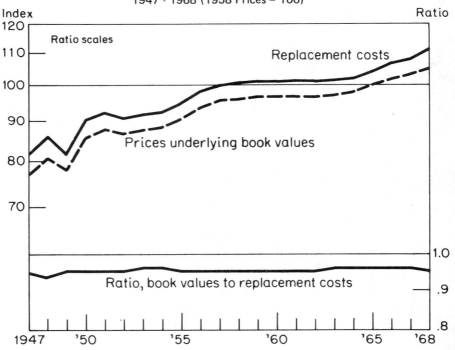

Whether the adjustment for hetero-temporality made by the IVA's lowers the level of reported profits more or less than would a general price level adjustment alone depends on the behavior of the ratio of the prices of the goods handled on an inventory basis to the prices of goods in general. When this ratio falls, as was the case during 1947–68, according to OBE estimates of the replacement costs of goods drawn from inventories (Chart 5), there is a loss from differential price movements.[19] The IVA then makes for a lesser downward adjustment of profits than would the general price level adjustment we want.

Chart 5

Indexes of the General Price Level (IPI) and of Replacement Costs Per Unit for Inventory Withdrawals and for Depreciation Charges, 1947 - 1968

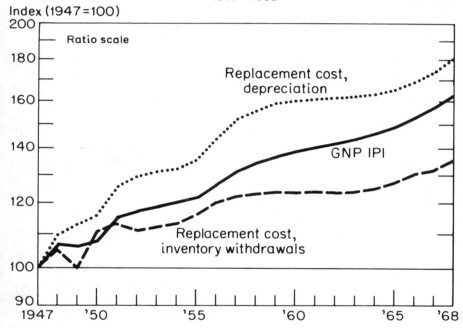

The IVA adjustment for the period 1929-68 as a whole[20] averages to -2.8 percent of profits before tax, and about double that for profits after tax. For the period beginning with 1953, the ratio is less, but still of some significance. This suggests that an adjustment for hetero-temporality of the price level may be worth looking into further.

---

[19]The decline in the ratio is not surprising. The average price of movable goods (which is essentially what the WPI measures) fell between 1947 and 1968 in relation to the IPI (which measures changes in the prices of services and construction, as well as movable goods). (See Chart 1.)

[20]This ratio is a weighted average calculated by first deflating each year's profits and each year's IVA, and then taking the ratio of the sums.

The importance of the IVA, relative to profits, varies considerably among industries. There are two reasons — variation in the relative importance of materials in total cost, and variation also in the relative volatility of the prices of the materials used by each industry. We cannot be sure, therefore, that the industrial variation in the IVA adjustment tells us what we want to know. But, as before, it is at least suggestive — perhaps more than merely suggestive, for, as might be expected, the IVA is most important for wholesale and retail trade (averaging 7 or 8 percent of profits after tax, during 1953–67). It is least important for the public utilities (averaging about 1 percent of profits after tax, during 1953–67).

DEPRECIATION AT REPLACEMENT COST

Studies by the NBER [7], Goldsmith [15], and more recently, by the OBE [31,32] provide us with information on historical cost, constant-price cost, replacement cost depreciation, and related price changes. Chart 6 gives one set of the relevant price indexes — replacement (current) costs and the prices underlying depreciation charges — and the ratio of the one index to the other. These were calculated on the assumption that depreciation charges are distributed in accordance with the straight-line formula, using the Treasury Department's Bulletin "F" depreciation rates [30].

Over the years, the straight-line formula has been partially superseded by several "accelerated depreciation" formulas, and depreciation rates above Bulletin "F" levels have been permitted [31 and 32, 27].

However, the picture would be similar were the other depreciation formulas followed, using rates up to a third above those in Bulletin "F." This is true also for an alternative replacement cost index used by the OBE in its calculations. For the present purpose, then, Chart 6 tells the story reasonably well.

Because pre-World War I levels were still heavily imbedded in the books of account even as late as 1929, the prices underlying depreciation charges in the year were still below replacement costs. This was the case, in fact, in all the years covered except for the lowest two of the Great Depression years. The gap was greatest, roundly 35 percent of the replacement cost, in 1948. The difference between depreciation prices and replacement prices then gradually diminished until it reached about 15 percent in 1968. (Under the double-declining, shorter life formula, the difference was about 25 percent of replacement cost in 1948 and 10 percent in 1968.) During the whole of the post World War II period, changes in the general price level (which took

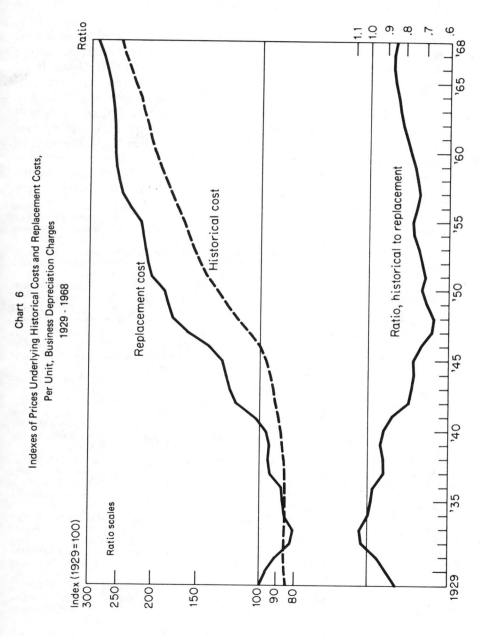

Chart 6

Indexes of Prices Underlying Historical Costs and Replacement Costs,
Per Unit, Business Depreciation Charges
1929 - 1968

place before, as well as during the period) caused profits in current prices to be overstated — by an amount equal, of course, to the difference mentioned.[21]

Just as with the IVA, a shift from historical to replacement cost would exclude (unfortunately, for our purpose) the contribution to profits of changes in relative prices. In this case, the cost of replacing capital plant and equipment rose in relation to the general price level over most of the period (Chart 5).[22] This means that holders of plant and equipment gained something from the differential price movement — a gain that is excluded from adjusted profits by replacement cost accounting. A shift to replacement costs would thus bring the level of profits down somewhat more than we would want for our purpose.

As in the case of the IVA, industries differ with regard to the correction required for the hetero-temporality of depreciation charges.

[21]Whether the liberalization of depreciation practices that took place after 1940, mentioned above, has provided an offset to the over-statement of profits caused by a rising general price level is discussed below in the final section entitled, "Errors in the Use of Unadjusted Accounting Reports."

It has sometimes been argued that an offset is provided also by the technological changes that improve the quality or productivity of plant and equipment — changes that also complicate the problem of measuring changes in the general price level, as already noted.

The point can be put as follows: When inflation occurs, depreciation charges calculated at original cost become insufficient to finance the replacement of capital assets at the expiration of their service lives. (Calculations useful in this connection have been provided by Evsey Domar [6].) Capital cannot be maintained, except by using funds taken out of profits as these are ordinarily computed. This is why we say that profits are overstated when inflation occurs. However, if technological change causes the capacity to produce, per unit of plant and equipment, also to rise — at a rate that is equal to the rate of increase in the price level — depreciation calculated at original cost will be sufficient to finance the maintenance of capacity.

But the depreciation charge on a capital asset is not designed to measure the decline in its capacity. The purpose is to measure the decline in the value of the asset. This value is a function not only of capacity, but also of the number of years of remaining life and of the other factors listed in an earlier footnote. Under certain assumptions — of which the "one-hoss-shay" assumption is only one — the capacity of a machine to produce may remain constant until the day the machine collapses into junk. But its value will nevertheless have been falling with the passage of time.

For some purposes, of course, it is capacity to produce rather than value of assets that is relevant. (That is why the capital-output ratio, which has more to do with value than with capacity, is an inadequate criterion in development planning.) But this purpose is not our purpose. (Is it necessary to add that if the rate of inflation should exceed the rate of improvement in the quality of capital goods, depreciation changes would be insufficient to maintain even capacity?)

Closely related is the suggestion that growth in the volume of capital assets provides an offset to inflation. Growth keeps low the fraction of depreciation charges (or of expenditures on capital assets) required for replacement. Depreciation charges are then in excess of the amount required to maintain capacity. But the presumption that this provides an offset to the understatement of depreciation caused by inflation, is correct only if the objective is to measure changes in capacity, not changes in value.

[22]Mention was made above of an alternate replacement cost series — "Price Series 2." Price Series 2 has risen less rapidly than Price Series 1, but the difference is not great. However, it is not negligible and further corrections that have been proposed would enlarge the difference. (Substitution of the plant and equipment replacement cost series used by the OBE in its national accounts by a series that rose less rapidly would affect also the IPI; but the proportionate adjustment would be very much smaller.)

This, as is well-known, is because the average length of life of capital assets and the relative importance of capital assets vary among industries.

PROFITS IN CONSTANT PRICES

We put the preceding estimates together, blinking our eyes to the problem of relative price changes, in Chart 7. The result gives us at least a notion of what corporate profits would look like — were depreciation charges calculated consistently on a straight-line basis, at Bulletin "F" rates — if adjusted for changes in the general price level.

Chart 7
Profits After Tax, Nonfinancial Corporations,
Before and After Adjustments for Changes in the General Price Level
1929 - 1968

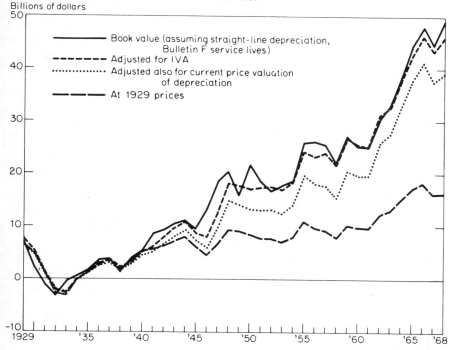

The series in the chart relate to all nonfinancial corporations combined. They are, then, weighted averages of the series for individual companies. All companies have experienced essentially the same changes in the general price level, but the impact on their profits has not been the same. The profits of some companies must have been less affected, and those of other companies more affected, than the average pictured in the chart. Comparisons among companies of levels of profits and of changes in profits are in some degree defective.

CORRECTED RATES OF RETURN

Economists making comparisons of the profit rates of different companies or industries have thought price level changes to be sufficiently important to warrant drawing attention to the probable effects on the comparisons. Recently, George Stigler made an effort to correct for these effects [25]. The corrections are necessarily rather crude, for even had the required details been available, which was not the case, it would have been too burdensome a job to use the details to make special corrections for each of the many industries being compared. However, even these estimates provide some sense of the difference made by price adjustments. (See Chart 8.)

The rates of return calculated by Stigler refer to net profits after taxes as a percentage of total corporate assets (excluding investments in other companies). The estimates are for twenty-three groups of manufacturing industries. As is desirable, Stigler corrects separately

Chart 8

Rates of Return on Assets, at Book Value and at 1947 Prices,

Manufacturing Corporations, 1938 - 1958

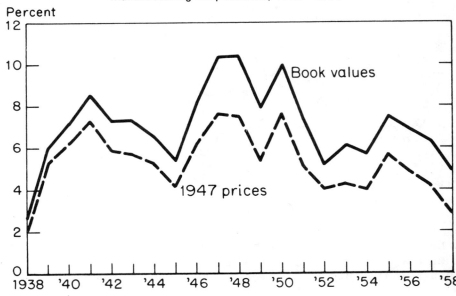

both numerator and denominator of the profit ratio. The price data used are essentially the same as those in the OBE's capital stock study and the corrections are therefore in terms of replacement cost rather than in terms of the general price level.

We may note, first, that the rates of return in 1947 prices are lower than the rates of return according to "book" in every year covered in Chart 8. In 1947 the corrected rate for manufacturing as a whole was 7.6 percent, for example, as compared with the book rate of return of 10.4 percent. In 1957 the two rates were 4.1 and 6.3 percent, respectively. Second, the difference between the two rates varied considerably among the 23 industries included in the analysis. The median difference in 1947 was 2.4, with an interquartile range of 1.1. In 1957 the variation was less, but so was the median profit rate. Chart 9 gives the full information.

It should be remembered that the industry figures hide whatever intra-industry variation there may be. Undoubtedly such variation exists, and the occasional calculations that have been made suggest that it is considerable.

ERRORS IN THE USE OF UNADJUSTED ACCOUNTING REPORTS

LIBERALIZED DEPRECIATION PRACTICES: AN OFFSET?

The question with which we are concerned is the bias in conventional accounting reports caused by the neglect of changes in the general price level. And we are concerned with the question because errors can result when these biased reports are put to the uses they are intended to serve. These errors would be of little consequence, however, were the reports subjected to other adjustments — adjustments that, although not aimed directly at the price-level problem, had the effect of meeting it.

Reference has already been made to what some observers view as a source of such an offset. This is the liberalization of depreciation practices permitted by the Treasury Department after 1940.

The liberalization of depreciation practices, as accountants well know, took two main routes. One involved granting permission to taxpayers to use depreciation methods — the double-declining balance method and the sum-of-the-years'-digits method — to recover more of an asset's cost in the early years of its life than would be possible with the straight-line method. These accelerated depreciation methods became applicable under the Internal Revenue Code of 1954. The

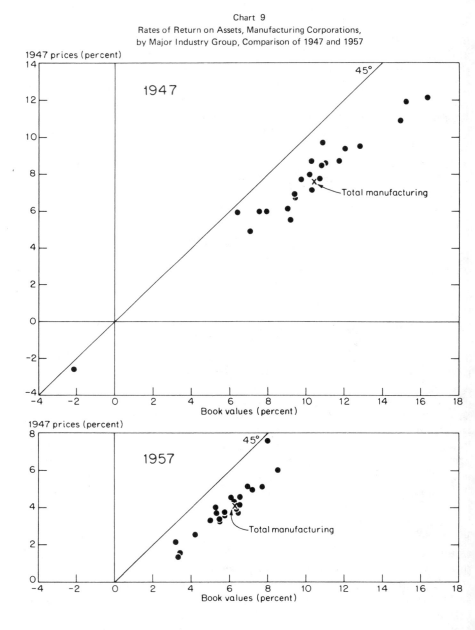

Chart 9
Rates of Return on Assets, Manufacturing Corporations,
by Major Industry Group, Comparison of 1947 and 1957

other kind of liberalization, which began with a Treasury Decision
in 1934, allowed taxpayers to use shorter service lives than had

formerly been permissible.[23]　The details of the various changes in the rules and regulations, and estimates of their effect on depreciation charges (to which I shall refer in a moment), are set forth in Allen H. Young's valuable articles [31, 32].

It can be shown, to begin with, that liberalization of depreciation practices can take care of the problem created by a changing general price level (if that is its objective) only temporarily. A shortening of service life or a shift to a "faster" depreciation formula will obviously raise depreciation charges above what they would have been under the prior practice. And this increase in depreciation charges could reduce reported profits to the level that would have been reached were appropriate adjustments made for inflation. It could even push profits below that level. But were inflation to continue, the offsetting effects even of further reductions in service life and of shifts to still faster depreciation formulas must eventually vanish. At the limit, when existing capital assets had been fully depreciated and newly purchased capital assets were all being charged off immediately and fully to current operations, even these current write-offs would not be sufficient to keep profits at an appropriately deflated level. A rising (real) capital-output ratio could postpone this result, but there are obvious limits to the continuation of such an upward trend.

Perhaps more important, in practice, is the strong likelihood that steps in a policy of continual depreciation liberalization would not — and could not — be geared to the rate of inflation and still less to changes in this rate. Only by chance, therefore, could liberalization provide a reasonably appropriate offset to the current rate of inflation in any particular fiscal period. Also, as a general rule, the effectiveness of depreciation liberalization in redressing the bias caused by inflation would vary among industries, making industrial comparisons of rates of return most difficult.

But we need not confine ourselves to these general remarks. Young's calculations of depreciation charges for nonfinancial corporations under varying assumptions make it possible to be specific about the quantitative effects of liberalization [32]. We focus our attention on the depreciation calculated under two main assumptions, and to the years as shown in Table 1.

Consider the depreciation charged in 1958, 21.3 billion dollars. This closely approximated the depreciation that would have been charged at historical cost valuation on a straight-line basis, using Bulletin "F" service lives; plus another 5 billion estimated by Young to show more liberalized depreciation practices.[24]　Were depreciation

---

[23]The investment tax credit, first enacted in the Revenue Act of 1962, is also relevant, but I shall not try to deal with its effects.

[24]The 21.3 billion includes oil and gas well drilling and exploration costs charged to current expense, plus certain other minor items specified by Young [32, Table 1].

TABLE 1

	1929	1948	1958	1966
	(unit: billion dollars)			
Straight-line depreciation, Bulletin "F" service lives				
Historical cost valuation	4.4	6.4	16.7	29.8
Current price valuation	5.4	9.9	23.0	35.0
Double-declining balance depreciation, .75 Bulletin "F" service lives				
Historical cost valuation	5.4	8.5	21.6	37.8
Current price valuation	5.9	11.2	26.0	41.2
Depreciation actually charged	4.1	6.8	21.3	37.0

estimated on a straight-line, "F" service lives basis, at *current* price valuation, considered to be the more appropriate charge, the amount would have been 23.0 billion. It is clear, in this case and for this year, that liberalization came fairly close towards permitting, in effect, depreciation to be charged on a current-price basis. In 1966, depreciation under the liberalized regulations actually exceeded the current-price amount estimated on the basis of straight-line, "F" service lives. (In 1929 and 1948, liberalization played little or no role.) But in neither 1958 nor 1966 did liberalization serve to convert current-price depreciation charges or calculated profits to a constant purchasing-power basis. As Chart 7 indicates, this is the most important step in meeting the problem of inflation.

Shifting our attention, suppose the double-declining balance method, with 75 percent of Bulletin "F" lives, were considered to be the appropriate way to determine depreciation charges at historical cost. In that case, actual charges (including liberalization) in 1958 would have provided no offset whatever to the error resulting from determining the charges at historical rather than current prices. And, as in the case of the straight-line, Bulletin "F" practice, no allowance would have been made for changes in the general price level.

We have been assuming what some people seem to suggest, that the sole objective of the liberalization of depreciation practices was to deal with the problem of inflation. If this was indeed the objective, it is evident that liberalization is an inefficient and erratic way to reach it. In fact, however, it is questionable whether the assumption is entirely or even partly warranted. Some proponents of liberalized depreciation may indeed have had in mind its offset to the effects of inflation. It is also possible, however, that liberalization was designed to permit the abandonment of an unrealistic depreciation formula and table of permitted service lives already obsolete even in the 1920's. Or, alternatively, the purpose may have been to recognize that formulas and depreciation rates realistic enough before the war required revision in an era in which technological change, and the obsolescence to which it leads, was proceeding at an accelerated pace. To turn in still another direction, the objective could have been to provide a tax advantage to private capital formation simply in order to help sop up unemployment and raise the rate of economic growth. If so, we can say that inflation tended to nullify the steps taken in pursuit of this policy.

Whatever its objective, we may conclude that liberalization of depreciation has provided only a partial, if any, offset to the failure to adjust accounting records for inflation. Further, what offset it provided must have varied from one year to another, and from one industry or firm to another.

THE INEVITABILITY OF ERROR

Given that certain measurements are biased, it does not necessarily follow, as a matter of logic, that users of the measurements are seriously misled by them. All users might be aware, some even well aware, of what is going on. They might be able to make the adjustments themselves with "sufficient" accuracy, and indeed be in the habit of doing so more or less automatically. It is hardly conceivable, in any case, that all users of the unadjusted accounts would take them at their face value. On the other hand, it is equally doubtful that all users of the unadjusted accounts could entirely avoid being misled by them. Some degree of error is inevitable.

That the error must be limited hardly needs to be argued. It is not possible to take seriously a model of the economy in which money illusion is universal and persistent despite significant and continuing changes in the general price level. Although accountants may fail to adjust their reports for inflation, their reports are not the only source of information on what is happening. Nor is everybody unable to pay for and use this additional information. Nor, to pursue the question further, is it reasonable to suppose that users of this information would fail — in the very act of using it — to convey to others the implications of what is happening. In one way or another, and sooner or later, people learn from experience. I started out by saying that labor unions enter wage negotiations carrying briefcases crammed with consumer price indexes (as well as unadjusted profits figures!).

That error will not be entirely eliminated, however, is almost as obvious. Try to imagine an economy in which failure to adjust the accounts for inflation would have *no* significant effect on the decisions of users. Such an economy would need to have something like the following characteristics:[25] (1) Changes in prices, and therefore also in the general price level, would be open, not suppressed. No governmental regulations or private arrangements to control prices or foreign exchange rates or otherwise hide the effects of inflation, would be in force. (2) The general price level would be changing at a constant rate, and would have been doing so for a long time. There would be no "stop and go" in the policies and the other factors (including "exogenous" factors) that determine the general price level. (3) The denizens of this economy would all have finally learned what was happening, would know the past and current rate of inflation, could and would anticipate with confidence what the rate would be in the future, and would be accustomed to taking this "fact of life" into account in all their calculations and decisions. If some people lacked the capacity to acquire the knowledge and develop the habits appropriate to living and working in an inflationary economy, there would be enough competition to make those fully acquainted with the facts bring even the most ignorant up to par with the knowledgeable. Arrangements such as escalator clauses to cope with inflation could have become universal.[26]

These make up an obviously extreme set of assumptions. But they are even more extreme than they appear at first sight. Consider, for example, a fact to which we have already pointed — that every economy experiences technological change. For an economy to have the characteristics that have been specified, technological change would have to be absent. But technological change does take place, and as it does, shifts occur in the composition and durability of the equipment held by each company, and also, therefore, in the degree of hetero-temporality in every company's accounts. It would not be quite accurate, then, for the user of a company's accounts to lower the level of the company's reported profits (in order to express them in fully current dollars) by using the same proportional correction that he had been using in the past — even though the rate of inflation has not changed in the slightest. He would have to keep up with changing facts. He could not act in a routine manner.

Further, it is a fact that in few economies has inflation ever been entirely open, so that people could fully appreciate what had been happening. Rents, for example, tend to become fixed by laws setting ceilings, and foreign exchange rates to be controlled by quotas, special taxes, or other means. Sometimes, even, the published consumer price

---

[25]See Milton Friedman's Bombay Lectures [12].
[26]Compare Amotz Morag's "inflation-proof economy" [22].

indexes become biased through the "judicious" selection of the commodities being priced, or simply through failure to correct the sample of prices for obsolescence.

Nor, to turn to another of the assumptions, has inflation ever proceeded at a constant pace in any economy. Monetary and fiscal authorities are never able to offset accurately and quickly the effects of changes in exogenous factors. And no government has been able to stay in power without doing something — sooner or later, big or little, sensible or otherwise — about the inflation that is taxing so many, and thus causing the rate of inflation to change.

We could extend this list of the characteristics of an imaginary economy in which errors in the use of unadjusted accounting reports are largely absent. But I have said enough to make it clear that such an economy would not possess the characteristics of the economy with which we have to deal. It would be as unbelievable as an economy with persistent money illusion.

I have pointed to these models of imaginary economies in order to highlight some of the characteristics of the real world that must make for error, yet limit the degree of error, when accounting reports are unadjusted. Of course, the major source of error is inability to forecast. No improvement in the historical or current data could make forecasts errorless. But forecasts are surely better when founded on adequate records of the past and present. We do need to be concerned about the possibility of errors resulting from the use of unadjusted accounting reports.

The question, indeed, is not whether errors are entirely absent, or whether there is nothing but an irrational or ignorant faith in the unadjusted dollar or in the accounting reports that are made public. The question is, how much error is there? No clear answer is yet possible.

One could ask people what they know about inflation and how they take it into account in making their decisions. I suppose surveys of this kind have been made and that they provide some kernels of useful information. But I suspect, also, that the results are often ambiguous and difficult to interpret, as is attested by the experience of economists with surveys over many years.

Much better — at least potentially — would be an analysis of economic behavior in which one of the independent variables was the rate of change in the general price level. Whatever people may believe or say about themselves and their actions, what we want to know is how they actually behave when the general price level is steady or rising, or is rising slowly or rapidly, or is changing at a rate that varies from year to year. How different is the fraction of income saved, or a decision to invest or to hold cash, for example, in these different circumstances? Only in a few studies have fairly clear-cut results been obtained.[27] Recent work has been largely experimental, as is natural when the statistical data are still seriously limited in scope and often defective, and the emphasis has been mostly on technical econometric problems.

CONCLUDING COMMENTS

We are left, at this juncture, largely with opinions on the extent of the error resulting from the use of unadjusted accounting reports. But these opinions are not entirely arbitrary. To state explicitly what has already been implied, it is difficult to believe that many people can make their own adjustments to the accounts; or that when they try, that the results come at all close to being as accurate as they would be if accountants did the work; or that the social cost of making the adjustments would not be greatly reduced if the work were done by accountants for the use of all readers of company reports. In a word, it is reasonable to expect that business decisions would be sounder if the accounts were adjusted before reports were released.

The need for recognition of inflation extends beyond the sphere of corporation reports. The accounts of the federal, state, and local governments would also be substantially more useful, and subject to far less misunderstanding, if supplementary tabulations were appended to them setting forth the effects of price level changes. These tabulations need not be elaborate.

Adjustment of accounting reports for changes in the general price level would mean an improvement in only a small portion of the almost endless information needed for sound decisions. These decisions are of great importance, however. Improvement in any part of the information would be worth more than its cost.

---

[27]Mention may be made of Cagan's study of the demand for cash balances during periods of hyper-inflation [4], and of Friedman and Schwartz's study (among other things) of the lag between the changes that have occurred in the trend of the general price level and the effects of these changes on price expectations and interest rates [13].

BIBLIOGRAPHY

[1] American Institute of Certified Public Accountants. "Reporting the Financial Effects of Price-Level Changes." *Accounting Research Study No. 6.* New York: American Institute of Certified Public Accountants, Inc., 1963.

[2] Braithwaite, Stanley N. "Real Income Levels in Latin America." *The Review of Income and Wealth,* Series 14, No. 2 (June, 1968), pp. 113–82.

[3] Burns, Arthur F., and Wesley C. Mitchell. *Measuring Business Cycles.* New York: National Bureau of Economic Research, 1946.

[4] Cagan, Phillip. "The Monetary Dynamics of Hyperinflation." *Studies in the Quantity Theory of Money,* edited by Milton Friedman. Chicago: University of Chicago Press, 1956.

[5] Deane, Phyllis (editor). *Studies in Social and Financial Accounting.* International Association for Research in Income and Wealth. Income and Wealth Series IX. London: Bowes and Bowes, 1961.

[6] Domar, Evsey D. "Depreciation, Replacement, and Growth." *The Economic Journal,* Vol. LXIII (March, 1953), pp. 1–32; reprinted in Evsey D. Domar, *Essays in the Theory of Economic Growth.* New York: Oxford University Press, 1957.

[7] Fabricant, Solomon. *Capital Consumption and Adjustment.* New York: National Bureau of Economic Research, 1938.

[8] —————— . "Business Costs and Business Income Under Changing Price Levels." *New Responsibilities of the Accounting Profession.* New York: American Institute of Accountants, 1948; reprinted in Study Group on Business Income. *Five Monographs on Business Income.* New York: American Institute of Accountants, 1950.

[9] —————— . "The Varied Impact of Inflation on the Calculation of Business Income." *Current Business Studies.* New York: Institute of Trade and Commerce Professions, 1949; reprinted in Study Group on Business Income. *Five Monographs on Business Income.* New York: American Institute of Accountants, 1950.

[10] —————— . "Capital Consumption and Net Capital Formation," in Conference on Research in Income and Wealth. *A Critique of the United States Income and Product Accounts. Studies in Income and Wealth,* Vol. 22. Princeton: Princeton University Press, 1958.

[11] —————— . *A Primer on Productivity.* New York: Random House, 1969.

[12] Friedman, Milton. *Dollars and Deficits; Living with America's Economic Problems.* Englewood Cliffs, N. J.: Prentice-Hall, Inc., 1968.

[13] —————— , and Anna J. Schwartz. *Monetary Trends in the United States and the United Kingdom: Their Relation to Income, Prices, and Interest Rates.* National Bureau of Economic Research (in preparation).

[14] Gainsbrugh, Martin R., and Jules Backman. *Inflation and the Price Indexes.* Studies in Business Economics No. 94. New York: National Industrial Conference Board, Inc., 1966.

[15] Goldsmith, Raymond William. *A Study of Saving in the United States.* Princeton: Princeton University Press, 1955.

[16] Grose, Lawrence, Irving Rottenberg, and Robert C. Wasson. "New Estimates of Fixed Business Capital in the United States, 1925–65." *Survey of Current Business,* Vol. XLVI, No. 12 (December, 1966), pp. 34–40.

[17] Hastay, Millard. "The Cyclical Behavior of Investment," in a report of the National Bureau of Economic Research, Special Conference Series No. 4. *Regularization of Business Investment.* Princeton: Princeton University Press, 1954.

[18] Hotelling, Harold. "A General Mathematical Theory of Depreciation." *Journal of the American Statistical Association,* Vol. XX, No. 150 (September, 1925), pp. 340–53.

[19] Keynes, John Maynard. *A Treatise on Money.* London: Macmillan Co., 1930.

[20] Kuznets, Simon S. *Capital in the American Economy; Its Formation and Financing.* A Study by the National Bureau of Economic Research. Princeton: Princeton University Press, 1961.

[21] Moonitz, Maurice. "The Basic Postulates of Accounting." *Accounting Research Study No. 1.* New York: American Institute of Certified Public Accountants, 1961.

[22] Morag, Amotz. "For an Inflation-Proof Economy." *American Economic Review,* Vol. LII, No. 1 (March, 1962), pp. 177-85; reprinted in Amotz Morag. *On Taxes and Inflation.* New York: Random House, 1965.

[23] Price Statistics Review Committee of the National Bureau of Economic Research. *The Price Statistics of the Federal Government.* General Series No. 73. New York: National Bureau of Economic Research, Inc., 1961.

[24] Scitovsky, Anne A. "Changes in the Costs of Treatment of Selected Illnesses, 1951–65." *The American Economic Review,* Vol. LVII, No. 5 (December, 1967), pp. 1182–1195.

[25] Stigler, George J. *Capital and Rates of Return in Manufacturing Industries.* A Study by the National Bureau of Economic Research. Princeton: Princeton University Press, 1963.

[26] Study Group on Business Income. *Changing Concepts of Business Income.* Report of the Study Group on Business Income, American Institute of Accountants. New York: The Macmillan Company, 1952.

[27] Ture, Norman B. *Accelerated Depreciation in the United States, 1954–60.* National Bureau of Economic Research, Fiscal Study No. 9. New York: National Bureau of Economic Research, 1967.

[28] U.S. Department of Commerce, Office of Business Economics. *The National Income and Product Accounts of the United States, 1929–65; Statistical Tables,* a supplement to the *Survey of Current Business.* Washington: 1966.

[29] U. S. Department of Labor, Bureau of Labor Statistics. *Handbook of Labor Statistics 1967,* Bulletin No. 1555. Washington: 1967.

[30] U. S. Treasury Department, Bureau of Internal Revenue. *Bulletin "F," Income Tax Depreciation and Obsolescence; Estimated Useful Lives and Depreciation Rates* (Revised January, 1942). Washington: 1942; reprinted as *Tables of Useful Lives of Depreciable Property.* Washington: 1955.

[31] Young, Allan H. "Alternative Estimates of Corporate Depreciation and Profits: Part I." *Survey of Current Business.* Vol. XLVIII, No. 4 (April, 1968), pp. 17–28.

[32] —————— . "Alternative Estimates of Corporate Depreciation and Profits: Part II." *Survey of Current Business.* Vol. XLVIII, No. 5 (May, 1968), pp. 16–28.

[33] —————— , and Claudia Harkins. "Alternative Measures of Price Changes for GNP." *Survey of Current Business.* Vol. XLIX, No. 3 (March, 1969), pp. 47–52.

APPENDIX 1. CHARTS

1. Indexes of the General Price Level in the United States, 1913–1968.
2. Rates of Change in the General Price Level (IPI), 1929–1968.
3. Inventory Valuation Adjustment Relative to Profits after Tax, Corporations, Annually, 1929–1968.
4. Indexes of Prices Underlying Book Values and Replacement Costs per Unit, Nonfarm Business Inventories, 1947–1968.
5. Indexes of the General Price Level (IPI) and of Replacement Costs per Unit for Inventory Withdrawals and for Depreciation Charges, 1947–1968.
6. Indexes of Prices Underlying Historical Costs and Replacement Costs, per Unit, Business Depreciation Charges, 1919–1968.
7. Profits after Tax, Nonfinancial Corporations, before and after Adjustment for Changes in the General Price Level, 1929–1968.
8. Rates of Return on Assets, at Book Value and at 1947 Prices, Manufacturing Corporations, 1938–1958.
9. Rates of Return on Assets, Manufacturing Corporations, by Major Industry Group, Comparison of 1947 and 1957.

APPENDIX 2.   SOURCES OF CHART DATA

1. The NNP IPI (Net National Product Implicit Price Index) is an unpublished series calculated at the National Bureau of Economic Research by Simon Kuznets [20], appendixes A and C for 1913-1942, and extended through 1946 by Milton Friedman and Anna Schwartz. The GNP IPI (Gross National Production Implicit Price Index) is from the Department of Commerce [28] and more recent issues of *Survey of Current Business*. The CPI and WPI are from the Bureau of Labor Statistics [29] and previous issues, and recent issues of *Monthly Labor Review*.

2. The rates of change in the General Price Level are computed from the OBE IPI mentioned above. The business cycle phases are as defined by the NBER [3] and unpublished data.

3. The IVA and the Corporate Profits after Tax (and before IVA) are from [28] and more recent issues of *Survey of Current Business*.

4. The implicit deflators are unpublished estimates prepared by the OBE, Department of Commerce.

5. See sources for Charts 1, 4 and 6.

6. The Historical Cost and the Replacement Cost indexes are from the OBE, Department of Commerce, Capital Stock Study; see Grose, Rottenberg, and Wasson [16]. The data are estimated on the basis of straight-line depreciation, using Bulletin "F" service lives, and the first of the two current price indexes prepared by the OBE.

7. The IVA is from [28] and more recent issues of *Survey of Current Business*. The Profits, Adjusted for IVA, the Depreciation Value Adjustment, and the Profits, Adjusted also for current price valuation of depreciation, are from Young [31 and 32] for 1929-1966; and estimates have been made for 1967 and 1968, based on Grose, Rottenberg, and Wasson [16]. The depreciation value adjustment is depreciation at current (replacement) cost less depreciation at historical cost. The data are estimated on the basis of straight-line depreciation, using Bulletin "F" service lives, and the first of the two current price indexes prepared by the OBE.

   The Profits, at 1929 prices, are the Profits after the above adjustments, deflated by the GNP IPI.

   The Profits, Book Value, are the Profits, Adjusted for IVA, less the Inventory Valuation Adjustment.

8. The Rates of Return are from Stigler [25], Table B-1, p. 203 and Errata, Table 5, p. 8. They are adjusted net profits after taxes divided by total corporate assets excluding investments in other companies. There was a slight change in the industrial classification between 1947 and 1948, which does not affect the figures given here.

9. The Rates of Return are from Stigler [25], Tables A-36 to A-59, pp. 170–202 and Errata, Table 1, p. 4.

"I believe . . . that general price-level information is required at this time for a fair presentation of the financial position of business enterprises—if not in the basic statements, then at least in supplementary statements."

INFLATION AND CURRENT ACCOUNTING PRACTICE: AN ECONOMIST'S VIEW

BY SOLOMON FABRICANT

"THE effects of inflation in the United States are not considered sufficiently important at this time to require recognition in financial accounting measurements." So reports the Accounting Principles Board of the American Institute in its statement on current accounting practice.[1]

I beg to differ. In my opinion—and the opinion of many other economists, I believe—the effects of inflation are indeed "sufficiently important." As is clearly recognized in the Board's report, inflation affects the basic unit of measurement in terms of which financial statements are made and thus distorts the information on which users of financial reports rely. But, as accounting practitioners fail to recognize, the distortions caused by general price-level changes are considerable "at this time" and have been considerable for years now. Further, it would be flying in the face of all that is known about the politics and economics of this age to presume that general price-level changes will be negligible in the future—if that is what the accounting profession is counting on.

At the very least, it seems to me, the reports of independent certified public accountants should do two things. First, they should mention the change in the general price level over the period covered by the financial statements that are being certified.

Second, they should draw the significance of this price change to the attention of those who rely on these financial statements. I would hope, however, that public accountants could decide to go further than this. To assist the share owners and the public at large, who must make far-reaching decisions on the basis of accounting reports, public accountants should ask management to provide supplements disclosing the effects of changes in the general price level or insist on doing so themselves.

The Accounting Principles Board has already recommended such supplementary disclosure.[2] Were the leaders of the profession to set the example of following this recommendation, the profession at large would find it easier to move ahead. These supplementary statements would be valuable even if they were not as detailed as the "basic historical cost statements," and even if they were labeled "approximate"—as they should be.

Perhaps, ultimately, accountants will see the need to go whole hog, and introduce a price-level adjustment in the basic financial statements. But this will never happen if the initial steps I have mentioned are not taken first.

I have been brief (I hope not to the point of curtness) in order to put sharply and quickly before the readers of THE JOURNAL my main reaction to the accounting practices described in the Board's

---

[1] Statement of the Accounting Principles Board No. 4, "Basic Concepts and Accounting Principles Underlying Financial Statements of Business Enterprises," October 1970, p. 64.

[2] Statement of the Accounting Principles Board, No. 3, "Financial Statements Restated for General Price-Level Changes," June 1969, p. 12.

Statement No. 4. With this done, let me now try to be rather less brusk.

RECENT TRENDS OF INFLATION

Inflation continues to be a serious problem of the day. After the 12 months of recession that began in November 1969, during which unemployment was pushed up to around 6 per cent and the percentage of capacity utilized in manufacturing was pressed below 75 per cent, the general price level was still rising, and rising at the exceptionally rapid rate (for a recession) of 5 per cent per year. Now that business is recovering, past experience with business-cycle expansions offers little promise of a stop to the rising general price level.

It is possible that the "worst of inflation is behind us," as the President said in April 1971. The rate of advance in the general price level seems indeed to have stopped accelerating. But this is not to say that inflation will soon be over. To judge from the private talk of its officials, the Administration does not look forward with confidence to anything that may fairly be called a stable price level. As *The New York Times* reported in May, a "high and knowledgeable" source in the Administration agreed then that "anyone who thinks the [wage] settlement in steel will be less than the can settlement is out of his mind." As we all now know, the steel settlement did match the high increases given in the can settlement. And the steel wage settlement was promptly followed by a substantial steel price increase. It is not surprising that in recent testimony before a Congressional committee, the chairman of the Federal Reserve Board said that "neither the behavior of prices nor the pattern of wage increases as yet provides evidence of any significant moderation in the advance of costs and prices."

Also revealing is the Executive Order on wage-price stabilization in the construction industry. The Order does not even pretend to be the first step in a rollback of the large wage and price increases that have already been made in that industry. Nor, if the wage settlements already approved under the Order provide a sign of what is to come, will an attempt be made to hold future wage increases in the industry to just the normal rate of increase in national productivity.[3] This means that construction costs will continue to mount.

A "significant moderation" in the rate of inflation may yet come. Most of the economic projections made outside the federal government (as well as those made inside), available at midyear 1971, do indicate a decline in the rate of inflation after the first half of 1971. But none of the nongovernmental projections puts the rate of inflation (measured by the GNP implicit price deflator) even a year and a half later as low as 2.5 per cent per annum. The projections for the second half of 1972 range from 2.7 per cent to as much as 4.7 per cent per annum, with the average equal to 3.6.

Nor would it be reasonable for anyone, inside or outside the Administration, to see an early end to large wage increases or to an appreciable degree of price inflation. The pressures in Washington to reduce the fiscal deficit and the rate of increase in money supply appear no stronger than the pressures to raise them. Further, when some of the current unemployment is sopped up (as the Administration has avowed is one of its prime objectives) and higher output begins to strain available capacity in a widening range of firms, industries and regions, the general price level may again tend to accelerate even if government policy remains as anti-inflationary as it now is.

As for the longer term, the "secular," trend—looking beyond the present cyclical expansion—perhaps it is sufficient to say that the immediate costs, in terms of unemployment and otherwise, of a strong anti-inflationary policy seem to many people to have turned out to be greater than expected, and greater than they feel to be tolerable. As a result, it is becoming harder for them, and even for those who minimize the costs and maximize the benefits of anti-inflation policy, to be even faintly optimistic about a horizontal trend in the price level. More and more wage contracts, price contracts and financial dealings are including escalator clauses, built-in wage or price increases, high interest rates, and conversion and other equity privileges. The public is adjusting itself not only to past inflation but also to the likelihood of future secular inflation. It is noteworthy that the majority on the Joint Economic Committee of the Congress, after a close examination of the problem, including listening to much testimony from all sides, found itself willing to settle on a "long-term objective" for

SOLOMON FABRICANT, Ph.D., *is professor of economics at New York University. He was formerly director of research and is now a member of the research staff of the National Bureau of Economic Research. Dr. Fabricant was a member of President Nixon's Task Force on Science Policy in 1969 and of the President's Commission on Federal Statistics in 1970-71, and has served as a consultant to various federal and state government agencies. He is the author and coauthor of numerous books, and has been a frequent contributor to* Studies in Income and Wealth *and has written articles for several professional journals. Dr. Fabricant received his doctorate from Columbia University.*

[3] Most of the approvals have clustered in the 6 to 9 per cent range—far in excess of the normal rise in national productivity, which is around 3 per cent per annum.

the nation that allows for an annual increase in the GNP deflator of "no more than 2 per cent."[4]

Also reflecting general thinking on the prospects ahead is the public demand for improved understanding of the process of inflation. Where there is a demand, a supply comes forth, as we economists say, so television programs are being offered to explain inflation to the layman. And more economists are turning their attention to the scientific study of inflation. There will soon be held, for example, a conference of research economists on "the economics of secular inflation"; and the Life Insurance Association of America recently provided financial support for an intensive study by the National Bureau of Economic Research of "the effects of secular inflation on financial markets."

The wage-price freeze and other actions taken, and proposals made, by the President on August 15, 1971, can (in my opinion) lead to no more than a slowing down somewhat of the rate of advance of the general price level. I seriously doubt that a significant degree of inflation is now only a thing of the past.

It should be noted further that even if and when the price level does stop rising, many years will elapse before the effects on the accounts of the inflation of earlier years become negligible.

THE APB's FUNDAMENTALS STATEMENT

It is natural, therefore, that when an economist picks up the "Fundamentals Statement" of the Accounting Principles Board—its Statement No. 4— he should turn first to what the Board reports on the current treatment of rising price levels. Of course, this is not the only item of interest to economists. Of all those outside the accounting profession, economists are the most keenly aware of the host of problems that confront accountants when they try to determine the flow of income and the stock of capital in a dynamic economy. Economists know how technological and other changes —in population, tastes, natural resources, economic institutions and international trade—complicate the task of accountants. But a discussion of what the APB has to report on all these perennial problems would hardly fit into my limited space. I concentrate on the question of inflation, because the distinctive feature of our era, from the accounting

viewpoint, is its tendency toward secular inflation.

The fundamental question to be put to a fundamentals statement, then, concerns the unit in which financial statements are to be expressed. On this, we read what is implied by current accounting practice in the Board's Statement quoted at the outset. What is offered to justify this answer? Very little, if anything, I am afraid. Nor could much be offered by anyone. The view of the accounting profession that is reflected in its current practice cannot be reconciled with the objectives and the criteria of good financial reporting that are set forth elsewhere in the Board Statement. Nor can the view of the profession be reconciled with the facts on price-level changes and their effects on financial statements.

In an inflationary era, it seems to me, the public is entitled to expect something better than this. It is not unreasonable to expect that accountants will recognize inflation's serious effects on the business accounts they certify, and will help the users of these accounts to assess these effects. We can hardly be satisfied with what may too easily be regarded as pussyfooting.

Consider, first, the criteria for adequate financial information set forth in Statement No. 4, criteria that are presumably widely accepted by the accounting profession.

The function of accounting, according to the Statement, is "to provide quantitative information, primarily financial in nature, about economic entities that is intended to be useful in making economic decisions" (p. 17). This information "is needed to form judgments about the ability of the enterprise to survive, to adapt, to grow and to prosper amid changing economic conditions" (p. 33). Financial statements must be comparable between periods, and these comparisons will be more informative if "changes in circumstances . . . are disclosed" (p. 39). Since economic decisions "involve the process of choosing among alternative courses of action," including choosing among enterprises, an effort must also be made to achieve greater comparability among the financial statements of different enterprises (pp. 35, 39).

Now, "the effects of economic activities are measured in terms of money in a monetary economy." However, "fluctuations in the general purchasing power of money cause problems in using money as a unit of measure" (p. 29). Even "moderate inflation or deflation," if it persists for several years, may cause "the general purchasing power of the dollars in which expenses are measured" to "differ significantly from the general purchasing power of the dollars in which revenue is measured" (p. 65). Presumably—though this is not spelled out in so

---

[4] The statement in full is as follows: "The President and the Congress should adopt as a long-term objective the twin goals of an unemployment rate no higher than 3 per cent and an annual increase in the GNP deflator of no more than 2 per cent." Report of the Joint Economic Committee of the Congress of the United States on the February 1971 Economic Report of the President, 1971 (92nd Congress, 1st Session, Senate Report No. 92-49, p. 35).

many words—even moderate inflation or deflation, if persistent, may cause the general purchasing power of the dollars in which a company's net income or net worth is measured at one time to differ significantly from the value of the dollars in which its income or worth is measured at another time. And it may be said, in addition, that the dollars in which the accounts of different companies are measured may differ significantly and, to that extent, be incomparable.

The Board's Statement makes clear the understanding by accountants that accounting principles "change in response to changes in economic and social conditions, to new knowledge and technology, and to demands by users for more serviceable financial information" (p. 12). To meet the need for "adequate disclosure" to facilitate understanding and avoid erroneous implications (p. 41), therefore, we may expect the Statement to go on to report the use by most, or at least by many, or at any rate by some, firms of at least supplementary disclosure of general price-level information. Yet, after the presentation of what amounts to a case for doing at least that much—even when inflation is only "moderate"—the Statement offers no comment on the fact that information on general price levels (supplementary or otherwise) is not provided in current accounting reports in the United States.

The Statement does mention, first, that Lifo and accelerated depreciation of plant and equipment, "which tend to minimize" the incomparability of revenue and costs caused by change in the general price level, have become generally accepted and widely used in this country. However, general acceptance and wide use are not *universal* acceptance and use. Nor, as I shall indicate, would their universal acceptance and use be sufficient.

Second, the Board does state that "methods of restating financial statements for general price-level changes . . . are not now used in the basic financial statements in the United States" (p. 65). To this a footnote is appended mentioning that Accounting Principles Board Statement No. 3 recommends supplementary disclosure of general price-level information. But Statement No. 3 states only that "general price-level information *may be* presented in addition to the historical-dollar financial statements . . . " (emphasis supplied). This seems to place the emphasis on the statement immediately following, that "general price-level financial statements *should not* be presented as the basic statements" (emphasis supplied). It is hard to read these sentences as "recommending" supplementary disclosure of general price-level information, which is how the footnote in Statement No. 4 refers to them. Rather, I read the recommendation

as focused on avoiding the use of general price-level information in the construction of the basic financial statements.[5] But even by the more favorable interpretation, the Board is only recommending a supplement, not requiring one. In any case, as I have already said, few (if any) such supplements are in fact being provided in the United States.

LESS THAN "MODERATE" INFLATION?

After reading the main body of Statement No. 4 and the immediately preceding Statement No. 3, I find it difficult, as an economist, to understand this hesitation of practitioners to follow through. And, I ask, what reason might be given for it?

Can it be that recognition of changes in the general price level would provide only insignificant information—since "financial reporting is only concerned with significant information?" (p. 11 of Statement No. 4). I have already quoted the Board's statement that even moderate inflation can mean significant incomparability of revenue and costs, and presumably, therefore, significant misstatement of income; and I shall present some figures in a moment to support the view that the inflation we have experienced not only can mean, but has meant, significant misstatement of income.

Can it be that estimates of change in the general price level, and statements using them, would be too imprecise and subjective for accounting purposes? But every accountant knows that "financial accounting involves approximation and judgment" (p. 41). And while there is no absolutely precise or even unique index of the general price level, the difference between the changes revealed by the indexes generally used—the GNP deflator and the consumer price index—is at most the difference between 4 and 5 per cent per annum. Either estimate is surely better than the assumption of zero change in the general price level. Also important is the general agreement, among the companies participating in the field test authorized by the Board some years ago, that "with proper preparation, practical problems should not present a signifi-

---

[5] In this connection, mention should be made of some of the "Proposals for Change," reported toward the end of Statement No. 4. These are suggestions to use current replacement prices, for example, as the basis of measurement in the basic financial statements; and in these statements to recognize changes in the general level of price (p. 104). The proposals are followed by the caution that "brief mention of . . . these proposals . . . does not, of course, imply a degree of present acceptance nor constitute a forecast of future acceptance. Reference to them in this Statement does not give them substantial authoritative support" (p. 103).

cant barrier to preparation of general price-level financial statements."[6]

Would a shift to purchasing power units, either in the basic financial statements, or in the supplements, violate the criterion of consistency between financial statements at different times and thus reduce comparability? But comparability requires, among other things, that "changes in circumstances" (p. 39) be disclosed. Surely changes in the purchasing power of money—the fundamental unit of measurement—constitute such changes in circumstances. To stick to an unadjusted dollar is analogous to refusing to make corrections for changes in temperature when using metal rules, or in elevation when calculating boiling points.

Would the correction for changes in the general price level during a period of inflation violate the convention of conservatism? On the contrary. The level of change in profits is, as a rule, overstated, not understated, when the general price level is rising. And rates of change in profits also are overstated.

Implicit in the thinking of the accounting profession, it seems, is the assumption that inflation in the United States has been (and promises to be) less than "moderate." So we come to the crucial question: What are the facts?

THE ACTUAL PRICE RISE

During the year preceding the publication of the Board's Statement No. 3, in 1969, the price level rose by 4 per cent, according to the GNP implicit price index. Between June 1969, when Statement No. 3 was published, and October 1970, the date of publication of Statement No. 4, the price level moved up by more than 6 per cent. Over a two-year period, then, the general price level had risen by 10 per cent, measured by the GNP implicit price deflator, and about the same when measured by the consumer price index. Is this negligible? Looking a bit further back, to 1963, when the American Institute published its Accounting Research Study No. 6,[7] the general price level has risen by 30 per cent. Since 1948, when the Institute set up its Study Group on Business Income,[8] which had a good deal to say about general price-level changes, the price rise has been 75 per cent.

The effect of inflation on the unit of measure-

ment in financial accounts cannot be shrugged off by anyone who ponders these quantities. And these price-level changes can hardly be news to accountants. Statement No. 3 contains the GNP deflator series for 1929-1968; and every month or quarter the new figures on these and on the consumer price indexes are reported in the daily newspapers. It is surely in recognition of these changes that the Board (in Statement No. 3, p. 12) expressed the opinion that "general price-level financial statements or pertinent information extracted from them present useful information not available from basic historical-dollar financial statements." It is puzzling to find accounting practitioners, as reported in the Board's subsequent Statement No. 4, considering the effects of inflation in the United States to be not "sufficiently important."

Perhaps accountants believe that Lifo and accelerated depreciation, to which the Board referred, can meet the problem of changing general price levels. If so, they are mistaken. First, not all enterprises do in fact use Lifo and accelerated depreciation, as I have already pointed out. Second, and more important, even at best these practices can only partially meet the problem of inflation. Viewed as variants of replacement-cost accounting, Lifo and accelerated depreciation attempt only to lessen the incomparability between the revenues and costs ascribed to a particular fiscal period—that is, to take care of the problem of "heterotemporality." But this step fails to be followed by the second step necessary to put the revenues, costs and incomes of different periods into the comparable terms of a general price level *constant over time.*[9] Third, Lifo and accelerated depreciation are inefficient and erratic as a means of meeting even the problem of heterotemporality. In the case of Lifo, this can be seen if one considers the effect of fluctuations in the physical volume of inventories. In the case of accelerated depreciation, it is obvious that steps in the liberalization of depreciation practices would not—and could not—be geared to the rate or to changes in the rate of inflation. Fourth, the effectiveness of Lifo and depreciation liberalization in redressing the bias

---

[6] Paul Rosenfield, "Accounting for Inflation—A Field Test," JofA, June69, p. 50.

[7] Staff of the Accounting Research Division, American Institute of Certified Public Accountants, *Reporting the Financial Effects of Price-Level Changes*, Accounting Research Study No. 6, 1963.

[8] Study Group on Business Income, American Institute of Accountants, *Changing Concepts of Business Income* (New York: The Macmillan Company, 1952).

[9] I pass over the question of whether changes in relative prices should be introduced into accounts, as they are handled by the usual replacement-cost procedures. On these, see my paper on "Inflation and the Lag in Accounting Practice," in R. R. Sterling and W. F. Bentz (editors), *Accounting in Perspective: Contributions to Accounting Thought by Other Disciplines*, Accounting Colloquium I, cosponsored by the University of Kansas School of Business and the Arthur Young Foundation (Cincinnati, Ohio: The South-Western Publishing Company, 1971), pp. 121-126; also Accounting Research Study No. 6, pp. 29-31, and Statement No. 3, Appendix D.

caused by inflation must vary among industries and firms, making interfirm and interindustry comparisons difficult.[10]

INADEQUATE MEASURES

We can estimate the extent to which the ameliorative effects of replacement-cost accounting, and accelerated depreciation, if these were universally accepted and applied, would fall short of adjusting aggregate net income for the full effects of inflation.[11] In 1970, the "inventory valuation adjustment" of the Department of Commerce, which in effect assumes a Lifo or equivalent adjustment for those corporations that do not use Lifo, equaled almost $5 billion. A corresponding "depreciation valuation adjustment," which no corporation makes, would be of the order of $8 or $10 billion.[12] Together, these total $13 to $15 billion, or almost 30 to 35 per cent of the reported after-tax profits of 1970. The corresponding percentages for 1960 are only about 16 to 23 per cent. As for changes between 1960 and 1970, reported profits in 1970 were 73 per cent higher than reported profits in 1960. After the adjustment for heterotemporality just mentioned, the rise is about 45 per cent. Adjustment for the change in the general price level further reduces the rise in profits between 1960 and 1970 to only about 12 per cent.[13]

These figures relate to aggregates, and therefore

provide a notion only of the average effect of the incomparabilities over time caused by inflation. The degree of incomparability could be a good deal more for many individual corporations. In any case, because companies differ in balance sheet structure, in the rate of turnover of assets and in the timing of new acquisitions of assets, there must be wide differences in the extent of the effects of inflation.[14]

CONCLUSION

To some people, these effects of changes in the general price level in the recent past may seem negligible. To me, and to many other people, they do not appear negligible. Nor, to repeat, does it seem to be reasonable to expect them to become negligible in the future. I believe, therefore, that general price-level information is required at this time for a fair presentation of the financial position of business enterprises—if not in the basic statements, then at least in supplementary statements.

When it is said—or at least implied—that ignoring this information is in conformity with generally accepted accounting principles in the United States, I cannot help but raise my eyebrows. When it is said further that conformity with these principles is sufficient for a fair presentation of the financial position of business enterprises, I must rise to disagree, and say that it is high time that these principles were revised. "Substantial authoritative support" should be given to recognizing the importance of general price-level information.

A major objective of financial accounting is to provide information useful in making economic decisions. For accountants to avow this, and then in effect to stop short of doing what needs to be done to reach the objective, is to expose themselves to the charge of nonfeasance. If I were an accountant, I would not want to be subject to this charge.

Statement No. 3 provides a useful guide to the preparation and presentation of "general price-level financial statements." Accountants should begin to use this guide to prepare and present this information. The foreword to the Statement emphasizes that "presentation of such information is not mandatory." But I can see no good reasons for not presenting such information; I can see many good reasons for doing so.

---

[10] A more adequate discussion of these various points appears in my Kansas paper.

[11] Estimates for each year, 1929-68, are given in my Kansas paper. I am indebted to the Office of Business Economics, Department of Commerce, for the additional data for 1969-70, as well as for a good part of the earlier estimates.

[12] The higher figure assumes that depreciation is generally calculated on a straight-line basis, using Bulletin F service lives. The lower figure assumes that depreciation is generally calculated according to the double-declining balance method, using 75 per cent of Bulletin F service lives.

[13] The rise in reported profits is about the same, 45 per cent, after the adjustment for heterotemporality, whether the adjustment is based on the straight-line Bulletin F assumption or on the double-declining balance 75 per cent of Bulletin F assumption. If it is assumed (to allow for the trend toward liberalization) that the former assumption applied to 1960 and the latter to 1970, the rise after adjustment for heterotemporality becomes 57 per cent, and, after further adjustment for changes in the general price level, about 20 per cent.

The new rules on depreciation put into effect by the Treasury in June 1971 would reduce reported after-tax profits for 1971, and thus cut the rise between 1970 and 1971 in reported after-tax profits by an amount estimated to be in excess of the amount needed to correct for the inflation between 1970 and 1971. But the liberalization would do little to make up for the inflation in prior years. Further, because its effect on reported profits in 1972 and immediately following years would be roughly constant, the rules change could not correct for any inflation during

---

subsequent years. The Treasury's new regulation exemplifies the inefficient and erratic character of depreciation liberalization as a solution for the problem of inflation.

[14] An idea of the average difference among industrial groups, drawing on estimates made by George J. Stigler, was given in my Kansas paper. Individual companies may differ still more, as Rosenfield's sample study, commissioned by the Accounting Principles Board, has indicated.

ACCOUNTING BY BUSINESS FIRMS

FOR INVESTMENT IN RESEARCH AND DEVELOPMENT

Summary

by

Solomon Fabricant*

* The full report is in three sections, as follows:

Section I: Business Accounting for Investment in Research and
            Development

            by Solomon Fabricant and Michael Schiff

Section II: An Examination and Analysis of Information on
              Accounting for R&D

              by Joseph G. San Miguel

Section III: The Literature on Accounting for Innovation

             by Shahid L. Ansari

The report is available from the National Technical Information
Service of the U. S. Department of Commerce. It was originally
published by New York University in August 1975 in a limited
edition. Financial support for the study was provided by the
Office of National R&D Assessment of the National Science
Foundation.

ACCOUNTING BY BUSINESS FIRMS
FOR INVESTMENT IN RESEARCH AND DEVELOPMENT

Summary

In this exploratory study of accounting for research and development,
we deal with the quantity and quality of the available data--which leave
much to be desired. We limit our attention to accounting by business
firms, excluding accounting by governmental and nonprofit private institutions, for company-sponsored innovative activity. While we are concerned
with investment in innovation generally, most of our discussion of necessity
deals with innovations resulting from what is conventionally thought of as
R&D. With respect to R&D, we inquire into current practices of accounting
and disclosure, and the character of the data they yield; review changes
in thinking and practice; and consider the factors involved in these
changes. We also note tendencies toward further change, some already
under way; and indicate what we believe the direction that change should
preferably take. Finally, we suggest lines along which further research
in the area might profitably be undertaken.

The particular subjects to be examined in a review of accounting
for investment in innovation are the same as of accounting for any form
of investment. They are:

(1) The activities identified as innovational, or more narrowly
    as R&D -- the question of concept and definition;

(2) The elements of cost charged to R&D;

(3) Whether these costs are charged to current expense in the
    fiscal period in which incurred or defferred in whole or in
    part to later periods, and if deferred, on what basis;

(4) The information disclosed in published financial statements.

Accounting for investment in innovation by business firms is in a primitive state. In fact, financial officers responsible for company accounts and public accountants who audit them have only begun to record this type of investment. The word, "innovation", cannot even be found in their vocabulary. Certain kinds of innovative investments, it is true, may sometimes appear in the balance sheets of business firms under such intangible-asset titles as patents, trademarks, deferred costs, and goodwill. It may also be inferred, from the accounting treatment of designing, engineering and other costs incurred in the initial stages of construction and operation of new plants and processess -- beyond the pilot plant stage -- that even plant and equipment may include some investment in what may properly be called innovation. But when these innovational investments do get into the balance sheet--which is infrequent-- they are usually combined inextricably with other investments or deferred costs that lack the features characteristic of innovation.

In the income account of a company (inclusive of supplementary schedules and notes) the only item that may be closely identified with investment in innovation is the expenditure on R&D expensed, or the amortization of capitalized R&D. It appears that most companies (small as well as large) that make significant investments in R&D do record these investments in separate accounts. Public reporting of R&D, however, is largely a recent development, required of companies under the jurisdiction of the Securities Exchange Commission only as recently as 1970, and then only when material by SEC standards.

However, no specific definition of R&D has been given by SEC or, for that matter, by professional accounting organizations until very recently--in fact, too recently to affect currently available figures. Most large companies, and some small companies, must have become familiar with the definition used by the National Science oundation in its surveys, but then may have departed from it in one way

r another. This has led to variation, of uncertain degree, that disturbs

omparisons not only between industries, but also between companies within

ndustries. And, we have discovered, the definition has not always been

onsistent over time even for the same company. Further, while classification

f R&D by operating division is required in the "charts of accounts" that

e have seen, hardly any company has subclassified its R&D expenditure in

ts published report. When the content or composition of this investment

as been occasionally described, it was only in rather general or merely

llustrative terms in the text of the report preceding the financial state-

ents.

With regard to the elements of cost charged to R&D, the main

uestion concerns the treatment of general and administrative expense.

robably most enterprises include in their R&D costs the "direct" over-

ead of the division or divisions conducting research and development.

ew appear to include the general and administrative expense incurred

utside the R&D divisions in supervising and servicing them. Very few

nterprises charge to R&D any interest on the capital invested in the

angible assets used in R&D activities. We conclude that reported R&D

osts, whether expensed when incurred or amortized in subsequent periods,

o not cover the full amount of the investment in R&D. The degree of short-

all varies among enterprises, but the understatement is unlikely to be

f large consequence in most cases.

Finally, except for a relatively few companies, and these mainly in

he so-called development stage, R&D expenditures have been largely expensed,

ot capitalized. Most enterprises that do capitalize R&D costs when incurred

imit this practice to certain of their R&D activities; they expense the rest. In some companies deferral of the R&D costs is temporary, pending determination of the fruitfulness of the R&D activities, at which time the costs are either expensed or capitalized. Capitalized R&D costs are generally amortized over a period of about five years or less, or if incurred in developing a new product, over the units of production or sale expected.

There are several, interrelated, reasons that may be offered for the scanty recording and disclosure of investment in innovation broadly conceived. One reason, probably most important, is the difficulty of defining innovation and distinguishing it from the other investment or current costs with which it is often combined. Another reason may be the fact or presumption that even now, in many--perhaps most--going concerns the expenditures on innovation (apart from R&D) constitute a modest ("immaterial") fraction of total expenditures or even of total investment expenditures. A third may be the difficulties of deciding whether to capitalize, and if so what amortization rates to apply, coupled with the traditional "conservatism" of financial accounting. The resulting practice of expensing lessens the incentive to distinguish expenditures on innovation (other than R&D) from other current expenditures. There is also the fact that beginning with 1954 the Internal Revenue Service has permitted expensing of R&D--under a mandate by Congress to encourage this sort of investment--despite R&D being clearly a capital investment and the IRS refusal to extend its permission to the expensing of other kinds of intangible capital investments. Formerly, when R&D was much less important than it was in 1954, the IRS took no definite stand, although there is evidence that the courts, as well as accounting authorities, viewed the capitalization of R&D as the appropriate accounting practice.

Looking to the immediate future, financial accounting standards for
R&D costs were promulgated in October 1974 by the Financial Accounting
Standards Board, the successor to the Accounting Principles Board of the
American Institute of Certified Public Accountants. They are effective
for fiscal years beginning on or after January 1, 1975. In our view, however, the new standards go against the available evidence, against logic,
and not of least importance, against the opinions and wishes of the
great majority of the accountants and business firms commenting on the
proposal, according to our analysis of the "position papers" presented
to the Board.

The new FASB standards are confined to R&D only. "Other similar
costs" -- costs of marketing research, promotion, start-up, and relocation
and rearrangement -- which were distinguished from, but coupled with, R&D
in the FASB's Discussion Memorandum, are to be considered by the FASB only
at a later date. The definition of R&D is broader than that of NSF, in
that it covers the social sciences. But the FASB definition is not broad
enough to encompass certain other kinds of R&D. Not only market research is
excluded but also, for example, "engineering follow-through in the early phase
of production." Design, construction and operation of pilot plants is
covered, but not detailed construction drawings of new plants that also
may involve innovations. Nor are expenditures in which R&D is not the "primary"
objective. No detail is required or expected; consideration of R&D by lines
of business is also postponed by FASB.

R&D must be reported as a separate item only if material; but when
material it must be reported by every company.* The elements of cost to be
identified with R&D activities include direct costs of materials, personnel,
and services performed by others. The entire costs of equipment, facilities
and intangibles acquired or constructed for a particular R&D project, and

---

However, there is as yet no current accepted definition of "material" or
"materiality." The FASB has issued a Discussion Memorandum on the subject and
expects to hold public hearings in early 1976. If the past is an indicator, a pronouncement on materiality will not be available until 1977 at the earliest.

having no alternative future uses (in R&D projects or otherwise) are also
to be included; only when there are alternative future uses is the cost
charged to be the depreciation or amortization of the equipment, facilities
and intangibles. As for overhead, a reasonable allocation of indirect
costs is to be made to R&D, excluding however both general and administrative costs not clearly related to R&D activities and interest or other cost
of capital.

Most striking is the elimination of the option of capitalization and
amortization now open. It is denied entirely, even to development stage
companies. Indeed, any R&D capitalized in the past must be written off by
a "prior period adjustment" on the effective date of the new standards.
The only exception to the expensing rule are R&D costs deferred by govern-
ment-regulated enterprises.

It seems, then, that the new FASB standards go further than present
practice in that they cover all companies, not only those under the jurisdiction of SEC; and that an explicit (although still somewhat vague)
and broader definition of R&D is specified. They mark no advance in the
information required on the composition or R&D. Elimination of the capitalization of R&D is a backward step, taken despite the recommendation in
the AICPA's Accounting Research Study No. 14 for capitalizing investments
in R&D that meet certain specified criteria. More important -- to us,
at least -- the FASB's action ignores the fact that the costs of R&D
being invested by many companies now constitute too large a fraction
of their capital outlays to be treated differently from investment in
tangible capital in their books and financial statements. The previously
available option to expense R&D permitted--and the new standard requires--
financial statements to provide substantially less information to stock-

holders and others, and impose substantially less discipline on management, than the statements can and should.

We review in some detail the bases offered by the FASB for its decision to require expensing of R&D costs when incurred. Briefly, the practical problems of deciding on R&D amortization -- difficult as they are -- strike us as essentially no different in kind, and on the whole not sufficiently different in degree, from the difficulties associated with other investments to warrant this exceptional treatment. The objection that an adequate basis for systematic amortization of R&D is lacking might have been valid a generation ago, but it is much less plausible today. We find it difficult to believe that the systematic bases and procedures for investment decisions that have been developed and that provide the necessary information, are not now being widely applied, especially in the larger companies that do most of the R&D, to the kinds of activities that make up the bulk of company sponsored R&D. Even where a decision on total R&D is based simply on a percentage of sales or the like, it is likely that the allocation of this sum to particular projects could be and is justified more rationally. These justifications would provide the information required for capitalization.

Other objections to capitalization can also be met. One is that R&D involves uncertainties that make capitalization of R&D inappropriate; but uncertainty is unavoidable in all investment. The argument that expensing of R&D is more "conservative", seems to us to confuse conservatism in finance, which may merit praise, with conservatism in accounting, which leads only to the omission of significant information and hardly deserves to be called conservative. The objection that capitalizing R&D would make for less precision in the accounts amounts to preferring an accurate esti-mate of a theoretically untenable item for a tenable item that can be esti-mated roughly. And still other objections fail to stand up to close inspection, in our opinion.

The new standard set by the FASB--that all company-sponsored R&D shall be charged to expense when incurred--strikes us as a choice of the least rather than the most appropriate of the alternative methods of accounting for R&D considered by the Board.

Worth noting, also, in thinking about the future, is the fact that the Federal Trade Commission has managed to get approval, at least for a limited period and sample, of its "lines of business" reporting of R&D and certain other items, including sales, income, and plant and equipment. The powerful Cost Accounting Standards Board, charged by Congress with setting standards in connection with defense contracts, has expressed an interest in the manner in which R&D is accounted for. The Industrial Research Institute also is concerned, particularly with the question of definition and subclassification.

As should be evident from the above, there is little prospect that much information on the content of R&D or on other sources of innovation will be available on a wide basis in the near future. For R&D, the FTC lines of business inquiry may mark a significant step forward, as did the earlier NSF efforts in this regard; but apart from this industrial classification, and the NSF three-fold subclassification of R&D (which is often estimated, when reported at all, by the respondent companies) there is no present prospect of anything but aggregative information.

What is needed, if knowledge concerning investment in innovation is to be expanded, and particularly if private and social accounting for innovation is to be improved, is an intensive and large-scale series of surveys to which our and other studies under the auspices of the NSF, are designed to pave the way. We simply do not yet know enough about the specific

objectives of R&D and other innovational activities, and the dimensions of
the resources devoted to each. Among the questions to which we need answers
are these: What have companies been doing to learn about, to produce, and to
market new or better products; and learn about and apply new or better
processes, materials and components,or new forms of organization to the
production of old or new products? How and at what points in the process
do they make the necessary decisions? How do they budget as well as
account for the expenditures involved -- the state of their records? How
do they evaluate their innovational efforts?

More of this sort of information is required before sound proposals
can be made to financial officers and accountants on how to improve the
accounting records on innovation by business firms, and also before anything like a comprehensive survey can be made that will generate a consistent and otherwise satisfactory set of statistical data concerning
investment in innovation.

We conclude with the observation that just when economists are
moving toward a more satisfactory treatment of intangible investments in
the national accounts and in other economic calculations, accountants
are moving in the opposite direction. Sooner or later, accountants will
have to back up if they are to go forward.

Economic Calculation Under Inflation: The Problem in Perspective

Solomon Fabricant

I

Our subject is economic calculation under inflation, not the whole problem of inflation. But it is well to start with some discussion of the larger problem, for the importance of our particular subject derives from the importance of that problem.

We cannot recall too often, these days, Lord Keynes' warning:

> There is no subtler, no surer means of overturning the existing basis of society than to debauch the currency. The process engages all the hidden forces of economic law on the side of destruction, and does it in a manner which not one man in a million is able to diagnose . . . [The] arbitrary rearrangement of riches [caused by inflation] strikes not only at security but at confidence in the equity of the existing distribution of wealth. . . . All permanent relations between debtors and creditors, which form the ultimate foundation of capitalism, become so utterly disordered as to be almost meaningless; and the process of wealth-getting degenerates into a gamble and a lottery.

Writing shortly after World War I, Keynes of course had in mind the severe wartime inflations, a few of which were already escalating in Europe into "hyperinflation." Inflations today here and abroad have been less rapid than those of World War I, or World War II. But they have persisted over a longer period. Their cumulative effects have too frequently already reached orders of magnitude similar to those of wartime. And they show no encouraging signs of coming to an end.

Chairman Arthur Burns of the Federal Reserve Board sees good reason to echo Keynes' warning. His remarks, pointedly entitled "The Menace of Inflation," also deserve to be quoted:

> Concerned as we all are about the economic consequences of inflation, there is even greater reason for concern about the impact on our social and political institutions. We must not risk the social stresses that persistent inflation breeds. Because of its capricious effects on the income and wealth of a nation's families and businesses, inflation inevitably causes disillusionment and discontent. It robs millions of citizens who in their desire to be self-reliant have set aside funds for the education of their children or their own retirement, and it hits many of the poor and elderly especially hard.
>
> In recent weeks, governments have fallen in several major countries, in part because the citizens of those countries had lost confidence in the ability of their leaders to cope with the problem of inflation. Among our own people, the distortions and injustices wrought by inflation have contributed materially to distrust of government officials and of government policies, and even to some loss of confidence in our free enterprise system. Discontent bred by inflation can provoke profoundly disturbing social and political change, as the history of other nations teaches. I do not believe I exaggerate in saying that the ultimate consequence of inflation could well be a significant decline of economic and political freedom for the American people.

In the light of these warnings, we can begin to see the social and political implications of our subject—a subject that at first sight might seem purely technical, and narrow even in that regard. Consider, for example, the reluctance, or at any rate the failure, of corporate officials to correct reported business profits for inflation, or to supplement the conventional figures with figures expressed in terms of general purchasing power; or of the auditors who certify corporate financial statements to draw attention to this lapse. As a consequence, during recent years the daily newspapers have published a flood of reports of large percentage increases in profits, almost always to new highs. Because these reports are generally limited to prior-year comparisons, newspaper readers are not reminded of the cyclical and other factors that make for large fluctuations in reported profits. The blinkers thus placed on them contribute to the impression of "unseemly" gains in profits. During most of the postwar period, however, inflation has been the major source of overstatement of profits.

It does not help the situation that the public reports on business income are in striking contrast with public reports on other kinds of income.

Efforts to measure and report labor income free of the effects of changes in the prices paid by workers have, in fact, a long history. Indices of food prices at retail became available in the United States around 1900. Comparison of changes in wages and salaries with changes in the food component of the cost of living promptly followed. A more comprehensive measure of change in consumer price levels, covering also non-food items, was demanded and became available during the great inflation associated with World War I. This consumer price index, applicable to urban wage earners and clerical workers, has been available on a regular basis ever since, and it has been gradually improved in coverage and accuracy. Indices of wage and salary income are now as a matter of course accompanied by this index of consumer prices and attention is paid not less to real than to money labor income in discussions of the changing economic status of labor. In a word, "deflated" wages and salaries are a commonplace.

Systematic allowance for change in prices paid when assessing the economic wellbeing of farmers came later, in the 1930s, when the "parity" idea was introduced and implemented under the Agricultural Adjustment Act. Like labor income, farm income—the return from capital investment and "entrepreneurship," as well as labor—is now regularly reported in constant as well as current dollars.

In contrast, corporate reports on profits earned during the year or quarter, whether made to stockholders, tax collectors, public utility commissions, "cost of living councils," or the public at large, are calculated on the basis of "generally accepted accounting principles," on which the dollar is assumed to be a stable unit of measurement.

Even the information on profits that is currently prepared by economists and statisticians for use in following the changing economic situation is deficient in this regard. The first appearance of a deflated corporate profit series in the monthly *Business Conditions Digest* and other publications of the Department of Commerce occurred only a couple of years ago. (Even this series exaggerates the rise in profits, because it is profits *before* the inventory valuation adjustment that the Department of Commerce makes in its national accounts.) No deflated corporate profit series yet appears in *Economic Indicators*, prepared by the Council of Economic Advisers for the Joint Economic Committee of the Congress. This monthly periodical, distributed to all members of Congress, and presumably widely used by them, publishes deflated income series only for labor and farmers. Such components of property income as dividends, interest, and rents are shown, in both *Business Conditions Digest* and *Economic Indicators,* deflated not separately but only in combination (along with labor and farm income) in the aggregate of personal income.

It is hard to overestimate the impact on public opinion of the exaggerated reports on profits. Indeed, the situation may have become such that the belated rush to the "last-in-first-out" (LIFO) method of costing inventory withdrawals could even strike some citizens, reading one news story after another about it, as only a subterfuge to conceal excessive profits and evade corporate income taxes. In any case, the well-nigh universal failure to adjust business financial statements for the depreciation of the dollars in which they are expressed can hardly have been other than misleading. It must have contributed to the public misunderstanding of the causes and consequences of our current economic situation. And to the extent that it did, it has made more difficult the task of choosing wisely and applying effectively government policy to deal with inflation—a task that would have been difficult enough under any circumstances. The consequences, social and political as well as economic, must be viewed as serious.

II

The sharp warning that debasement of the currency disturbs the economic arrangements and calculations that underlie our society suggests another and broader theme. The theme is complex as well as broad, relating as it does to a number of major historical developments. Economic historians have made these developments crucial factors in their delineation of the process of economic growth.

There is, first, the introduction and spread of money in the economy. As Wesley C. Mitchell put it in his beautiful essay, "The Role of Money in Economic History":

> By giving economic activity an immediate objective aim, and by providing a common denominator in terms of which all costs and all gains can be adequately expressed for business purposes, the use of money provided a technically rational scheme for guiding economic effort. . . .

The spread of the money was accompanied by—indeed, it stimulated—technical and managerial innovations that brought greater precision of measurement, greater ease of calculation, and vastly improved economic information. Werner Sombart's enthusiastic emphasis on one of these advances, the rise of systematic bookkeeping, as a decisive factor in the development of capitalism—"the complete rationalization of economic life became possible only through the advent of double-entry bookkeeping"—is now taken with a large grain of salt. But he did succeed in drawing attention to the significance of rational economic calculation. Max Weber widened the view of the development of economic calculation to include also such items as the final acceptance in Europe during the fifteenth and sixteenth centuries of Arabic numerals in place of the Roman.* And John A. Hobson widened it still further:

---

* Weber's comment on the displacement of Roman by Arabic numerals is worth a footnote: "It was at first viewed as a disreputable means of securing an immoral advantage in competition, since it worked in favor of the competitors of the virtuous merchant who disdained its use. Consequently it was first sought to exclude it by prohibitions. . . ."

The development of bookkeeping accompanied as it was by a wide general application of rational and mathematical system throughout commerce in the shape of exact measurement of time and place, forms of contract, land surveying, modern methods of weights and measures, city plans, public accounts, was at once an indispensable tool and an aspect of modern industry.

An economic historian writing today would, I suppose, want to mention that the chart of accounts of today's large business corporation is rather different from the simple bookkeeping set forth in Pacioli's famous treatise. Pointing to the greater power and precision of modern methods and means of measurement and calculation, he might update the list of examples to include such items as operations research, electronic computers, and the marketing and other surveys that utilize small sampling techniques. And he would not fail to draw out the implications of these developments —for example, the increase in the average size of business enterprise and the economies of scale to which this increase contributes.

An economist, looking over the historian's shoulder, would remind him of the contribution of economic theorists. He would at least mention their recognition of the complementary character of supply and demand in determining price, their discovery and refinement of marginal analysis, and the distinction they draw sharply today between social and private benefits and costs. And the economist would point also to the invention and improvement of such economic tools of analysis as index numbers, national accounts, and econometric models.

Another development related to these was the widening of economic, and inevitably also political, freedom. In Mitchell's words:

When money is introduced into the dealings of men, it enlarges their freedom. For example, when a personal service is commuted into money payment, the servitor has a wider choice in the use of his income. By virtue of its generalized purchasing power, money emancipates its users from numberless restrictions upon what they do and what they get. As a society learns to use money confidently, it gradually abandons restrictions upon the places people shall live, the occupations they shall follow, the circles they shall serve, the prices they shall charge, and the goods they can buy. Its citizens have both a formal and a genuine freedom in these respects wider than is possible under an organization in which services and commodities are bartered.

In turn, freedom makes for greater efficiency, for in a free society, as was pointed out above all by Mises and Hayek, individuals have the authority and the incentives to use the particular knowledge which they—and only they —possess to adapt most economically to the incessant changes that go on in a dynamic world.* This stock of

---

* Many people are familiar with the idea that capitalism is efficient and free, at any rate relative to other systems, but not with the idea that capitalism is efficient in substantial part because it is free. The idea helps us to understand the difficulties encountered by Soviet Russia in its effort to reach a "Western"—a capitalistic—level of economic efficiency. I cannot resist the temptation to comment on it.

The analysis by Mises, mentioned above, was made shortly after World War I, in the course of a theoretical examination of the possibility of rational economic calculation in a socialist economy. Soviet Russia's experience since then has provided some concrete information on the relation between rational economic calculation and economic and political freedom, something that Hayek also had very much in mind, and to which Burns referred in his warning of the menace of inflation. Understanding has grown in Russia of the limitations of a centralized planning agency in acquiring and utilizing effectively all the information about consumer demand and production possibilities that is needed for the efficient allocation of resources. There has consequently been a good deal of discussion there about the desirability and feasibility of a system of decentralized decisions, and even some hesitant movement towards something like a profit incentive and freer price system. The trend has been hesitant because it is also real-

knowledge includes detailed information that no central
authority could ever hope to gather, digest and apply in
formulating its plans and making its decisions. It is precisely
because inflation biases the information in the hands of
individual economic units and renders this information
less useful, that inflation makes for inefficiency in the allocation of resources and inequity in the distribution of income
and wealth.

Improvement in the technical means of economic calculation and in the information utilized in economic calculation
has been made almost continuously over the centuries, and
even at an accelerated pace in recent generations. In one
significant respect, however, there has been little progress.
The pecuniary unit, a necessary element in all economic
calculations, has not been kept stable; and this instability has
been generally ignored in business accounting. The contrast
with the improvements made in other aspects of economic
calculation is striking. The most sophisticated calculation
using the latest generation of electronic computers cannot
yield a truly rational result if the data fed into the computers
are expressed in unstable units. "Garbage in, garbage out"
has become a tattered cliché among computer men. But,
worn and vulgar as it may be, it states our problem vividly,
if not quite accurately.

III

The overstatement of increases in business profits because of inflation—or understatement of decreases—has

---

ized that such a move would lead to, and its success require, a degree of
economic freedom incompatible with the tight control Party stalwarts feel
to be essential.

worried thoughtful citizens. They are concerned about the implications of this overstatement for business decisions generally, investment in particular, and taxation, price and wage controls, and economic forecasting.

This concern has, of course, been intensified by the very rapid inflation that the American economy has been experiencing in recent years.

The failure of conventional accounting practice to deal adequately with changing price levels is an old worry, however. Over twenty-five years ago two outstanding accountants, George May and Percival Brundage, organized a "Study Group on Business Income" under the auspices of the American Institute of Certified Public Accountants (then called the American Institute of Accountants). Ten years ago the Accounting Research Division made another study of the question. Five years ago the Accounting Principles Board of the AICPA issued its "Statement No. 3" recommending—but not requiring—supplementary statements disclosing the effects of changes in the general price level on the financial accounting measurements. Yet these studies and statements have had hardly any effect on current accounting practice.

Only very recently has the accounting profession as a whole begun to recognize the need to allow for changes in the general price level, in business accounts, and to do something about it. Four years ago the Accounting Principles Board could still say that "the effects of inflation in the United States are not considered sufficiently important at this time to require recognition in financial accounting measurements." Now, however, its successor, the Financial Accounting Standards Board, considers it possible as well as desirable to propose a Statement of Principles that "would require supplemental disclosure of accounting information restated for changes in the general purchase power of the dollar." A similar proposal has been made in Britain and Canada. In a few countries—not many—some sort of adjustment for changes in the price level is already in fairly general use, as a recent compilation by Price Waterhouse indicates.*

The FASB's action, and the behavior of others throughout the economy, implies, of course, acceptance of the idea that inflation is and will remain "sufficiently important" for some considerable time in the future. It is worthwhile, however, to take a moment to clarify our notions of the magnitude of the inflation we have already experienced and of the prospect of inflation in the years ahead.

Over the 10 years since 1964, when the current inflationary episode is often said to have begun, the Consumer Price Index has risen by 66 percent. This seems like a big enough rise to be considered substantial by any standards. Its relative magnitude may be better appreciated, however, if we compare it with the increases associated with the two World Wars. In the inflation associated with World War II, counting from 1939 to 1946, the consumer price level rose by about 40 percent. In the inflation associated with World War I (1913–1920), the consumer price level rose by 100 percent. If the period associated with World War I is extended to 1922, the sharp decline after 1920 puts the net increase (1913–1922) at 70 percent. The price increase since 1964 compares "favorably"—if that is the right word —with the two wartime increases.

---

* Another valuable compilation is provided in George Lent's paper prepared for the International Monetary Fund.

However, the Consumer Price Index was rising before 1964. In fact, the period of inflation since 1964 is only the latest episode of a history that dates back to the period starting before World War II. Every one of the calendar years after 1939, except only two—1949 and 1955—saw a price index higher than it had been in the year before. With respect to the price level, our generation's experience has been almost nothing but inflation. The cumulative effect since 1939 has been a rise of 270 percent in the price level, equivalent to a reduction of almost 75 percent in the purchasing power of the dollar.

This suggests another comparison—namely, with the inflation dignified as "the price revolution" by historians. It resulted from the great transfer of gold and silver to Europe following the discovery of America, along with a substantial debasement of the currency. Despite reservations made necessary by the paucity of comparable data—only some wholesale prices are available for the early period—as well as by the vast difference in stages of economic development, the results are worth presenting. Over the sixteenth century, according to indices assembled by Anna Schwartz, wholesale prices in France and England rose at an average annual rate of only about 1 percent in terms of silver, and about 2 percent in terms of money on account. The latter, the more relevant, is much less than the 3.3 percent we have experienced over the 36 years since 1939. The whole of the sixteenth century saw a wholesale price level increase of some 600 percent. We have already come close to this —500 percent—in the twentieth century, despite the precipitous price decline during the Great Depression. And our century is not yet over.

Looking ahead, the prospects for a quick end to inflation

appear rather dim. If there are still some optimists among us, they should ponder the reaction of the country to the recession under way since 1973. Inflation is no longer the nation's "number one" economic problem.

The rate of inflation will probably decline as the effects of the spurt in petroleum and grain prices recede, and the recession worsens, before efforts to turn the economy around are agreed upon, are actually applied, and their results finally materialize. Looking "over the valley" to the expansion ahead, however, it is likely that the policies to bring about revival in employment will also prevent the rate of inflation from declining during expansion. These policies may even result in some acceleration of inflation before or after revival. Even if anti-recession policy should somehow prove neutral with regard to inflation—which is hard to believe—the coming expansion phase of the business cycle will tend for other reasons to be accompanied by a rise in the rate of change in the general price level, as Geoffrey H. Moore has shown to be typical of cycles in the postwar period, just as it was of the more violent business cycles before World War II.

The application of some form of incomes policy involving controls over individual prices and wages at some later date is, I suppose, not altogether out of the question, despite Administration denials. But even a strong set of controls, vigorously enforced, would have to be relaxed—perhaps after a brief "freeze"—to permit some increases in prices and wages. "Hardship cases" and other exceptions to "catch up" will abound. Experience provides little reason to expect that efforts to slow up wages that are already ahead of the crowd, or to reduce the prices of industries in which productivity is rising rapidly and costs per unit are declining, will be successful—if they are attempted at all. Yet these slowdowns or reductions are necessary in order to offset valid increases if the general price level is to remain stable.

What I see ahead, through 1976 and well beyond, then, is a rising long-term trend in the general price level, around which will be cycles of retardation and acceleration in the rate of inflation. Progress toward stabilization will gradually diminish the amplitude of cycles in the rate of increase of the price level and lower the level of the average rate of inflation. But I do not see inflation soon vanishing or the amplitude of fluctuations in the rate of increase in prices soon becoming negligible. Whether there would, in fact, be progress—a reduction in the amplitude of fluctuation and in the average rate of inflation—is not certain. It depends on how soon and to what degree anti-inflation policy is relaxed during a slowdown or recession. It depends on whether, and how strongly, the need to fight inflation is kept in mind during the earlier as well as the later stages of business expansion. It depends on the means used to moderate inflation and inflationary expectations. It depends on the success of continuing efforts to remove already notorious structural obstacles to price declines and fuller employment; to improve governmental organization; to expand tested economic knowledge; and to add to the flow of current information required to apply this knowledge effectively. And all this depends, in turn, and fundamentally, on how well the public is taught to understand the problem of inflation.

IV

My earlier remarks about the failure to adjust current business accounting in order to allow for inflation were not meant to imply that this adjustment is altogether simple and straightforward. I want, rather, to say the contrary.

Various problems, many of which are difficult, arise when one attempts to correct financial statements for inflation. The *Business Conditions Digest*'s simple deflation of the reported profit series is, no doubt, a major step toward recognizing changes in the value of money. The rise in corporate profits before taxes between 1966 and 1973, for example, reported in current prices as 40 percent, is under 10 percent when measured in constant prices. But how thoroughly this deflation corrects for reduction in the value of the dollar is a matter of considerable controversy. The *Business Conditions Digest* deflated series is derived simply by deflating profits as accountants calculate these profits.*

Four groups of questions arise about the validity and accuracy of the result. One concerns the current-dollar profit figure, reported in the usual corporate income account or profit and loss statement, that is deflated. Another concerns the deflator, that is, the index that measures the decline in the purchasing power of money. The third concerns the purchasing power gains or loses, realized or not, on monetary and non-monetary assets and liabilities when the value of money changes—gains or losses not covered in the deflation of the reported profit series. And the fourth concerns "current value accounting," a subject on which questions properly arise when the price level is stable, questions which—for good reason—become more intense

---

* More exactly, the Department of Commerce distinguishes between the two components of profits—dividends and undistributed profits—and deflates each separately. Dividends are deflated by the national consumption implicit deflator. Reported undistributed profits are deflated by the gross capital formation implicit deflator. The two deflated series are then combined to yield the deflated profit series.

when inflation occurs and the subject of "general purchasing power accounting" is brought up. All four groups of questions overlap, and are therefore difficult to keep apart. But it would be worse to consider them all together.

Reported profits, such as are shown in annual or quarterly reports and mentioned in the daily press, are not good measures even of profits expressed in current prices. The reason is well known to economists and accountants. Certain important elements of current cost are calculated in the prices paid in earlier periods, not in current prices or in original cost prices adjusted for change in the general purchasing power of money. When price levels are moving up, original cost prices may be significantly below the prices appropriate to the current period, the period for which profits are being measured.

One such element of cost is withdrawals from inventory of material, components, goods in process, and the like, in producing the goods or services sold. With the "last-in-first-out" method of costing inventory withdrawals, the charge to current operations is at something reasonably close to current prices. But LIFO is in fact used only to a limited (but, recently, a rapidly growing) extent in calculating corporate profits. When prices are rising fast, the underestimation of the cost of withdrawals from inventory may be large. In 1973 this cost may have been understated by some $15 billion.

Similarly, depreciation and obsolescence charges are generally based on the prices prevailing in earlier periods —indeed, periods far more remote than the corresponding periods for inventory. Yet accountants make no effort, when calculating business profits, to substitute for the original purchase price and equipment the current replacement price, or the original price adjusted for change in the general price level. The difference between original and current prices of capital equipment used up in any year may be greater or less than the difference in the case of inventory withdrawals; it depends on the course of the price level up to that year. In 1973 depreciation and obsolescence charged at original prices understated the current cost also by about $15 billion.

In the national income and outlay accounts prepared by the Department of Commerce, the cost of withdrawals from inventory is adjusted (approximately) to the current price level by means of the department's "inventory valuation adjustment" that I mentioned earlier. However, even in the national accounts an adjustment is not yet made for the fact that under current accounting practice depreciation and obsolescence are charged at less than current cost or original cost adjusted for inflation.

Returning to the profits reported in corporate financial statements, it appears that 1973 profits before income tax, reported as $118 billion, must have been overstated by as much as a third. Further, the degree of overstatement of profits in 1973, measured in 1973 prices, was greater than the degree of overstatement of profits in 1972, measured in 1972 prices. The deflation procedure followed in *Business Conditions Digest* putting profits in all years on the same price basis—that of 1958—does not correct this upward bias in the rate of change in profits.

Conventionally measured profits may suffer also from biases in the opposite direction—biases that understate rather than overstate both the levels and the rates of change of profits. If sufficiently strong, the downward bias could even provide some offset to the bias that results from calculating inventory withdrawals at original cost, although this offset could hardly be important in years when inflation is very rapid.

One such offsetting factor is provided by "accelerated" depreciation and obsolescence, which the Internal Revenue Service has permitted in recent decades. Speeding up the deduction for depreciation and obsolescence reduces the lag between the time when capital goods are acquired and the time when depreciation is charged, reducing also the difference between original and replacement cost. But accelerated depreciation does not make it possible to recoup more than the original cost. The difference can be reduced, not eliminated. Accelerated depreciation serves to eliminate *some* of the profits that reflect merely a rise in the general price level (profits on which corporate income taxes would otherwise have to be paid) but doe snot eliminate *all* the "profits" or the taxes due on these "profits." In addition, there is a question whether the accelerated charge for depreciation and obsolescence really represents a departure from the appropriate charge. In one view, which I tend to share, the accelerated charge is closer to and more representative of the underlying facts on depreciation and obsolescence than the charge permitted under IRS rules before the revision of these rules.

A more subtle and perhaps more powerful offset that some economists have worried about results from technical change. This tends to reduce the cost of maintaining the capacity of capital equipment to produce a given volume of output to less than the depreciation charged. They have worried also about growth in the capital stock. This growth also serves to make current depreciation charges higher than the amount needed to maintain current capacity on a replacement accounting basis. The issue, as I see it, is whether technical change and capital growth do in fact offset the understatement of depreciation and obsolescence in the calculation of business profits, if depreciation and obsolescence are viewed as measuring reduction in the private value of plant and equipment rather than reduction in the capacity of plant and equipment to produce. The issue involves a difference between two points of view, the social and the private. The issue merits more attention than it has received.

V

The second group of questions concerns the deflator used to convert business profits in current prices to profits in constant prices.

In a dynamic economy, prices are always changing in response to shifts in demand and supply. The prices of some products will tend to decline in relation to the prices of most other products when the industries producing them enjoy exceptionally rapid increases in productivity because of breakthroughs in technology, for example, or because cheaper sources of supply of materials have been discovered. The relative prices of some products will tend to rise when productivity in the industries manufacturing them advances less rapidly than in the nation as a whole. And the prices of still other products will tend to move with the general price average when productivity in the industries producing them keeps up with the national average. "Change in the general price level," then, must mean some sort of average of many different price changes. The problem of defining and measuring this average led to the invention of index numbers.

Many index numbers of prices have been devised. They

differ in the markets to which they refer, in the mathematical form of the averaging process used, and in the weights used to allow for differences in the relative importance of the various commodities and services—an importance that changes over time as the economy develops.

One of the issues here is what index should be used in deflating profits. If a single index is to be used for all companies, should it be the GNP Implicit Price Deflator or some alternative to it? Alternatives sometimes suggested are the implicit price deflator for private GNP, the "fixed weighted price index" for gross private product, the Consumer Price Index, the all-commodity wholesale price index, and the industrial-commodity wholesale price index. Most of these indices differ significantly over long periods as well as short. The two alternatives most often considered are the GNP Implicit Price Deflator and the Consumer Price Index, which differ rather slightly, on the whole. The error made in choosing between them, if any, is a trivial matter compared with the error of not deflating at all.

Another issue is whether a single deflator should be used for all companies, or deflators be tailored to the particular situation of each company. In the case of wages and clerical salaries, the common deflator used is the national Consumer Price Index, which reflects change in the average level of prices paid by all those in urban areas receiving this kind of labor income. It is known, however, that consumer price indices in different parts of the country do not move exactly parallel to the national average. Nor is it likely that consumer price indices applicable to workers at different income levels even in the same city would be identical. The question has usually been avoided, presumably on the ground that the differences are not large. Now, however, it is attracting attention because of the plans of the Bureau of Labor Statistics to broaden the coverage of its price index.*

A similar question arises in the case of profits. Companies differ considerably with regard to the goods and services on which their profits are expended—by stockholders with their dividends, and by the companies themselves with the money they retain to replace and enlarge inventory and capital goods as well as for other purposes. These differences among companies in the composition of expenditures must be far wider than among workers. The range is from the small, specialized firm in one tiny corner of the United States to the vast multinational conglomerate doing many different kinds of business in many different countries, countries in which price levels change at diverse rates, and between which exchange rates may fluctuate widely.

The use of deflators specific to each company would, however, tend to eliminate some of its profits or losses caused by changes in relative prices. The possibility raises another complicated issue. It involves a difference between those who think of the real profits of a company as measuring its contribution to the real national income and those who think of these profits as measuring the company's

---

* Old families living in their own homes with the mortgage paid off will not experience the same degree of inflation as young families in rented apartments, or only now acquiring their own homes.

Involved here is an important and difficult problem, but one seldom mentioned. If the price of housing services is based on rental equivalents in the case of owner-occupied houses, there will be no great difference in the prices paid (or imputed) for such services between owners and renters. But there will then be a difference in the income received (or imputed). It is, in other words, difficult to determine the effect of inflation on the economic position of a family without paying attention to its income as well as to its expenditures. The same difficulty arises in the case of business firms.

share in the real national income. Interestingly enough, the issue was raised in the very first Income Conference held by the National Bureau of Economic Research almost forty years ago, as well as in later conferences. But there continues to be much confusion about it—in the economic as well as the accounting literature.* The appropriate treatment in financial statements of changes in relative prices, when making adjustments for inflation, raises another issue that would warrant careful analysis.

VI

We turn to the third set of questions about the deflation of profits. In addition to the effects of inflation on the costing of inventory withdrawals and depreciation and obsolescence, economists and accountants naturally think also of the effects of inflation on other items in the income account and balance sheet.

Besides inventories and plant and equipment, the asset side of the balance sheet includes holdings of non-depreciable tangible assets such as land. Land and other tangible assets are carried on the books at original cost, less accumulated depreciation in the case of assets subject to depreciation. But their market value, or their original cost adjusted for inflation, may have risen substantially. This rise in value is not included in the conventional measure of profits until it is "realized." Realization may be through sale of the asset itself, as in the case of land. Or it may be through sale of the products, to the cost of which have been charged the

---

* Recall the Department of Commerce's deflation of undistributed corporate profits, referred to earlier, by the implicit deflator for gross capital formation rather than GNP.

materials drawn from inventory and the depreciation of
the plant and equipment used in producing the products.
The issue, here, hinges on whether realization of a profit
(or loss) during a fiscal period is considered crucial in the
decision to include it in the period's profit. The issue is old,
but it draws more than the usual amount of controversy
when inflation (or deflation) is rampant.

There are also monetary assets and liabilities, the "real"
values of which change when changes occur in the purchasing power of the money in which they are expressed.
Much the same issue arises in the case of monetary items as
in the case of non-monetary items. To illustrate: Is the loss
on the purchasing power of a bond investment to be charged
to the period in which the decline in purchasing power
occurs, or to the period in which the bond is finally re-
deemed? The answer to this question has implications for
the treatment of the interest received on the bond.

Let us suppose that inflation proceeds at a constant rate,
that it is fully anticipated, and that the coupon rate is therefore sufficiently high to offset the loss of purchasing power
of the principal. Suppose further that it is decided to charge
the purchasing power loss on principal to the last period.
The interest received in any period must then be considered
subject to a depreciation charge, which is to be credited to
a reserve for the depreciation of the principal's purchasing
power when it is finally realized. Even the precise form of
the method of depreciation is implied; it must be such as
to yield a net interest income constant in terms of purchasing power. If the treatment of the interest received,
under general purchasing power accounting, is made consistent with the treatment of the loss on bond investments,
it will not matter which of the two alternative answers is

given to the question posed. The point I have been making applies equally, of course, to the treatment of debts and interest paid on them.

In this discussion of the effects of inflation on the balance sheet, and through it on the income account, I have been concentrating on the accounts of business firms. The same questions arise—or should arise—also about the "accounts" of wage and salary workers and farmers. Although not as often pointed out in popular discussions of labor or farm income as they should be, to recipients of these types of income also, the balance sheet or wealth effects of inflation are of concern. Questions about capital gains, for example —real or nominal, realized or unrealized, and their bearing on income and income tax status—must give trouble to citizens receiving various kinds of income and standing at various levels in the size distribution of the nation's income.

VII

Another set of questions about the adjustment of profits for inflation revolves around the issue of "current value" accounting. The questions are essentially the same as those we have already discussed about the valuation of assets, but they are usually discussed in somewhat different terms and may therefore be worth some separate consideration.

Advocates of current value accounting would abandon the principle of historical cost and would value all assets and liabilities at current prices. Because the difference between current value and historical cost widens during inflation, the issue is brought closer to the boiling point.

Advocates of current value or historical cost accounting could and probably would agree on the usefulness of general purchasing power accounting. Those who favor current value accounting would make the adjustment for change in the purchasing power of money after converting historical costs to current values. Those who hold to historical cost accounting would make the adjustment for change in the general price level without converting historical cost to current value. If all prices moved closely together, the results would be essentially the same. But all prices do not move closely together. The results will therefore differ. However, they will differ by not nearly so much as they might if general purchasing power accounting did not eliminate a major part of the difference between current value and historical cost.

In the end, when assets are sold or have become fully depreciated, and when liabilities are finally settled, current values will have entered the books under either system of accounting, whether historical cost or current value.* But the periods in which current values are recognized and recorded will not be the same. Under historical cost accounting, the recording of any difference between original cost and current value will be delayed until final "realization." Under current value accounting, the gain or loss will enter the calculations in every period in which prices differ from those of the preceding period, whether "realized" or not. The issue, I might mention, is not one of conservatism, for under historical cost accounting acceptance of unrealized losses as well as unrealized gains may be postponed.

Although current value accounting and general pur-

---

* However, the rise or fall in value of a non-monetary asset that is neither sold nor depreciated periodically, such as land or an investment in common stocks, will never appear on the books or be taken into the financial statements unless explicitly revalued.

chasing power accounting deal with rather different questions, the distinction between them is not always drawn sharply. Most of the published estimates of what corporate profits, or such items as depreciation charges, would look like when adjusted for inflation (including those I have mentioned earlier) combine the adjustment to current value and the adjustment for change in general purchasing power without drawing any special attention to that fact. One reason has already been mentioned. When inflation is substantial, it does not matter much whether conversion to current value is made before or after correction for change in the general price level, considering the rough character of the published estimates. There is another reason. Most of the estimates mentioned are prepared by economists who generally favor current value accounting, and are often impatient with those, particularly accountants, who prefer the precision (and verifiability) of historical cost to the relevance of current value, which must necessarily be estimated.

It is possible that readers of financial statements expressed in units of general purchasing power, when these become available, will not always understand that the adjusted values shown are not current values, despite explanations to the contrary. Indeed, I expect some considerable confusion. Should it arise, it will strengthen the hands of the advocates of current value accounting. They will insist that the only way out of the confusion is for accountants to go all the way towards recognizing changes in prices— not only changes in the average level of prices but also changes in relative prices. My own view is that adjustment for the general price level alone in effect puts financial officers and accountants in an uncomfortable and untenable halfway house, from which they will have to advance or retreat. Given the inflation we have already had, and the prospect of more inflation, retreat is out of the question.

VIII

I have not yet addressed directly another question, one important enough to be raised and considered explicitly. This question bears on the extent to which users of conventional financial statements may actually be misled by them.

The users in mind when this qustion is put are present and potential stockholders, creditors, and the like. It is hardly conceivable that all these users of the unadjusted accounts, or the financial analysts who serve some of them, would take the conventional accounts at their face value. On the other hand, it is equally doubtful that all users of the unadjusted accounts could entirely avoid being misled by them. Some degree of error is inevitable. That this is so may be seen if we consider the extreme assumptions that must be made to conclude otherwise.

To suppose that the unadjusted accounts would be taken at their full face value is to suppose that our economy is suffering from universal and persistent "money illusion" despite continuing and substantial changes in the general price level. Accountants may fail to adjust their reports for inflation, but their reports are not the only source of information on what is happening. Nor is everybody unable to pay for and use additional information. Nor, to pursue the question further, is it reasonable to suppose that users of this information would fail—in the very act of using it—to convey to others the implications of what is happening. In one way or another, and sooner or later, people do learn from experience. To assume complete money illusion is quite inconsistent with all we know about the world.

To suppose that all users of the unadjusted accounts could entirely avoid being misled by them is equally untenable. It would be to suppose that the users of the reports know all that is going on—that they know the past and current rate of inflation, that they can and will anticipate with confidence what the rate will be in the future, and have at their disposal the detailed information about individual companies necessary to determine the effects of inflation, past and prospective, on these companies—and that they will be accustomed to taking all this into account in all their calculations and decisions.

These make up an obviously extreme set of assumptions. To be valid, the assumptions require, at least, an economy in which all changes in prices are open, none are suppressed; and in which the general price level is changing at a constant rate and has been doing so for a long time.*

The users we have been discussing are not the only users, and not the only important users. There are also the "users" to whom I referred at the the start. These are the great bulk of our citizens, the majority of the electorate. They worry not about investments in corporation shares and bonds, but about their rising cost of living. They hear about record profit levels and feel they are suffering an in-

---

* A constant rate of inflation is not necessary. It would be sufficient if the rate of change in the general price level were to follow some reasonably clear pattern of fluctuation. Fairly adequate adjustment to inflation could then take place, as it does in the case of seasonal fluctuations in prices, production and employment. But, for various reasons, inflation is a highly erratic phenomenon.

justice. They demand to know what governmental authorities intend to do about those who are profiteering from the
price rises. They, and many of their representatives also,
are misled by the conventional profit reports—if not by
reading the reports themselves, then by reading the newspaper accounts of them, or the government statistics in
which they are summarized without adequate allowance
for inflation. The sense of injustice thus engendered is not
mitigated by those who take advantage of the political possibilities opened up by these widely publicized reports.

IX

The variety of ways in which inflation disturbs the calculations and affairs of business is enormous. It is enough to
say that inflation acts on prices and costs, and on profits
and taxes. It undermines the basis on which past commit-
ments were made, creates current and urgent pressures,
and it clouds expectations about the future. It disturbs relations with customers, labor, suppliers, financial institutions,
and governmental agencies, and internal relations within
business firms. And the particular impact of inflation in
each of these respects, whether favorable or not, differs
widely among firms, depending as it does on the nature of
a firm's business; the age, size and form of its organization;
its location; and the way it customarily does its business.
But in every company, when inflation is as rapid—and as
variable—as it is now, its impact can be serious and must
be dealt with. And this in turn requires a variety of adjustments, the efficacy of which must always be in some doubt
because so many of the adjustments must be new. The fact
that inflation obscures and makes dubious the financial

accounting data with which every business executive must work when making his plans and decisions, is only one source of the problem posed for rational calculation by inflation.

True, a private enterprise system will adjust to change— if left to itself—including change in the purchasing power of money. But flexible as it is, it can do so only at a cost and only with a lag. We may presume that the costs in such a system will generally be lower, and the lags shorter, than in any other. But while the costs may even be at a minimum, in some sense, they will not necessarily be low. And the lags may be shorter but not necessarily short.

Nor will the costs be distributed evenly, nor the lags uniformly throughout the economy. Inequities of all sorts will be discovered. Private enterprise may therefore not be "left to itself." Incomes policies, price fixing in this or that particular industry, quotas on imports and exports, formal or informal rationing, foreign-exchange controls, taxes on excess (or "windfall") profit in selected industries or even across the board—these and other actions, or threats to take action, by government will abound. The cumulation of changes of this sort forced on the economy is bound to alter its character and efficiency. Taking them into account in business calculations when they happen— and before they happen—cannot be easy or their consequences costless to economic efficiency.

The difficult problems of financial management caused by inflation and its variability are exacerbated also by the innumerable and wide-ranging laws and regulations, both federal and state, already in existence which restrict, or slow down, or even prevent, adjustment to the situation. Built into these rules are assumptions that simply are not

valid in a period of inflation—assumptions that the dollar
is a stable unit, for example, and that anything over six
percent is a usurious rate of interest. Alterations in these
are sometimes made, but then only grudgingly and not
everywhere they are needed. Regulatory agencies permit
price increases, but not quickly, and when they do they may
limit the increases to certain cost "pass-throughs." Banking
authorities are slow to permit competitive interest rates.

Not only business firms but also individuals and families
encounter these difficulties in adjusting. Even if they were
as well equipped as business firms to deal with inflation,
which they are not, individuals would not find it easy, or even
possible, to care properly for their savings, for example. If
nothing else, the variety of governmental and other restrictions on the directions in which they can channel their funds
must hamper their adjustment to rising price levels and
disparate interest rates.

Governmental units also have their difficulties, caused
by constitutional, legislative, bureaucratic, and political limitations on their ability to deal with inflation. Not all state
and local governments have yet shifted from property taxes
to income and sales taxes as the major source of their revenue. To cite another example, salaries in the higher ranks
of the federal civil service are still lagging, as are the salaries
of many judges at all levels of government. The consequences for the quality of service provided, and even for the
discouragement of corruption, may not be trivial.

Nor is this all. To see the ramifications of the effects of
inflation on the calculations of governments (and of those
they deal with), consider the fact that in much penal legis-
lation on the statute books, fines are still at prewar dollar
levels. Since the fines were designed to impose costs on

criminal behavior, this lag means that the real costs have been lowered. Research in the area of law and economics supports the presumption that these costs do enter the economic calculations of potential and active criminals. The implications for the crime rate are not far-fetched. Further, where fines are set as alternatives to jail sentences, as they often are, the "trade-off" between the two has been shifted radically by inflation. The real cost of confinement in jail has risen with the average level of real wages, but the real cost of a fine has declined because of inflation. This has serious implications for the equity as well as efficiency of our penal system.

Examples of the effects of inflation on the economic calculations that influence behavior are easily found in still other areas of government regulation and taxation. A "trade-off" shift similar to the one that has occurred in our penal system has taken place also in tariff schedules. In this case it is the relation between ad valorem and specific tariff rates that has been altered by inflation. The result is a change in the costs confronting importers and in the relative degree of protection offered producers of different commodities.

X

Adjustments to inflation in economic transactions and arrangements do take place, of course, despite the difficulties. The adjustments provide some hints of the character and content of the underlying calculations. They appear in abundant variety: escalator clauses of all sorts—in wage contracts and in contracts for materials, components, construction, and rents; variable-rate mortgages and bonds; "equity kickers" in loan contracts; variable-annuity type pensions; the shortening of the term of contracts; renegotiation of long-term contracts already in force; the introduction of different first-, second-, and sometimes also third-year wages, in labor-management contracts; the use of alternatives to price, wage, or interest rate increases (especially when the option to make such increases is foreclosed) such as changes in other terms—credit, delivery, compensating balances, tied sales, fringe benefits; the postponement of payment when the conventional discount for prompt payment or the penalty for delay becomes obsolete; the speed-up in money velocity. The list is endless, reflecting as it does the ingenuity and enterprise of people anxious to protect themselves from the ravages of inflation or to profit from the opportunities they see inflation opening up for them. But we know little about the present extent of these forms of adjustment and how quickly they have spread.

It would be particularly interesting to survey the different efforts to use escalator clauses and determine how these have changed in character and extent as inflation has continued and accelerated. We know something about the number of labor-management contracts that include cost of living escalators. Concerning other contracts, such as materials and construction, however, we know little more than that they exist, and that the particular price indices used vary widely. The question—why escalator clauses have been so few, even in wage contracts, and even today, in this country —is puzzling.

"Escalation," as a general policy now being rather widely discussed, deserves a word here. One question concerns the relation between the proposal to make financial reports in units of general purchasing power, and the proposal for general income and debt escalation. The two are not quite the same, but the difference is not clear to many people and it needs to be spelled out. There are other questions about escalation that would be interesting to pursue in a thorough discussion of economic calculation under inflation. For example, there is a question about the risks of escalation— in the case of wage contracts, the risk to the wage-earner if stability of real wages comes to be regarded as desirable even when productivity is rising; the risk to the employer and consumer if the stability of real wages comes to be tolerated even when national productivity declines.* And one can only speculate on what the distribution of national income would look like—during the period of adjustment and afterward—if escalator clauses were introduced on a comprehensive scale, as some economists have been proposing.

XI

Recently the Financial Accounting Standards Board published its Discussion Memorandum presenting and analyzing the issues related to "Reporting the Effects of General Price-Level Changes in Financial Statements." The issues I have listed, and more I have not, are all covered in the Board's comprehensive review. The only exceptions are those issues in my list that would be raised by economists viewing the

---

* I say "national" productivity advisedly. The relation between wages in an industry, on the one hand, and the industry's productivity and national productivity, on the other, is not well understood. The subject is not entirely outside our area of concern. It is important in incomes policies and therefore enters wage calculations and negotiations when incomes policies are being followed and even when they only appear in the offing.

problem of inflation accounting strictly from a social standpoint.

A public hearing by the Board was held on the subject
in April 1974, and at year-end 1974 the Board published
an Exposure Draft of its proposed statement of financial
accounting standards, "Financial Reporting in Units of
General Purchasing Power." With this Exposure Draft the
Board revealed its decisions on the accounting issues—
subject only to its second thoughts in the light of further
discussion. The Board proposed to require financial reports
in units of general purchasing power as supplements to conventional reports. Change in general purchasing power is
to be measured by change in the GNP Implicit Price Deflator on the ground that it is the most comprehensive index
available. Current income, measured in units of general
purchasing power, is to include the gains (or losses)—also
in terms of general purchasing power—from the holding of
monetary assets (or liabilities). Gains or losses on non-
monetary assets and liabilities are to be reflected (implicitly) in the determination of income only when the non-
monetary items are charged or credited to income—for
example, when plant is depreciated or sold. Current value
accounting, then, is put aside; it is to be considered at a later
date in another project now on the Board's agenda.

The issues will not be closed, of course, by the decisions
set forth by the Board. We may expect many differences of
opinion to be conveyed to the Board before the period for
public comment on the Exposure Draft ends—comments on
the choice of deflator, the postponement of a decision on
current value accounting, the cut-off date selected (one of
the issues I did not mention), the decision to update

("roll forward") successive annual statements, the incon-
sistencies that will arise between successive annual statements because of revision by the Department of Commerce
of its GNP Deflator, and still others of large or small moment. Later, experience with the application of the new
principles will undoubtedly stimulate still other discussion
and controversy.

This conference of ours, coming as it does at a propitious
moment in the move to modernize "generally accepted
accounting principles," can contribute to the discussion of
the technical issues involved.

Perhaps we can do more. The problem of business accounting and business financial statements under inflation
is important. However, business is not the only sector of the
economy in which accounting problems arise under inflation. Nor is accounting the only kind of economic calculation. We may serve also if we set the problem in an
economic, social, and political context wider than is usual.
This, at any rate, has been my objective.

To conclude: The problem of rational economic calculation in an era of inflation raises many issues. Some of the
issues involved are of very real substance, and also complicated; research is needed for their resolution or clarification.
Some are of real substance but not important, although
what is "material" depends on the circumstances and one's
point of view.* Some are only the result of misunderstanding
or ignorance of what the experts agree on. All, however,

---

* During World War II there was widespread complaint about the accuracy
of the Consumer Price Index, which was being used under the "Little Steel
Formula" to adjust money wages for the wartime inflation. An estimate
was therefore made by a government committee of the bias in the index.
The published estimate of the correction factor had subsequently to be

require education of the public. On the people's understanding or misunderstanding of the issues depends, in significant degree, the kind of society in which all of us will be working and living in the years ahead.

---

revised, however, when a "rounding error" in it was discovered under the close scrutiny to which the estimate was subjected by all parties concerned. Had not the "trivial" error been corrected, something on the order of a hundred million dollars more per year would have gone into the pay envelopes of workers, and a corresponding amount would have been taken out of the income of employers.

Bibliography

References in the text are to the following publications:

Accounting Principles Board. Statement No. 4. "Basic Concepts and Accounting Principles Underlying Financial Statements of Business Enterprises," October 1970.

Burns, Arthur F. "The Menace of Inflation," Address at the 141st Commencement Exercises, Illinois College, May 26, 1974.

Financial Accounting Standards Board. FASB Discussion Memorandum, "Reporting the Effects of General Price-Level Changes in Financial Statements," February 15, 1974.

Financial Accounting Standards Board. Exposure Draft, "Proposed Statement of Financial Accounting Standards, Financial Reporting in Units of General Purchasing Powers," December 31, 1974.

Hayek, F. A. "The Use of Knowledge in Society," *American Economic Review,* September 1945. Reprinted in A. Klaasen (ed.), *The Invisible Hand,* 1965.

Hobson, John A. *The Evolution of Modern Capitalism,* rev. ed., 1926.

Keynes, J. M. *The Economic Consequences of the Peace,*

1920, pp. 235–7. Reprinted in *Essays in Persuasion,* 1931.

Lent, George E. "Adjustment of Taxable Profits for Price Changes," International Monetary Fund, Fiscal Affairs Department, multigraph, December 31, 1974.

Mises, Ludwig von. "Die Wirtschaftsrechnung im sozialistischen Gemeinwesen," *Archiv für Sozialwissenschaften,* 1920; translated by S. Adler and reprinted as "Economic Calculation in the Socialist Commonwealth," in F. A. Hayek (ed.), *Collectivist Economic Planning,* 1935.

Mitchell, W. C., S. Kuznets, and M. G. Reid. "Report of the Technical Committee Appointed by the Chairman of the President's Committee on the Cost of Living, June 15, 1944," in Office of Economic Stabilization, *Report of the President's Committee on the Cost of Living,* 1945. Reference is to p. 295, footnote 17.

Mitchell, Wesley C. "The Role of Money in Economic History," *Journal of Economic History,* 1944, Supplement. Reprinted in F. C. Lane and J. C. Riemersma (eds.), *Enterprise and Secular Change,* 1953.

Moore, Geoffrey H. "Slowdowns, Recessions and Inflation: Some Issues and Answers," National Bureau of Economic Research, Xerox, January 20, 1975, to be published in *Explorations in Economic Research.*

Price Waterhouse International. *Accounting Principles and Reporting Practices, A Survey in 38 Countries,* 1973.

Schwartz, Anna J. "Secular Price Change in Historical Perspective," *Journal of Money, Credit and Banking,* February 1973.

Sombart, Werner. *Der Moderne Kapitalismus,* 2nd ed.,

1916, translated and reprinted in part in Lane and Riemersma.

Weber, Max. *General Economic History,* translated by F. H. Knight, 1927.

A few portions of the text have been drawn from the following writings of the author:

"Inflation and the Lag in Accounting Practice," in R. R. Sterling and W.F. Bentz (eds.), *Accounting in Perspective,* 1971.

"Inflation Accounting: Issues for Research," in National Bureau of Economic Research, *54th Annual Report,* September 1974.

"The Problem of Controlling Inflation," paper at the November 11, 1974, meeting of the Academy of Political Science and the Lehrman Institute, Columbia University, New York City. [To be published in the proceedings of the meeting.]

ACCOUNTING FOR BUSINESS INCOME UNDER INFLATION: CURRENT ISSUES AND VIEWS IN THE UNITED STATES*

BY SOLOMON FABRICANT

New York University and National Bureau of Economic Research

To adjust business accounting for inflation, one current proposal is to convert all dollar figures in existing financial statements to units of fixed general purchasing power. A widely offered alternative is to retain the dollar units but replace the historical-cost figures by current values. The two alternatives would yield very different results. After reviewing these and variant proposals, the analysis concentrates on certain major issues: the unit of measurement; the treatment of capital gains; the concept of capital maintenance; and the treatment of changes in the purchasing power of debt. Current value accounting would not correct for changes in the general price level and would involve far more difficult problems of concept and measurement than general purchasing power accounting. The latter is therefore preferable.

1. INTRODUCTION

As its title indicates, the present paper concentrates on the financial statements of business in the United States. I review the discussion going on among accountants, financial executives, and the others concerned, of how to adapt business accounting and reporting to inflation. As might be expected, however, many of the questions raised apply also to accounting for the income and wealth of families and other nonbusiness entities, and in countries other than the United States. And they apply, as well, to some of the adjustments for price change made—or not made—in the official national accounts.

In recent years, with the discussion of inflation accounting in the U.S.—as elsewhere—more intense than ever before, helpful calculations illustrating the various estimates of business income and net worth that would emerge from one or another decision or compromise on the various issues have been accumulating. What is worrisome, however, is the extension of the discussion beyond the topic of inflation accounting *per se*. It is not being limited to the application, to conventional financial statements, of a correction for the decline in the purchasing power of the accepted unit of reckoning, the dollar. Now embraced and subject to questioning are other "generally accepted accounting principles" (GAAP), in accordance with which conventional statements are prepared. Differences of opinion about these "generally accepted" principles were by no means dormant before inflation became serious. However, the issues have become more acute in its presence, especially (though not entirely) because of

*Paper presented at the Fifteenth General Conference of the International Association for Research in Income and Wealth, August 21, 1977, York, England.

The author's current work on the subject of economic calculation under inflation is being done as a part of the research program of Liberty Fund, Inc., of Indianapolis, to which grateful acknowledgment is made.

1

the predilection in many quarters towards "current value accounting" as the solution of the inflation accounting problem. The purposes to be served by financial accounting and reporting, and with regard to these purposes, the degree to which financial statements can at the same time be made more relevant yet still remain reasonably reliable, understandable by their users, and also conservative—such fundamental matters have come under closer scrutiny.

The effort to reach a consensus on inflation accounting is proceeding at a stronger pace than some years ago, as I have noted. But if its success requires a resolution of many of the fundamental issues opened up by an examination of the conceptual framework of accounting, doubt arises whether it will soon be attained. Whether this resolution is necessary to meet the problem posed by inflation is itself a question, however. The distorting effects of inflation are serious. The need to deal with them is urgent. Is it worthwhile—considering the cost of delay—to take the time to come to terms on many other issues; and—as solutions involving current values would require—to burden management with the task of making the estimates that would necessarily remain rough and subjective even if a large collection of price and other data were amassed?

As the reader will have gathered, I do not think so. True, a change in GAAP aimed solely at correcting the accounts for decline in the purchasing power of money cannot help but raise questions about some of the other accounting principles. But to deal reasonably well with these questions does not require rewriting the entire constitution that underlies financial accounting and reporting. We need not neglect altogether the effects of inflation on financial statements while the nature and advisability of steps to provide a comprehensive reformulation of GAAP are debated.

2. Generally Accepted Accounting Principles: the Current Situation

Before sketching the developments in the United States that have brought us to this point, it is well to recall the principles to which currently published financial statements are expected to conform and which therefore guide their preparation and certification. Of prime importance among these principles, in the present connection, are use of the dollar as the unit of reckoning, and devotion to historical costs. Also involved in the discussion of inflation accounting, however, are the principles of postponing the recognition of operating revenues and expenses and non-operating gains and losses until they are realized, and of including realized gains and losses in current net income. It therefore becomes necessary to consider these principles as well.

It should be understood that GAAP allows certain exceptions, some of which will be mentioned, and (what is not the same thing) for a rather considerable degree of latitude—too considerable in some views—in the choice of the principles to be applied when they conflict, as they will on occasion. Further, GAAP is not fixed in time, which is why I specify "the current situation." Changes in the relative importance of the objectives to be served by financial statements may alter the trade-offs among the objectives and lead to changes in GAAP. And the principles are eventually adapted to important general changes in circumstances, such as the vastly increased importance of leases and pension systems. Inflation is, of course, the case before us.

The income reported in financial statements conforming to GAAP reflects the end result of a calculation involving a mixture of current values and historical costs, measured in dollars subject to change in purchasing power. All changes in prices (with the exception, noted below, of gains never realized) are sooner or later reflected in revenues and costs and gains and losses, and thus also in reported net income. More specifically, when prices are generally rising, certain effects follow: (1) The net income reported for a period is higher than it otherwise would be because of the lag of historical costs between the time of acquisition and the time of sale or use of goods sold or plant and equipment consumed through wear and tear and obsolescence. In other words, net income is overstated because the portion of revenue required to provide for the maintenance of capital is understated. (2) Net income tends to rise from one period to another at a more rapid rate than it would were price levels stable. Growth in "real income"—income in terms of purchasing power—is less rapid than growth in money income. (3) Reported net income reflects changes in the prices of inputs and outputs relative to the general price level, as well as changes in the general price level itself. When changes in relative prices are in a firm's favor, its net income will tend to rise more than it otherwise would; when in its disfavor, reported net income will tend to rise less.

What changes in GAAP are required to deal with inflation, in view of these effects?

The lag in historical costs requires that these costs be updated. But updated by what—an index of the general price level, or indexes of the particular costs concerned? Involved here is a question long familiar to economists. Is income to be measured by what can be spent after providing for the maintenance of financial capital or of physical capital? Under GAAP, it is the former that is "accepted" as the appropriate definition. An increase in the prices of inventory or plant and equipment, then, would be counted as adding to the capital invested in them, either immediately or later when realized. (The major exception under GAAP occurs when the "last-in-first-out" [LIFO] procedure is used for inventory accounting. More about this in a later section.)

To correct for the decline in purchasing power requires a shift from dollars to units of fixed purchasing power. But purchasing power over what? Should we substitute for the dollar unit a unit of fixed general purchasing power or a unit of fixed specific purchasing power? Specific purchasing power measures real income in terms of the bundle of goods and services on which the income of a particular firm is spent, rather than of the bundle of goods and services on which income in general is spent.

The question of "realization" troubles accountants more than it does economists, because accountants have had more and closer experience with optimistic and sometimes even shady businessmen. The issue here is whether unrealized revenues and expenses or gains and losses are to be recognized; and if so, how they are to be determined and by whom, and how presented in the financial statements. Under GAAP, because accountants prefer conservative and also objective and therefore verifiable estimates, these unrealized items are excluded. The rule is not to enter them in the accounts until they are finally realized, as by sale. A rise in the market price of an asset (for example, land) that is not sold or used up in current production will not be counted as income. Exceptions, made for consistency with the practice of accrual accounting and the doctrine of conservatism, apply mainly to expenses and losses. Inventories may be valued at the lower of cost or market, for example. The usual provisions for reserves against depreciation and obsolescence, bad debts and self-insurance, can also be thought of as exceptions; or, alternatively, as realized "by use". Occasionally, write-downs—but not write-ups—of assets will be made even when not realized through a transaction. The realization question is raised about changes in the real values not only of tangible assets but also of monetary assets and liabilities. When the general price level goes up, these gains or losses can be very substantial. Whether they may be viewed as realized and taken into the calculation of income, or as unrealized and put aside, is therefore an important question.

The final question we raise concerns the distinction made between operating and non-operating, or normal and abnormal, business events. The measure of operating income is presumed (on grounds open to some question, however) to provide an index of a firm's long-term earning capacity. This is the old question of the place of capital gains, especially those resulting from price and interest rate changes, in the determination of current income. Are realized capital gains to be treated as part of current income (although segregated in the income statements) as is the practice now under GAAP; or handled as direct adjustments of capital, as was the accepted practice some decades ago? And what of unrealized capital gains, if these are taken into the accounts?

3. DEVELOPMENTS TO DATE

Attention to the problem posed for the financial accounting and reporting of business firms by a persistently rising general price level became really serious in the United States only late in 1973, when the rate of inflation reached "double-digit" levels.[1] Early in 1974 a "discussion memorandum" on the subject was published by the Financial Accounting Standards Board, a non-governmental body set up by the American Institute of Certified Public Accountants with the participation of other interested groups and the approval of the official Securities and Exchange Commission. By the end of 1974, after digesting the many oral and written reactions to the memorandum, the FASB felt ready to state, in an "exposure draft" circulated for final review, the standard to which it was leaning.

The FASB's proposal to meet the problem was relatively simple and aimed directly at the point in question. The idea was to make only one change in the

---

[1] A brief sketch of developments prior to 1973 is given in my paper, "Toward Rational Accounting in an Era of Unstable Money, 1936–1976." See the bibliographical note below.

accounting principles generally accepted and followed in the preparation of the financial statements of business—a shift in the unit of reckoning—and one that could be implemented with reasonable dispatch and at modest expense. Under the proposed standard, business corporations would be required to supplement the financial reports they were already making in terms of dollars varying in purchasing power from year to year, with a parallel set of reports identical in all respects except that they were to be expressed in units of constant general purchasing power.

For monetary items, such as cash and debt in the balance sheet, and sales receipts and interest costs in the income account, this would mean merely dividing the amounts reported in the usual financial statements of a given year by the ratio of the given-year index of the general price level to the index of the year in terms of which the purchasing power unit was defined. It would be a bit more of a nuisance—though less later than at the outset—to convert to purchasing power units the reported historical costs of non-monetary items, such as plant and equipment and inventories and the current charges associated with them. These, having been acquired at various times in the past, were at different price levels. The year of each acquisition would have to be identified and the adjustment to base-year price levels of each vintage made accordingly. But this task would not be unduly complicated; and the necessary data had to be available in existing accounting records. As for the choice of the index of the general price level, only the Consumer Price Index and the GNP Implicit Price Deflator could be regarded as serious candidates. The FASB chose the GNP deflator.

Quite explicitly, then, the FASB was deciding against the proposal, often discussed in the U.S. and elsewhere, to adjust to the fact of inflation by converting historical costs to some sort of current values, with or without a further conversion of current values to units of fixed general purchasing power. The Board recognized that a shift to current values raised serious questions about the choice among, and reliability of, the various possible measures of current value, and involved also many other contentious questions about generally accepted accounting principles that went well beyond the immediate problem posed by inflation. These questions, the Board felt, should be set aside for separate (and later) consideration.

With the FASB's proposal out and, if approved, slated to become effective in financial statements for fiscal years beginning as early as January 1, 1976, the question of inflation accounting could no longer be treated as an academic matter. The figures that might be expected from application of the FASB's approach to financial reporting were therefore looked at more closely than before.

One lesson was that companies and financial analysts had difficulty in adapting their thinking to the new unit of account. As the FASB said later, the companies and analysts did not seem to understand how to use the data adjusted for inflation according to its proposal. But, second, it also appeared that many of those who thought they could make sense of the figures found the results surprising and disturbing. They were aware of the inflationary effect of a rising general price level on replacement costs, but had tended to overlook its opposite

5

effect on the purchasing power of long-term debt, which had come to bulk relatively large in many balance sheets during the post-war period. And it was felt, further, that the treatment of the monetary items proposed by the FASB, particularly of gains from the reduction in the purchasing power of this debt, could be interpreted as more than just a shift in the unit of reckoning— as, in fact, a departure from the general rule of not recognizing gains until realized.

In any case, critics of the FASB's proposed standard, with different ideas on how, or how far, or even whether, the problem posed by inflation should be met, and even those generally in favor of the new standard but questioning its details, sharpened their criticisms and protests. Many renewed their arguments for making allowance for inflation by substituting for historical costs their current money values or costs, rather than the original costs in general purchasing power units. But some would do this only for some items, such as depreciation and obsolescence charges and cost of goods sold, while others would substitute current values for all items. Of the latter, some would take also a second step and convert the current values, or their net change, to values in purchasing power units; others would not. As for those who agreed on an adjustment to purchasing power, either by itself or after the conversion to current values, some questioned whether the line between monetary and non-monetary items had been properly drawn, and whether the supplementary set of statements needed to be as detailed as the primary statements. And there were some, even, who believed that supplementary financial statements adjusted for inflation were unnecessary. In their view, sophisticated investors and financial analysts who could understand the adjusted figures had been making their own adjustments and did not need the supplementary figures; and those not so sophisticated had more than enough trouble making sense of the existing financial statements and could be expected to continue to depend on the others for advice. Opinions, it is clear, differed very widely.

In the midst of all this, in August 1975, the Securities and Exchange Commission entered the arena with a limited current-value proposal of its own. During 1973 and 1974 the SEC had been urging the disclosure, to be made in notes to the usual financial statements, of replacement costs of inventories and then also of plant and equipment, and of withdrawals from inventory and charges for depreciation and obsolescence. But to what turned out to be only "jawboning" by the SEC, there was little response. Now, with the FASB's proposed standard—about the priority of which the SEC apparently had its reservations—in the offing, the SEC proposed a regulation to require (not merely urge) such replacement cost disclosure by all the large corporations under the SEC's jurisdiction. First, the SEC's requirement would cover only the items specified, not all, in the income account and balance sheet. Second, the SEC asked for current replacement cost, not reproduction cost. And third, no deflation by an index of the general price level was required or even recommended. The SEC stated only that when implementing its rule, "some registrants may wish to use data regarding changes in the general price level as part of the analysis of reasons for changes in replacement cost." In effect, the SEC was supporting the position that income was properly measured after provision for

6

the maintenance of physical capital: any increase in replacement values per physical unit of inventory or plant and equipment would be counted as raising unit costs, but not as providing gains from holding these assets.

With the weather turned so harsh, in November 1975 the FASB decided to postpone the proposed effective date of its own standard. Time was needed, the Board said, for study of the many letters of comment received on the exposure draft and of the results it expected to obtain from an application—more extensive and detailed than hitherto made—of its proposed standard to the financial statements of a sample of large corporations for recent years.

Unlike the SEC's earlier proposals on the subject, the Commission's new proposal was not still-born. In March 1976 the replacement cost requirement became official, and effective with end-of-1976 financial statements. It was not surprising that soon after, in June 1976, the FASB announced its decision to postpone its 1974 proposal indefinitely. By way of explanation the Board reported the lack of understanding of financial data adjusted for inflation, already mentioned, and its resultant feeling that the cost of implementation did not (or did not yet) appear to be warranted. The Board also stated, however, that it had not itself yet come to a final conclusion about the merits of its proposal and—its mind changed—that the subject of inflation accounting would be considered within the FASB's broader project, already under way, on a conceptual framework for financial accounting and reporting. In December 1976, the FASB published a long discussion memorandum setting forth some of the major issues related to that broad subject, including those particularly pertinent to our present concern, with a promise of further memoranda on other issues at a later time.

Accompanying the discussion memorandum was a separate statement on the Board's tentative conclusions concerning the objectives, of financial statements of business enterprises, at which the conceptual framework should be aimed. Also issued at the same time was a booklet providing a "capsulized" view of the preceding documents, to which some remarks were added under the heading of "The Next Step?". These hinted that the process of formulating new standards to cope with inflation (among other things) and learning to live with the standards before they became "official" requirements for financial accounting and reporting, might stretch out well into the future—the implications of which will concern us later.

During 1976, in the meanwhile, many meetings of accountants, financial officers and economists had been devoted to the procedures and data involved in meeting the now official—and difficult—SEC requirements. In the case of plant and equipment, the SEC had made emphatic, the requirements were to report the cost of replacing existing capacity, which could be obsolescent, with equivalent capacity of modern design, not to report the cost of reproducing existing plant and equipment. The SEC itself felt compelled to issue several Staff Accounting Bulletins in order to assist accountants and financial executives to interpret and meet the new disclosure requirements. The complications involved became evident as these requirements were studied, and protests against the regulation mounted. But the SEC held fast, and during the Spring of this year annual reports and the more detailed 10K reports to the SEC providing such information have made their appearance. Usually, also, these reports have contained warnings about the difficulty of interpreting the replacement cost data—warnings often carried to the point of stating that the data were virtually meaningless and had been provided only at the SEC's insistence.

Noteworthy also is the "experiment" gotten under way early in 1977 by a Task Force of the AICPA, the results of which are to feed into the material to be considered by the FASB. For the experiment, as reported in April, the Task Force designed four "models" to accommodate what it felt were the major lines of thinking on concepts and measurement and their implications for the adaptation of financial accounting and reporting to an era of inflation. The models are to be applied by some thirty or more large corporations to their respective financial statements for 1975 and 1976, with such additional variations within each model as the companies believe desirable. In addition, of course, there will be the financial statements prepared in conformity with present GAAP. The experimental applications are due to be ready in October of this year.

To bring the story up to date: Compilations and preliminary examinations of the results of the SEC's requirements have begun to appear; in May the FASB completed and published its research report on financial statements in units of general purchasing power; written comments on the FASB's memorandum on the conceptual framework have been accumulating; hearings on the subject originally scheduled for one meeting in June, 1977, have been postponed to two meetings, one in August, 1977, and the other in January, 1978, with the latter date devoted particularly to the problem of inflation accounting; and the results of the AICPA's experiment should presumably be available (although barely, I would guess, considering the time required for collation and at least minimal analysis) in time for discussion at the FASB's meeting in January, 1978.[2]

4. THE VARIETY OF INFLATION ACCOUNTING MODELS

The AICPA's Task Force does not presume that its models have equal claims as candidates for acceptance. Nor does it appear that the choice among them and their variations will hinge on how the results look in relation to one another, though it is hard to believe that comparison of the results will not play some role in the preferences expressed. However, the results will reflect the outcome of a number of the more important proposals to which I have alluded and now need to specify. For this purpose it is sufficient to note the chief distinctive characteristics of the models, and mention how they differ in certain major respects from the "illustrations" provided by the FASB in an appendix to its discussion memorandum.

---

[2]Lack of space has precluded attention to certain proposals to deal with inflation made by the Cost Accounting Standards Board, established by the U.S. Congress about five years ago to set accounting standards for Federal Government procurement contracts. The standard that finally emerged in June 1976, effective October 1, 1976, will be discussed (along with other CASB standards) at an "evaluation conference" to be held in October 1977.

For a brief summary and critique of the proposals and the new standard, see the paper mentioned earlier. To what is said there, I should add the following: The CASB standard on inflation cannot be judged fairly without reference to its other cost accounting standards as well as to the Department of Defense's "guidelines for the profit standard" in defense procurement contracts.

The Task Force's Model A is essentially a set of financial statements made in accordance with the FASB's general purchasing power proposal, modified and condensed somewhat to meet some of the criticisms leveled at that proposal.

Model B goes to current values in calculating net income, but—as with the SEC's requirement—only for the cost of goods sold (which is to be on a LIFO basis) and charges for depreciation and obsolescence (using lower of reproduction and replacement cost). As a result, reported net income under Model B will be lower than the net income reported under GAAP by the difference between historical cost and current cost for these two items. (To the extent that LIFO is already used for inventories, as it may be under GAAP, the calculation of net income already uses the current cost of goods sold.) Increase in the unit value of the corresponding assets, inventory and plant and equipment, is not counted as income: the concept of physical capital maintenance controls the determination of income. Were the LIFO procedure applied to accounting for plant and equipment, as it is to be for inventory, the change in stockholders' equity would also be lower by the difference between historical and current cost of depreciation and obsolescence. But it is a peculiarity of the model that plant and equipment continue to be valued at their historical cost; the year's excess of current-cost over historical-cost depreciation is credited to a special equity account entitled "Accumulated Current Depreciation;" and the excess is eventually transferred to retained earnings when the depreciable fixed assets to which it relates are sold or retired, although it was not reported as earnings in the income statement.

Model C is closer to a full current value basis than Model B, and the current values are estimated somewhat differently. In the balance sheet, securities and land, as well as inventories and buildings and equipment, are stated in current values. However, as under GAAP, long-term debt is at par rather than current value; changes in the market value of debt are recognized only when the debt is liquidated at the market price. All value changes are excluded in calculating net income, which therefore differs from GAAP net income essentially as does Model B net income. Value changes are accumulated in the balance sheet under the headings of "Unrealized Value Changes" and "Retained Realized Value Changes," and appear as part of stockholders' equity along with retained operating income and contributed capital.[3] General price level changes are not recognized as such.

Model D goes still further to a current value basis in that long-term debt is reported in the balance sheet at market value. However, no changes in value are considered to affect net income. They are listed, along with the net income resulting from ordinary operations (which include some unusual transactions and events), in a special statement of changes in stockholders' equity, and in supporting schedules. An interesting inclusion in this statement is an estimate of "the amount required to recognize the impact on stockholders' equity of increase in the general price level during the year." In effect, the difference

[3]Except for presentation, the Task Force states, the model resembles in many respects the models proposed in the United Kingdom by the Chartered Accountants Exposure Draft 18 on "Current Cost Accounting."

between this amount and the reported sum of the value changes is the gain or loss due to value changes greater or less than the rise in the general price level. Inclusion of this estimate of the impact of general inflation is the closest the model comes to recognizing the decline in the purchasing power of the dollar units in which the financial statements are expressed.

The AICPA's current-value models (C and D) and the corresponding illustrations provided by the FASB differ in a number of respects. Two of these are important enough to be noted here, for they reveal how wide is the variety of models offered as deserving of consideration. First, the FASB includes purchasing power gains on monetary items and holding gains on tangible assets in net earnings (distinguishing them from earnings from operations). These value changes, realized or unrealized, are not credited directly to capital, as in the AICPA's models. Second, the FASB shows what the current value statements would look like after conversion of the money units in which they are expressed to units of general purchasing power.

5. THE UNIT OF MEASUREMENT

The problem of inflation accounting stems from the fact that the money units in which the accounts are kept are unstable in the sense that they decline in general purchasing power—in real value—as the general price level rises. The problem is exacerbated by the lag between historical cost and current cost, but it would exist even if the lag were of trivial importance or entirely absent. The solution requires deflation of the dollar figures, both historical cost (taking appropriate account of the dates to which the historical cost figures refer) and current cost or value, thus converting them into units of fixed general purchasing power.

But many, probably most, accountants and businessmen seem to think of the problem of inflation accounting as stemming from the fact that historical costs lag behind current costs and prices when price levels are rising. They see the solution as one of correcting for this lag. The historical cost dollar figures must, in other words, be inflated rather than deflated, and brought up to or in line with the current level of prices. This solution would serve also to provide financial statements that conform to established habits. The unit of measurement would continue to be the customary dollar unit; there would be no need to deal with an artificial or imaginary unit of fixed purchasing power.

Resistance to the idea of units of general purchasing power, and a correspondingly strong inclination towards current values in dollar terms, is clear. It is evident in the reactions to the FASB's exposure draft on general purchasing power accounting. It led the FASB, in its discussion memorandum on the conceptual framework, to raise the question whether current value accounting is "a foregone conclusion". More recently, it is indicated by the models chosen by the AICPA to illustrate the varieties of current thinking.

Why the resistance to general purchasing power units and the partiality towards current values in dollar terms, in the dialogue over inflation accounting? The idea of converting historical to current cost is not necessarily incompatible,

10

of course, with the idea of purchasing power units, since a second step can be taken to pass from the current dollar units to the purchasing power units, as is suggested in the FASB's illustrations. However, this is infrequent among the proposals being seriously considered.

Even economists might appreciate the trouble people have with a unit of measurement that is new to them, if they were to take a moment to recall their own difficulties with the metric system. Yet all that is required to switch from yards to meters is conversion merely by a fixed ratio, not by the changing ratio required in the conversion of dollar values to purchasing power units. Economists find it easy to think in terms of units of general purchasing power because they have been trained to do so. And economists are comfortable with the GNP implicit price deflator, which is used to convert dollars to purchasing power units, because they know its derivation and understand the significance of the words with which this measure of the general price level is denoted. These words—"gross," "implicit," and "deflator," if not also "national" and "product"—must often be puzzling to the layman.[4] Nor would the layman's plight be eased by the proposal in the FASB's exposure draft to "roll forward" the purchasing power financial statements from one year to another—that is, to shift the base period annually to the current year's last quarter, instead of sticking to a fixed base, as do most government statistics.

It is likely that many members of the general public have become fairly familiar with such measures as those of real wages. But these are almost invariably presented in the press in terms of changes (as in the AICPA's Model D) rather than base-year prices. The occasional reports of real wages, and other such measures as those of real GNP, have not accustomed people to think in terms of constant purchasing power units. The stress of daily life is always upon money units. Business is done in current dollars. What people see, pay, receive, are current prices in dollars, not units of general purchasing power. Indeed, to most people, inflation means rising prices of what they buy and have to pay for. When galloping inflation forces people to abandon the units in which they have been making their calculations, their recourse is to the stabler money of other countries.

Perhaps the idea of purchasing power units could be understood more readily by people were it applied to their own income and its command over the particular goods and services they purchase. In any case, the question raised earlier, "Which purchasing power?" must be answered.

---

[4]This is one reason why the Consumer Price Index might be better than the GNP deflator as the measure of the general price level. The CPI has also the advantage that it is not subject to revision (at least in a way that would require "prior period" adjustments), as is the GNP deflator. On the other hand, the GNP deflator is more comprehensive; it covers the prices of capital goods as well as of consumption goods, and of all consumption goods, not only those consumed by urban wage-earners and clerical workers. This is why the FASB chose it. Even the forthcoming broadened CPI, covering consumers now omitted, will be less comprehensive than the GNP deflator.

The Department of Commerce now also publishes a "fixed-weighted price index" for GNP, using 1972 weights. It differs only slightly from the GNP implicit price deflator, but is conceptually preferable to the latter as a measure of the general purchasing power of money. Its use for that purpose would also lessen the problem mentioned in the text above. The fixed-weighted index is available only beginning with 1958, but it could be extended further back without much trouble.

The notion of units of purchasing power specific to the expenditure patterns of particular groups appears most often in discussions of the real income of the aged, the poor, or some other social group, when the objective is to maintain or raise their standard of living in terms of the goods and services normally consumed by the group. But the idea of units of specific purchasing power is not entirely absent from the inflation accounting literature. Indeed, the definition of real net income as what can be spent after provision for the maintenance of physical capital is closely related to the idea of specific purchasing power. Here it may be sufficient to underscore the fact that a price index tailored to the expenditure pattern of a particular group is not a good measure of inflation. What it measures is a combination of inflation—change in the general price level—and the net up or down change in the relative prices of the goods and services bought by the group. The relative prices of concern to different industries, and even firms within industries, are bound to change at different rates as demand and supply conditions vary. The price indexes specific to each will therefore also change at different rates. And this will be so even when inflation is entirely absent, though inflation may contribute to the forces making for relative price change. What these relative price changes have been (and may be expected to be) are, like many other kinds of information, relevant to the decisions of businessmen and investors. But they have nothing to do with the accounting problem with which we are concerned. To eliminate from the accounts the distorting effects of inflation, the unit of measurement must be one of general, not specific, purchasing power.

In view of the obstacles already discussed (and some still to be discussed) to the acceptance of the FASB's general purchasing power proposal, or its slightly modified (and improved) form in the AICPA's Model A—and also the experience to date—we cannot be sanguine that it will be accepted as the solution to the accounting problem caused by inflation. However, before we conclude that it has little chance of being accepted, we should consider the problems posed by the alternative of current value accounting. Going to current value accounting raises questions serious and difficult enough to prevent current accounting from being a "foregone conclusion" or, at least, a conclusion that can be reached reasonably soon.

6. Which Current Value?

When it is proposed that historical costs be replaced by current values—whether or not this is to be followed by the translation of the money units of purchasing power—the question posed above immediately arises. It has two aspects. One concerns the choice of the concept of value; the other, how to measure the current value selected.

Current values can be defined and measured in a variety of ways. The FASB, for example, lists current cost, current exit (market) value, expected exit (net realizable) value, and present value of expected cash flows. And further distinctions are made among historical rate, current rate, and "some other" rate of discount; and between current cost of property, plant and equipment "in kind" (equivalent to current reproduction cost), and current cost of "equivalent productive capacity" (the SEC's replacement cost). Which current value is to be used for each of the several categories of assets and liabilities,[5] and which suits best the objectives of financial accounting[6] are questions on which opinions differ. This is why the FASB requests respondents to its discussion memorandum on the conceptual framework to answer these questions by checking off their opinions on the "matrix" form provided. (However, what information can be provided by the show of hands, beyond the fact that opinions differ, remains to be seen.)

Obviously, also, serious questions arise on what data to use when one can pick and choose, how to estimate from these data the current value selected, who is to do the estimating, and what information is to be provided in the financial statements to support the estimates.

No economist would object to shifting from historical cost to current values. Indeed, economists were the first to do so. Raymond Goldsmith's balance sheets and the national accounts prepared by the Bureau of Economic Analysis are in current as well as constant prices. But economists are keenly aware of how scanty and rough the information is; they take some comfort in the belief that the various measures of current value tend to converge; they use what is at hand; they are—have to be—content with crude approximations. But the differences among current value concepts and measures make for very real worries by accountants, who want verifiable estimates free from bias.

Consider the kind of information available on the current cost "in kind" of inventories and property, plant and equipment. Members of this Association are well aware of the wide gaps in the available compilations of price and cost data; their uncertain comparability over time because of the quality changes that the compilers are not able to allow for in making up their indexes; and the thorny theoretical, econometric and statistical problems encountered by economists attempting to deal with these quality changes by developing "hedonic" price indexes even to a limited extent.

If this particular variety of current value were to be accepted for use in current value accounting, it would be necessary to extend the price data now available. And to limit the cost of developing and using the data, it would be desirable (as has been suggested) to publish a set of price indexes, recognised as imperfect but generally accepted for the purpose, similar to the set of depreciation rates put together by the Internal Revenue Service in its old *Bulletin F* and its later guidelines to meet an equally difficult problem. The publication would

---

[5]Receivables, investments in marketable securities, inventories, property, plant, and equipment, and purchased identifiable intangibles, are included in the FASB's list of assets, to which might be added "home-grown" intangibles which may or may not be counted as assets under GAAP. Liabilities are classified into three groups: specified amounts of money payable at specified dates; estimated amounts of money payable at unknown times; and products or services to be delivered in satisfaction of an obligation. The classifications are designed for use in discussing various questions, including some I am passing over. One, for example, is the question whether a liability due at some future date, but on which no interest is charged, should be currently valued at an appropriate discount.

[6]The objectives of relevance, reliability, comparability, timeliness, and understandability, as well as "other", are listed by the FASB. These are drawn from the secondary literature abstracted in an Addendum to Chapter 7 of the discussion memorandum on the conceptual framework.

13

contain a reasonably detailed set of indexes, classified by industry and type of good, giving the ranges that would be acceptable. Every firm could use this set of conventional price indexes without trying to concoct its own, departing from them only when justification could be given, as in the case of depreciation rates. A precedent is provided by the set of indexes pertaining to department store inventories, regularly published by the BLS and acceptable by the IRS for LIFO. The indexes developed by some industry groups and a few individual companies to meet the requirements of the SEC may have added something useful to what is already given in government sources. But what is now available marks only a beginning in the compilation needed.[7]

Consider, next, the difficulties encountered in determining the current value of existing plant and equipment by turning to the current cost of equivalent productive capacity, as the SEC and others propose. There will be difficulties even when a new machine is identical in all respects except capacity with the old machine that is eventually to be replaced. Capacity and price are not proportionate to one another; doubled capacity is not necessarily at double the price. The SEC found itself compelled to discuss the relationship between size and price, in responding to companies trying to understand its replacement cost requirements, and took refuge in recalling some conventional rules of thumb about the relationship. Yet this is only one of the troubles encountered in pricing equivalent productive capacity. Very frequently the new machine will differ from the old machine not only in capacity, but also in the amount required (per unit of capacity), of labor, maintenance, fuel and power, and even material. These requirements not only may change; they are bound to change as technology improves, and as changes in the relative prices of the various inputs make it desirable to redesign equipment to use increasingly expensive inputs more economically.

The SEC was aware of this problem also, but merely asked registrants to report what consideration, "if any", had been given by them to the related changes in other factor costs. The SEC did not explain how to give this consideration. Even a cursory glance at the 10K's reporting replacement cost, following instructions from the SEC, reveals that many companies offered little more than a caveat to the effect that there would be such related changes and that the associated savings might be large.

The AICPA's Model D would explicitly require the respondent to estimate the future cost savings expected from the replacement of existing with improved capacity. The AICPA even lists "at least four possible ways" of accounting for expected cost savings. However, one of these ways is simply "to ignore them;" the others are not as easy to follow. In principle, of course, the differences among machines of different vintage with regard to the labor, etc., they require per unit of output could be estimated by a careful comparison—when the conditions under which they operate are reasonably similar. But this is easier said than done; and to go further and determine "expected" differences would encounter additional difficulties.

[7]Something like this is emerging in Britain. The Central Statistical Office has already issued the third edition of its "Price Index Numbers for Current Cost Accounting," and a fourth is in preparation.

Another problem in taking the current cost of equivalent productive capacity as the measure of current value arises because of past and projected changes in the demand for the products of the productive capacity. The current value based on some exit value, or an estimate of the discounted expected cash flow, would presumably take both cost and demand into account. But the problem of estimation is complicated. While the FASB lists the discounted cash flow variety of current value in its discussion memorandum, it also makes clear that it hardly expects any company to make a serious effort to use it should current value accounting become accepted. The AICPA is no less pessimistic. In one of its models the current value of plant and equipment that cannot or will not be replaced is to be estimated by the higher of discounted present value of cash flows and current net realizable value. But the AICPA notes that "since determination of discounted present value may be impracticable or impossible, the current net realizable value may be the only available information to use for valuing the asset." And even this value can be estimated only roughly from the scanty market data available.

The complexities encountered in current value accounting may be appreciated also when the relevance, to the measurement of current value, of the charge for depreciation and obsolescence is considered. When a decision to invest in plant and equipment is made, the calculation must allow (among other things) for the loss of value of the new assets as time passes. The annual series of charges for depreciation and obsolescence in effect consists of the estimates, made at the time of the investment, of the declines in current value that are expected to take place each year; and the corresponding net book values, the estimates of each year's current value of the asset. The estimates would admittedly be crude, refinement not usually being worth the trouble, when straight-line or some other simple depreciation formula is used; but this does not alter their nature or purpose. The estimates may hardly be expected to take account of inflation even in an age of inflation; presumably the calculations underlying the investment in plant and equipment are generally made in terms of relative prices, ignoring possible changes in the general price level. The original estimates of future current value, and change in current value, would then require adjustment each year for the year's rise in the general price level, as is proposed in the FASB's model.

But, of course, other things will have happened after the investment was made, besides a rise in the general price level. Are the SEC and those who propose to use replacement costs or discounted present values in effect asking for revisions in the original estimates—revisions made necessary not only by inflation but also by initial ("prior period") errors in the estimate and by subsequent changes in other conditions?

Such questions lead the discussion into a large area of controversy about the theory and factual basis of depreciation and obsolescence. What is the empirical foundation of the IRS's tables of acceptable depreciation rates and the variety of depreciation formulas its regulations allow? Is permitting accelerated depreciation for tax purposes merely an easy way (politically) to allow, in some degree, for inflation? If so, should this allowance be extracted, replacing accelerated depreciation by straight-line depreciation before going to purchasing-power

15

units? Or is permission to accelerate depreciation simply a way to reduce corporate income tax rates? Or, alternatively, does it bring the estimates actually closer to the realities of depreciation and obsolescence than does the prevailing straight-line depreciation formula? These unsettled questions, which I can only mention, are often discussed (especially by economists),[8] but seldom in connection with the problem of inflation accounting.

Not of negligible importance, in thinking about current value accounting, is the burden that would be imposed on management to provide current value estimates and justify them, should current value accounting become the generally accepted procedure for dealing with inflation. The fact that the burden of compliance with any change in accounting procedure tends to be over-stated by businessmen should not cause us to under-state it.

The great advantage of general purchasing power accounting is the modest demands it makes. Even the kind of current value accounting that would accept simple "indexing" would enlarge the task substantially. If the current values by which historical costs are to be displaced are anything like replacement costs with allowance for savings of other inputs, or discounted value of cash flows, the burden would be multiplied by a substantial factor.

As I have reminded the reader, a decision to invest in any piece of tangible capital involves a judgment whether the value of the item to the firm at least equals its cost. This requires not only assessing the immediate possibilities but also formulating expectations about the future. These will presumably be based on what solid information is available, but this information will never be sufficient. Recourse will be had also to judgments or guesses of all kinds, and these will be influenced, as they must be, by hopes and fears about the future. In small enterprises the calculation may therefore be extremely informal. In large enterprises, it may take the form of detailed justification on paper; but even in this case, the final selection among alternative investment possibilities will seldom be based merely on comparisons of the calculations of their expected payoffs. In any case, what calculation is made will be made internally. About all that will get into the financial accounts released annually, apart from general remarks by the president of the company, will be the costs incurred in making the investment and the depreciation and obsolescence that will be applied to the new assets. No ordinary stockholder will demand or expect a detailed justification of the investment decision.

Yet, to require that management calculate, publish, and be prepared to justify estimated current values, is in effect to demand and expect something of this sort. And not only once, but every year. It goes without saying that businessmen are always watching the course of events as closely as they can. They are always asking themselves whether to enlarge or to contract, whether to replace their capacity with the same or with different capital goods, and so on. But this monitoring is more often rough and ready than detailed and precise; and the results need not be, seldom can be, and even more rarely are, presented even in the remarks attached to the formal financial statements.

[8]Most recently, at a meeting on the measurement of capital held by the Conference on Research in Income and Wealth in Toronto, late in 1976.

7. The Capital-Maintenance Issue

Under GAAP, as mentioned earlier, net income reflects all changes in prices, relative as well as general. There will be lags in the response of expenses to price changes, because the expenses are charged at historical cost, but eventually all the price changes will enter the income statement and affect the net income it reports.

Conversion of the dollars in the accounts into units of general purchasing power will eliminate the changes in the general price level, but not the changes in relative prices. The real values of inventories (except for those under LIFO) and plant and equipment—and also intangibles if they are recorded—as well as the real costs of goods sold and depreciation and obsolescence, will reflect these changes in relative prices. The physical volume of inventories may remain quite constant, for example, yet its real value will be higher or lower than before if the prices of the goods in inventory have risen more or less than the general price level. And this change in value will be included in real net income. In short, real income (after taxes) is defined as the purchasing power available for dividends and net investment after deducting provision for the maintenance of real capital, not for the maintenance of physical capital.

However, some people think of capital in physical terms, when they worry about inflation accounting. They conceive of an enterprise as continuing in the same line of business indefinitely, and maintaining its capital only when its physical capacity to turn out or handle its usual line of products is maintained. They would exclude the effect on income of a change in the relative prices of inventory and plant capacity. This, in effect, is what would be done under current value accounting, when cost of goods sold and depreciation and obsolescence are charged at current cost, while changes in the current value of inventory and plant and equipment are excluded from the calculation of net income by relegation to a separate statement.

Is there any merit to this view?

It is true that businessmen are concerned about maintaining "their share of the market," and this concern may foster the notion that net income in some truly relevant sense is income that is left over after providing for the maintenance of physical capital, or even the notion that income or income available for dividends is what is left over after providing for the maintenance of the firm's share of the market, which may mean after expanding capacity. I suspect that the insistence on physical capital as the capital that is to be maintained originates in the confusion generated in an inflationary era by conventional financial statements that are based on historical costs measured in dollar units. The provision for replacing goods sold and plant and equipment used up that is recorded in the conventional statements is obviously insufficient for the purpose by any reasonable definition of capital maintenance. The book values reported for inventories and plant and equipment will rise more rapidly than the physical or real capital they represent, and may rise even when the physical or real capital is deteriorating. What is needed is an adjustment of the financial statements to eliminate the distorting effects of a rising general price level—in a word, purchasing power accounting.

17

To adjust the statements also for changes in relative prices would eliminate market signals important to businessmen for the efficient management of their affairs. For their primary interest, we must remember, is to maintain or increase their firm's capacity to "make money" in the most remunerative way. It is not merely, or necessarily, to make money in the accustomed way. Their concern with physical capital maintenance is simply a concern with one of several means of making money. Like any means, it will be discarded when it is no longer as attractive a source as other means available to them.

This must be so in a world of change in which new products and new materials displace old, in which factor prices change, in which new markets are opened up and old markets disappear. It is a world shaped by innovation and adaptation to innovation, as Schumpeter taught us long ago. The business that counts its profit after providing for the maintenance of its physical capital, and fails to innovate or adjust to the innovations of more enterprising businessmen, eventually goes under.

Except for the peculiarities attached to LIFO, accounting under GAAP is properly focussed on this objective of making money, and is devoted to measuring the degree to which this objective has been attained. General purchasing power accounting aims to measure the same objective expressed in terms that allow—as they should—for inflation.

The LIFO exception under GAAP to historical cost accounting is a consequence of the requirement, under the tax code, to use LIFO in the financial statements when LIFO is used in the tax return.[9]

In an inflationary period, LIFO has the effect of indefinitely postponing some of the tax on business income as it would be were income measured under GAAP without the benefit of LIFO. It therefore provides a way of adjusting the income tax return for inflation. However, the adjustment it permits is seriously incomplete because it applies only to inventories. Further, should the physical quantity of inventories decline, some or all of the postponed taxes would become due. The fact that under LIFO changes in the relative prices of inventories are excluded from income might be considered as only a minor defect in the way it deals with inflation.

8. The Monetary Items in Purchasing Power Accounting

Current value accounting raises controversial questions regarding the disposition, between net earnings and credits directly to capital, of gains from holding assets and owing liabilities; and when these holding gains are counted as part of earnings, regarding their inclusion in operating income or in nonoperating income. But purchasing power accounting is not entirely free of this problem. Holding gains on monetary items come into question. In the FASB's model, and the AICPA's variant, these gains are treated as part of net earnings; but they could be treated otherwise.

---

[9]In this respect, the requirement differs from the regulation governing depreciation and obsolescence. Accelerated depreciation may be used for tax purposes, but need not be used for the financial statements. The difference is set forth in a note to the statements.

18

The issue requires our attention, which we limit to the monetary items in purchasing power accounting.

Under GAAP, liquidation by a company of its own long-term debt, by purchase in the market at less than par value, would be considered as yielding a realized nonoperating gain, to be included in net income. Unrealized gains of this sort would be ignored. Under purchasing power accounting, however— adhering to GAAP in other respects—such an unrealized gain (measured by the change in the debt's purchasing power caused by a rise in the general price level) is not ignored. It is included in net income, under the category of nonoperating gains. Revising GAAP in what appears to be just one respect—a shift from dollar units to general purchasing power units—also results in counting as income what under GAAP would be viewed as unrealized gains and excluded from income. As I mentioned earlier, this implication has raised a stumbling block to the acceptance of purchasing power accounting. What can be said about it?

Consider, first, the situation in an era in which the general price level has been rising for some considerable time, is continuing to rise at a more or less constant rate, and is generally expected to rise in the future—in a word, an era of inflation. Both borrowers and lenders will take into account the prospective decline in the purchasing power of the principal, as well as of later interest payments. Debt floated in these circumstances will bear an interest rate that includes an allowance for the expected rate of inflation. From the point of view of general purchasing power accounting, the interest payment may be seen as a gross payment or receipt, against which is to be credited or charged a revenue or cost reflecting the depreciation in the purchasing power of the obligation. In the borrower's income statement, the net interest payment in purchasing power units would be the gross amount less the gain. As in the treatment of depreciation and obsolescence charges, the gain could quite sensibly be viewed as a realized operating-income item. With appropriate changes, the treatment in the lender's income accounting would be the same.

Sharply in contrast is the situation in which the general price level is more or less stable, and inflation is not seen as a possibility serious enough to be reckoned with. Interest rates on loans would be set at rates that include no inflationary factor. Should inflation erupt later and persist, interest rates will rise and market values of debt incurred earlier and still outstanding will decline. Because this decline would not have been anticipated in setting the original terms, it could with good reason be viewed as a capital or extraordinary gain rather than an operating revenue. And there is also justification, though that is not so clear, to consider the gain as realized, even though liquidation of the debt by purchase in the market has not taken place.

What I have posed are obviously extreme, essentially theoretical cases, in order to point up the issue. As usual, the actual situation is not as clear. Even before 1965, from which year the current phase of inflation is dated, memories of the post-World War II and Korean War rises in the price level had not completely faded away; the average rate of inflation had fallen to low but not to negative levels; the threat of inflation was considered by some lenders to be worth worrying about, and "equity kickers" were becoming fashionable. Interest rates may have contained only a modest inflationary factor, but whatever it was, it cannot be assumed to have been entirely negligible.

As for the situation after 1965, while the price level kept on rising, it did not do so at a steady pace—in substantial part because of "stop-go" efforts by government to dampen inflation. And interest rates on new loans moved up and fluctuated in resonance with the price level, responding also, of course, to the cyclical and secular forces that determine the real rate of interest.

It is not easy to determine the inflationary factor in interest rates in this situation, as economists making the attempt have come to realize. Yet we can be sure that the inflation factor in interest rates has been much greater in recent years than in the early 1960s; and that it is recognized as greater by more people. More the reason, therefore, to think of treating declines in the purchasing power of monetary items as elements of operating income rather than of nonoperating income, and certainly not to think of excluding the declines as unrealized. More than before, in other words, holding gains may be viewed as the result of "normal" business events that occur in an era of inflation, with which business-men must deal as best they can, just as they have to deal with changes in the prices of the goods and services they buy and sell.[10]

But this is not the view that everybody holds, and the differences of opinion remain to be thrashed out. The differences are especially strong on the question of realization when liquidation of debt by purchase has not taken place. Under purchasing power accounting, realization is presumed simply as a consequence of the rise in the general price level.

How gains or losses resulting from changes in the purchasing power of the monetary items are treated makes a material difference. As I mentioned earlier, there was a large increase in the proportion of debt to equity financing during the post-war period; and in the aggregate, nonfinancial corporations are net debtors today. As a consequence, gains on net monetary items may offset a good part of, or even overpower, the rise in the replacement costs of nonmonetary items in years when inflation is rapid. However, even for 1973 and 1974—years of double-digit inflation—most companies covered in the FASB Research Report sample had net income in purchasing power units that fell short of GAAP net income.

Interfirm variation in the effect of holding gains on net earnings needs to be stressed because a major purpose of inflation accounting is to improve interfirm comparisons of earnings. Under GAAP these comparisons can be very mislead-ing because of differences in balance-sheet structure. For 1972, not as inflationary a year as 1973 and 1974, the percentage decrease in net income expressed in purchasing power units, from GAAP net income in "mixed

---

[10]To recall Pigou's example, it is as if a country in which earthquakes are exceedingly rare, is transformed into a country in which they come as do changes in the weather. The damage done by earthquakes may then no longer be treated as capital losses, but must rather be considered as normal costs of doing business, to be provided for by insurance or otherwise, and taken into account in calculating operating income.

dollars," ranged from +61 percent to −36 percent in a sample of 58 firms.[11] Utilities and other firms making heavy use of funded debt show purchasing power income well above mixed-dollar income.

9. CONCLUDING REMARKS

Proposals to modify social arrangements in order to cope better with the new situations that inevitably arise in a dynamic world always encounter resistance. There will be those who oppose any change, for one reason or another; and those who agree that something must be done, but will differ on what to do, and how and when to do it. The case before us provides abundant illustration.

Surely persistent inflation is a new situation. Surely, also, it is important enough to require modification of the units in which economic calculations are made and reported. The general price level doubled in the United States during the past 15 years, and the outlook for soon attaining a reasonably stable price level is dim.

In a number of areas of economic life the problem of getting some agreement on a better unit of measurement is being overcome and the arrangements are being modified. Mention need be made only of the escalator clauses introduced in public and private pension systems and wage and other contracts on a widening scale.

Accounting for business income under inflation, however, is still only in the discussion and experiment stage. The exception—if it is an exception—concerns the limited and otherwise questionable requirements imposed by the SEC last year on the financial reports of large listed corporations. We are confronted, in official and unofficial sources, with a considerable variety of measures of business profits, or of the costs and value changes that go into the calculation of profits, adjusted in different ways for inflation. The adjusted estimates are radically different from one another, as well as from the unadjusted measures that appear in conventional financial statements or tax returns.

A glance at the current month's issue of the Department of Commerce's *Business Conditions Digest*, for example, reveals four widely different aggregates of business profits, all provided by the Bureau of Economic Analysis.[12] And

---

[11]The frequency distribution of firms by percentage decrease (increase) in net income from "mixed-dollar results" is worth presenting for 1972:

Percentage decrease	50 and over	40–49	30–39	20–29	10–19	0–9	(10)–(1)	(20)–(11)	Under (30)
Number of companies	2	3	6	10	21	7	2	3	2

Source: FASB, Research Report, Exhibit 2. Numbers within parentheses are negative.

[12]Profits after taxes, reported in the first quarter of 1977, relative to the previous peak in 1966, were as follows: according to the tax returns, up about 100 percent; the same in "1972 dollars," up about 10 percent; as reported on tax returns but with the BEA's inventory value and capital consumption adjustments (approximately equivalent to a shift from historical to replacement cost), up about 25 percent; the last, in 1972 dollars, down 30 percent. (The BEA's conversion to 1972 dollars is not quite an adjustment for change in the *general* purchasing power of the dollar, but it is not far from it.)

21

there are still other and different estimates of these aggregates, prepared occasionally by nongovernmental economists, that allow (as the BEA does not) for the reduction in the purchasing power of the monetary items that takes place as the general price level rises and also for holding gains on nonmonetary assets.[13] As for individual companies, the FASB Research Report mentioned earlier reveals wide variations in the degree to which their estimated earnings are altered by a conversion to purchasing power units. Application of inflation accounting procedures that involve a shift to current values as well as subsequent deflation shows a similar wide diversity of results.

Whatever doubts one may have about the choice of this or that concept and procedure, it is impossible to deny that the accounting problem raised by inflation is a serious matter. In some quarters, however, it is argued that it is best to let things alone, to stick with the "tested procedures that have served us so well in the past," rather than turn to untested concepts and measures that can serve only to confuse. No less strange is the argument that readers can make their own adjustments, in the financial statements that cross their desks, readily and cheaply enough to serve their purposes, and therefore nothing more is needed. It is difficult to treat this contention with any respect while loud complaints are being heard about the difficulties of preparing financial statements adjusted simply by a shift to general purchasing power units even when there is full access to the detailed books of account. Something more *is* needed.

No doubt GAAP has many features that require reconsideration. The validity of the dollar as the unit of measurement is not the only principle in question. But it is the question that is most urgent, the question that should be settled first.

The simplest and quickest way to deal with it is along the lines suggested by the FASB in its exposure draft two and a half years ago. Improvements might be made, and subsequent discussion has indicated some that deserve consideration. The use of a fixed base, such as 1972, instead of a shifting base rolled over from one year to another, would help people to think in purchasing power units more easily; and the term, "dollars of 1972 purchasing power" could then be substituted for the vaguer term, "purchasing power units." The line drawn between monetary and nonmonetary items might be shifted a bit. And the full detail suggested by the FASB might be replaced by a more concise presentation. It should be sufficient, however, to distinguish the several sources of change in income and stockholder's equity, measured in constant dollars, and to make possible a reconciliation of these with the corresponding changes in the GAAP statements. The purchasing power statements should be supplementary to the GAAP statements, at least at this stage. And they should be required, not left to the discretion of the management of each company.

Given these supplementary statements, all concerned groups—not only controllers, auditors and users but also the various governmental agencies involved, as well as the Congress, and the media—could begin to acquire

[13]Such estimates have been made by Shoven and Bulow, and by Kopcke (see the bibliographical note). These estimates would raise the level of 1977 adjusted profits, but apparently not enough to bring current profits in the aggregate (measured in general purchasing power units) up to their 1966 level.

adequate understanding of the nature of the accounting problem caused by inflation, and of what is required to deal with it. It would be a mistake even if it were possible, to supplant the present statements with a set based on purchasing power units (or a combination of current values and purchasing power units) before this educational process had run its long course. In any case, the present GAAP statements must continue to be available because many institutional and contractual arrangements—in bond indentures, tax returns, and public utility reports, for example—are geared to them, and while these will eventually change, they will change only slowly.

Later, further and more leisurely steps could be taken to pursue the questions about current value accounting and about other components of GAAP. These are not as urgent. Current value accounting is not a substitute for purchasing power accounting, and discussion of current value accounting tends to spill over into a discussion of the entire conceptual framework of financial accounting and reporting, concerning which there appears—to an economist, at least—to be some considerable confusion that will not be easy to clear up.[14]

To conclude: While I have argued that the solution to the problem of inflation accounting should be the one proposed by the FASB in its exposure draft, with some modifications, I am not very hopeful that it—or any other solution—will be accepted soon, if it is accepted at all. In its comments on "the next step," mentioned earlier, the FASB states that with regard to the question of measurement, "the Board cannot foresee the next course of action that it may take . . . Proposals for change in the attribute presently measured and presented may require more specific and detailed consideration than the Discussion Memorandum provides and might well require experimentation before a pronouncement is developed." So also the AICPA's Task Force, which, when describing the objective of its experiment, states that it considers "any present action toward a resolution of such fundamental issues as very preliminary . . . helpful [only] in pointing the way toward the next step. That step may well be in the form of further experimentation . . ."

To return to the FASB, its hesitation to move ahead decisively is apparent also in its "tentative conclusion" that for transitional purposes its pronouncements on concepts should initially not be statements of policy binding on AICPA members, according to which noncompliance by an audit client must result in a qualification of the auditor's report. A separate, nonbinding class of pronouncements by the FASB would "provide time to assess the impact of those concepts on existing standards and practices and the related transitional problems pending a definitive conclusion. Those policies would serve not only to

---

[14]An example is the distinction, of which much is made in the FASB's discussion memorandum, between the asset/liability approach to the measurement of earnings and the matching of revenues and expenses approach. So far as I can see, the two approaches differ only because of differences in the treatment of value changes and in the definitions of revenues and expenses. These differences have nothing to do with the approach. Given consistent positions on the treatment of value changes and the definitions mentioned, they would—should—yield identical results. More specifically, as I tried to indicate earlier, depreciation and obsolescence expense is—in principle at least—identical with the decline in the current value to the business of the assets subject to depreciation and obsolescence. Estimating the one implies estimating the other. The estimates may differ, but not because of a basic difference in concept, point of view, or approach.

guide the Board itself . . . but also to guide financial statement preparers, auditors, and users in understanding and applying those standards and in resolving accounting questions for which no standards have been promulgated." The road ahead may stretch long into the future.

REFERENCES

American Institute of Certified Public Accountants, Task Force on Conceptual Framework for Accounting and Reporting, "Experimentation Program, Financial Accounting Models," April 1977.

Fabricant, Solomon, "Toward Rational Accounting in an Era of Unstable Money, 1936–1976," *National Report 16*, National Bureau of Economic Research, December 1976.

Financial Accounting Standards Board, "An Analysis of Issues Related to Reporting the Effects of General Price-Level Changes in Financial Statements," *FASB Discussion Memorandum*, February 1974.

———, *Public Record, 1974–Volume II, Part 1*: Position papers submitted in respect of Discussion Memorandum dated February 15, 1974; *Part 2:* Transcript of public hearing—held April 23–24, 1974.

———, "Proposed Statement of Financial Accounting Standards, Financial Reporting in Units of General Purchasing Power," *FASB Exposure Draft*, December 1974.

———, "An Analysis of Issues Related to Conceptual Framework for Financial Accounting and Reporting: Elements of Financial Statements and Their Measurement," *FASB Discussion Memorandum*, December 2, 1976.

———, "Scope and Implications of the Conceptual Framework Project," December 2, 1976.

———, "Tentative Conclusions on Objectives of Financial Statements of Business Enterprises," December 2, 1976.

———, "Field Tests of Financial Reporting in Units of General Purchasing Power," *Research Report*, May 1977.

Kopcke, R. W., "Current Accounting Practices and Proposals for Reform," *New England Economic Review*, Federal Reserve Bank of Boston, September/October 1976.

Securities and Exchange Commission, "Notice of Adoption of Amendments to Regulation S-X Requiring Disclosure of Certain Replacement Cost Data," Rule 3-17, Regulation S-X, *Accounting Series Release No. 190*, March 23, 1976.

Shoven, J. B., and Bulow, J. I., "Inflation Accounting and Nonfinancial Corporate Profits," *Brookings Papers on Economic Activity 3*, 1975, and 1, 1976.

PRODUCTIVITY IN ASIA'S DEVELOPING ECONOMIES: REFLECTIONS ON THE DESIGN, CONSTRUCTION AND ANALYSIS OF RELEVANT INFORMATION

Dr. Solomon Fabricant

1.1 Background

The 1979 Symposium or Workshop in Productivity Measurement was designated the third in a series. The idea of paying special attention to the measurement of productivity was discussed, and its pursuit approved, at the 13th session of the APO Governing Body in 1971. Recommendations on a large (but not, I believe, overly ambitious) framework were made by an expert group – of which I had the privilege of being a member – early in 1972. The recommendations centered on the measurement of "total factor productivity," in which output is compared with the combined input of labour and tangible capital, instead of with labour alone. But the expert group recognized the need for a step-by-step approach, beginning with the measurement of labour productivity in simple and then more complex ways, going on to measure capital productivity, and then total factor productivity, as the prior steps were mounted. The recommendations were considered by the APO Governing Body later that year. Subsequently, early in 1973, another expert group concentrated on the particular problems of productivity in agriculture, in which the productivity of land, as well as labour and reproducible capital, is especially important.

The first Workshop was approved, and then held in June 1973. After an assessment of its results in 1974, the Governing Body decided upon a Second Workshop, and this was held in 1975. In turn, after evaluation by the Governing Body, the third Symposium on Productivity Measurement was approved.

Let me present, by way of introduction to our deliberations, some reflections on the design, construction and analysis of the sort of information that is appropriate to our purpose.

2.1 The Purpose of Productivity Measurement

It is well to remember, first, that our task is not meant to be an exercise – mere gymnastic – undertaken for its own sake. The objective of productivity measurement is to develop information – more and better information – that, along with other information, will be helpful in the difficult task of improving the economic welfare of our fellow men. Productivity measurements, as with other economic information (including the insights or theories derived from economic measurement and analysis), are "instruments for the bettering of human life," as a great English economist put it long ago.

Anyone who looks around the world today, even casually, or has followed the course of economic development in some country, knows that the richer peoples of the globe are not rich because they work longer hours or work harder, or work both longer and harder. The situation is quite to the contrary. The rich work less, not more, and not as hard; the poor work more, not less, and they work harder. It is evident that the major source of the differences around the globe in average real incomes per capita is the differences in labour productivity. And more and more people are coming to appreciate also the fact that accounting for these differences in labour productivity are differences in capital per worker and in the efficiency with which labour and capital are used in production (measured by total factor productivity); and that still deeper, underlying these differences, are the incentives provided by the economic and social organization that induces men and women to save, to invest, and to seek means to greater efficiency. We need to know more about those differences – their levels and rates of change, and their sources – if policies and programmes to raise real income are to be effective.

It is with this need in mind that the APO has put stress on the quantitative measurement of productivity. The information sought is of a quantitative character because quantitative information is more useful than merely qualitative information. We organize this quantitative information in appropriate ways, and condense its content in the form of appropriate summaries. The summaries we make, by aggregation or averaging, are designed to enable us to grasp a mass of numerical details that could not otherwise be grasped. In the common language we use, we call these summaries index numbers. The nature of these summaries, and the terms or language in which we express them, have to be understood, if we are to communicate with one another easily. They must be learned by each of us. The language of productivity measurement, and the language of economics and statistics more generally, are not designed merely to impress outsiders.

I cannot be too emphatic in saying that productivity measurements are useful and important, so let me elaborate a bit.

It is no mere coincidence, for example, that the leaders of the communist countries as well as the free countries of the world constantly stress the importance of productivity and cite its measurements. Nor is it surprising that in the countries already well developed, as well as in the developing countries, whatever the regime, attention continues to be paid to productivity and productivity measurement. A recent hearing of the U.S. Congress's Joint Economic Committee was devoted to the subject of productivity because, as everyone agreed at the hearing, productivity growth is not only *a* source, it is the *major* source of a higher standard of living for the American people.

More explicitly, productivity measurements constitute vital elements in economic thinking and planning. Every long-term projection of real national product or of the product of a single region or industry, to illustrate, is derived, in the first place, by projecting two quantities. One is the number of workers or worker-hours; and the other is the productivity, that is, output per worker or hour of work of these persons. Further, because productivity is the more difficult to measure, more attention has to be paid to it and its sources. Refinements to take account of capital productivity and other sources are of importance precisely because they influence the level of labour productivity. Indeed, productivity measurements are among the considerations that enter into every plan for national or sectoral growth, every discussion of prices and wages, every conference on the problems of international trade and exchange rates, every calculation of the costs and benefits associated with or expected from public and private programmes and decisions, every debate on policy concerning employment and unemployment. The productivity level is among the considerations in every case because to understand and come to grips with these problems, and through dealing with them, to influence the level and distribution of income, requires attention to past, current, and prospective levels and rates of change of productivity.

2.2 "Learning by Doing" Productivity Measurement: A Continuous Process

I started by placing the present workshop in the context of the APO's current plan for the series of meetings of which this is one. But, and this is my second main point, productivity measurement is not a one-time or one-shot affair. It is a continuing process of improvement of our measurements and deepening of our understanding of what these measurements signify. It is a process that began in the APO, as well as outside it, well before 1971. And such work has a history, particularly in North America and Europe, that is much longer.

We may expect, further, that work on productivity measurement will continue indefinitely into the future, and the APO has already made its own intentions clear in its Rolling Five Year Plan for 1979-83. Recently, a number of experts in the U.S., from the government, business, labour, and academic halls, spent a substantial fraction of their time over a year or more in discussing the productivity statistics and measurements available in the U.S. and how to improve them. Their recommendations will be published later this year. And still other current efforts with the same objective in mind could readily be mentioned.

The efforts in the future, as in the past, will aim at developing more comprehensive, more detailed, and better quality information. Efforts will be made to improve the theoretical and statistical basis of the underlying data, the methods by which they are organized and summarized, and the lessons which can be drawn from their analysis. Efforts will continue and grow, to understand the sources or causes of change in the rates of growth of productivity and of differences in levels of productivity among countries, industries and establishments. For, as we know from experience, in the production of productivity measurements, as in the production of goods and services, we "learn by doing." The very process of working with and using the productivity measurements reveals gaps, ambiguities, and other imperfections in the measurements that deserve correction. We will always be in the position of regarding our current measurements only as the best approximations to date, and therefore subject to improvement. We want and seek better measures of aggregate output and of individual inputs, and a finer sector and industrial classification of output and input. Further, needs not yet recognized as needs, and needs recognized but not yet met, or not well met, with the available information, emerge: the demand for more and better information grows.

Nor should we forget the essential job of training successive generations in the preparation, interpretation, and use of productivity measurements. It goes without saying, that this is a perennial task. As long as higher productivity is a central objective of men's efforts to improve economic knowledge and thereby raise efficiency and the standard of living — and no one can see interest in and concern with these diminishing — we may expect organizations such as the APO to play a significant role in the future, as they have in the past, in this continuing work of research and education.

2.3 Even Approximations are Useful

Having stressed that productivity measurement is a continuing process of approximation, of learning and improving, of progress — as is true of measurements in other areas of economics, and also in areas outside of economics — I must hasten to add a note of assurance. We need not, and we should not, wait until perfection is reached before we put our measurements to use. "Perfection is not for man," as a great English moralist expressed it two centuries ago, and "since perfection cannot be reached...... he who will not easily be content without it....will lose the opportunity of doing well in the vain hope of unattainable excellence."

My third point, then, is that even first approximations can be useful, crude though they may be. For example, suppose output per worker has gone up over the past decade by about 25 percent, according to our best estimates. These estimates, we know, are rough because the measure of output and the measure of employment come from two different sources and therefore lack close comparability. To express the range of uncertainty arising from this imperfect comparability, we may prefer to say that the 25 percent is simply the central estimate in a distribution ranging from about 20 to about 30 percent. We explicitly acknowledge the limits on our knowledge. Yet to know this much is to know that labour productivity, as we have measured it, has at least gone up; and we can say that it has gone up probably at something within sight of 2 percent per annum, and perhaps even as much as 2.5 percent per annum. Or, to change the example a bit, suppose we view the 25 percent increase in output per worker as a good enough estimate of itself, but only as an approximation to the increase in output per worker-hour. Knowing that hours have generally fallen slightly, even though the exact figure is unknown, we can legitimately say that output per man-hour has increased by at least 25 percent, and probably by a little more. We might even view the rise in output per worker as an approximation to the rise in total factor productivity, when we believe that capital per worker has not risen too rapidly, and that its weight in the calculation of total factor productivity is of the order of only 20 or 25 percent.

Our purpose here, further, is not only to learn how to measure productivity, or to measure it better. We want, also, to learn how to put the measurements to use, how to draw inferences or at least raise questions, on the basis of the figures. And we can proceed to do so. To continue with our initial example, an average annual increase of 2 percent in output per worker provides a statistic important in judging what may have been or will be likely by way of an increase in average real wages. An increase in real wages in excess of the increase in output per worker is not impossible, but it would mean a rise in the fraction of real national income going to labour, and a corresponding decline in the fraction going to capital. An argument urging an increase in real wages in excess of the increase in output per worker, then, should be accompanied by reasons why the fraction of income going to capital could be reduced without meeting serious political obstacles or, ultimately, without deleterious economic consequences.

A great deal can be learned also by comparing the rates of change in productivity among different industries and establishments. Rates that differ greatly from the average stand out and deserve special attention. Also, the industrial differences revealed have significant consequences for industrial differences in rates of price increase, employment, and other economic variables — one of the topics to be addressed in your papers, and to be discussed more fully in my later remarks.

Similarly for regional comparisons, and also comparisons among countries. The desirability of inter-country comparisons is the reason why the APO places emphasis on the comparability of the measurements among the member countries. In our discussions here our time will surely allow for comparisons of rates of productivity change among the countries represented at this meeting and also with countries not members of the APO. After we depart, however, there will of course be much more time available. You, and I hope the APO also, will consider making systematic comparisons of the results presented in the various papers prepared for the meeting. This would be in addition to the comparison of methods, such as appears in the helpful comments prepared by Professor Kurosawa on the papers submitted to the APO's Second Workshop on Productivity Measurement.

2.4 Recognition of Margins of Error

Measurements of productivity are approximations, if only because the basic data on output, employment, and so on, are necessarily rough. Even comprehensive census data seldom cover 100 percent of the population; and the data obtained in samples — which are increasingly coming to be utilized — are necessarily surrounded by margins of error. Nor can we be fully confident that the information reported in census or survey schedules are entirely accurate, for they depend on the records kept by the respondents, which are often incomplete, and on their recollections of past events, which are often dim.

This being the case it is well to avoid clothing our measurements with a spurious or false air of precision. We should not present the basic data to the last digit, or the indexes to two decimal points (as has been done in some of the papers delivered at earlier meetings) when the underlying data are simply not accurate enough to warrant it. It is misleading to do so. It is also wasteful of time and space to make the calculations and to typewrite the figures. A table given in digits or even thousands, when the important figures are in the millions, can be cut drastically without significant loss. All that is necessary is to use some judgment on the number of digits really required and to "round out" the residue in accordance with the standard rule of rounding. The results will also be easier for the reader to grasp and understand. This is not a minor consideration.

Another suggestion, relevant in this connection, concerns the variety of productivity measurements, such as those listed in the table on pages 18 and 19 of the August 1978 edition of "A Tentative Methodology of Productivity Measurement." One may wish to calculate the full list to see how different the index of output per worker is from the index of output per worker-hour, for example. But even for this purpose, it may often be quite sufficient, initially, to limit the calculations to the end-years of the period being covered, and stop short of a calculation for all years between, if the differences between the end-year results turn out to be miniscule. Also, when the full set of calculations is made, the presentation need not always be as full. The text tables need not reproduce the detailed worksheets. It may be quite enough to say, in the text or a footnote, that the detailed differences are too small to be worth presenting; and even when worth presenting, they could be relegated to an appendix and the main text can then concentrate on the major findings.

Because the basic data are always, in one way or another, approximate, they are subject to revision as information is added. The extent to which revision has been made is itself a useful piece of information. It is helpful in judging the degree of accuracy that may be ascribed to the basic data and the results based on them. When significant, the revisions are worth noting, at least briefly, and reasons for the revision provided, to the extent possible. Revisions can be expressed in absolute as well as relative form as we all know; the latter is more useful, but sometimes both may be worth attention.

Sometimes, flaws in the basic data are uncovered without revision being possible. This also should be mentioned, for as with the extent of revision, it is helpful to the user of calculations that must be based on the defective data.

Apart from defects and revision in the basic data, index numbers calculated from them may also come to be revised. This may happen as coverage is expanded, shifts made in the formula or base-period or weights used in combining diverse outputs, or for other reasons. Comparisons of the earlier and later estimates are then worth making, and notes on the revisions included if they are of sufficient importance. Otherwise, however, a very brief mention that the revisions are not important may be quite sufficient. Sometimes, as often happens in economic statistics, there is no clear choice between one formula or base or another; it may then be worthwhile to present the results of both to indicate by how much they differ; or, when that is the case, to mention that they do not in fact differ significantly.

3.1 Productivity Measurement a Cooperative Process

I have mentioned that productivity measurement is a process of learning, involving successive stages in the construction, analysis, and application of the measurements. It follows, then, that the persons in a country engaged in productivity measurement must be in constant communication with those of their compatriots who are charged with the responsibility for gathering the basic data and putting the measurements based on them to use.

By constant communication, I mean not only the exchange of reports, but also frequent dialogue leading to interaction. What is required is a "two-way street" at every stage.

Thus, the gatherers of data, stationed in the census or sampling establishment, should be kept informed of the use made of their data. They should be told of the results, including those that may raise questions about the accuracy of the data. Suggestions for improvement of the data on this and other accounts should be made to them; and they in turn should be asked to make suggestions to the productivity measurers on the best way to use the data. Such intercourse is not easy, with vested interests often differing, but the obstacles should be overcome. It would make for better data and better measurements. The gatherers will also be stimulated to do better, as they see the results of their work being put to use, rather than merely being relegated to dusty library shelves.

Similarly, there should be constant communication with those in the central bank or other government agency preparing the national accounts for the UN Statistical Office, in the planning agencies using the various figures, and the economists, statisticians, accountants, and engineers in the productivity and other agencies engaged at the industry and establishment levels in trying to improve productivity. The productivity measurements can and should be put to use, even at this stage, to measure progress, to point to backward areas or areas of stagnation, to set goals.

And, of course, a dialogue with those in the universities and other academic institutions, is highly desirable. A good deal of what is involved in productivity measurement is statistical theory, practical index number computation, and the relations between output and input set forth in the production functions of economic theory. Too many students learn only the abstractions of statistical and economic theory; they are not taught and do not learn how to compute a production index.

It is hardly necessary to add that exchange of ideas and information between countries also is useful. That is why we have joined together in this and other APO enterprises.

The interest of the APO and most of you here is, I gather, mainly in productivity at the plant and industry level. Yet measurements at these levels need to be reasonably consistent with those at the aggregate or macro level. In any case, what is learned at the lower levels of aggregation can help to explain some of the changes revealed at the macro level and vice versa. This is why it is important to understand the way in which index numbers at different levels of aggregates are related to one another.

We do have assembled here representatives from one or another of almost all of the groups I have mentioned. But not more than two or three such groups from any one country are represented here. I would like to be surer than I am, that when you return home, you will inform the others as fully as possible of what has been learned here. After all, these meetings can last only a few days. Their function is primarily to provide material for digestion at home. I recognize that not every country here needs to be reminded of the need I have been discussing, but perhaps one or two do, and trust the others will pardon me.

4.1 Special Problems of the Asian Countries

Mention has been made by the Governing Body of the need to develop techniques of measuring productivity "suitable for Asian countries." Westerners might confess to being surprised, on first reading this, by the implication that what is suitable for non-Asian countries is not the same as that which is suitable for Asian countries. They would ask, are we not all involved in problems of measurement that are, viewed scientifically, identical in all countries? Products will vary among countries – in Europe and elsewhere, as in Asia – they would say, and so will inputs, technologies, forms of industrial organization, levels of development, and the roles of government in guiding or regulating economic affairs. But these differences are, from the point of view of the technique of measurement, differences in details. The problems of measurement raised by the differences, they would say, are differences of degree rather than of kind.

Yet, on reflection, they would allow that these differences of degree deserve attention. Problems that would be minor in one situation, may be more serious in another situation because of these differences. There is, indeed, merit in the request made by the Governing Body, and I take a moment to discuss it. The problems associated with the differences mentioned may fairly be said to arise from differences even among the Western countries and even among the Asiatic countries, as well as between Asian countries as a group and Western countries. But I must concentrate on the latter, and because I must also be brief, I shall simply enumerate the more important problems and confine myself to a few remarks on each.

4.2 Nature of Data

A major difference, with obvious exceptions, between the Asiatic countries and the Western is in the quantity and quality of statistical data available for productivity measurement. Most Asiatic countries are, in this respect, at the stage that the more developed countries were generations ago. True, virtually every country now puts together an annual set of national accounts, something hardly any country had before World War I, and few before World War II. But these national accounts are too often based on data no better than the data available in the U.S. or Britain a century ago. It is because much of the Asiatic data are crude, that I stressed earlier in my remarks that even crude data can be useful, and we should do the best we can with them while making a serious effort to improve the data and widen their scope – one of the aims of the dialogue between those measuring productivity and those providing the data.

4.3 Scarcity of Personnel

The persons trained in the theory and practical aspects of economics, statistics, and accounting necessary in making productivity measurements are relatively scarce in most of the Asiatic countries. Again, it is with this in mind that I stressed the desirability of the dialogues mentioned earlier, and the need for practical as well as theoretical education, and why I feel that these meetings of ours and the Tentative Methodology provided by the APO are helpful. I would add only the observation that the Methodology could be even more helpful were the presentation in it put more in terms of plain English than in terms of symbols and formulas, with the latter relegated to second place, or even to a technical appendix. Even an experienced statistician, thumbing through the Methodology, might be repelled initially by what seems to be a formidable list of productivity indices, such as is provided on pages 18 and 19, and by the task of keeping in mind the meaning of the symbols used there. But of course, the August 1978 edition of the Methodology is clearly labelled "tentative," and we may expect to see improvements as it becomes more definitive.

4.4 Problems of Measurement

Because so large a fraction of output, in most Asiatic countries, is agricultural and for home consumption, or small-scale manufacturing, and so much of labour input is of a family type, the problems of measuring output and input, and deriving productivity indices, are more difficult than in the industrialized countries. The problems of measuring entrepreneurial and family labour arise there also – they are still vexing problems even in the U.S., for example but they are of relatively minor importance and the crude solutions to which we are all reduced do not seriously affect the final indexes of productivity in agriculture and manufacturing in the more advanced countries.

4.5 Effects of Development

The substantial relative importance of small-scale farming and manufacturing in the Asiatic countries causes special difficulties in measuring productivity. There is the further fact that this importance has been declining sharply as economic development has accelerated. This decline also has significant implications for the measurement and analysis of productivity growth, as is mentioned in the Tentative Methodology. A measure of output, input or productivity limited to the large-scale, commercialized or plantation type of farm or to the large factory, will provide an incomplete, and generally biased measure of change in farming or manufacturing as a whole. In the U.S., and Soviet Russia, for example, the bias has been substantial, entirely too serious to be neglected, and efforts have had to be made to deal with it. Further, the value of output per worker in small-scale agriculture or industry is almost always lower, on the average, than the value of output per worker in large-scale agriculture or industry. For this reason, the shift of workers and other resources from small to large-scale establishments that takes place during economic development contributes to the rise of productivity in the total of both small and large-scale establishments. This contribution has been great enough to be counted as a separate source of economic growth in the U.S. and other countries, under the caption of "Improved Resource Allocation," the term used by Edward Denison.

4.6 Double-deflation Method

Another problem, related to the imperfections of the data and to the small average scale of economic organization, causes difficulties in measuring capital input and material input even more than in measuring output and labour input. Thus, also, there are difficulties in measuring total factor productivity and output by the double-deflation method. The double-deflation method is not easy to apply, with sufficient accuracy, even in the countries with good statistics, for it is extremely sensitive to errors in the data. I would therefore put the double-deflation method low on the priority list of productivity measurements; and at a later point, I will suggest an alternative less subject to error, but still useful – perhaps even more useful for some purposes. As for capital input, as the Experts suggested in their memorandum of 1972, the problem is not insuperable. The national accounts at least provide a rough estimate of gross capital formation or investment. Estimates of depreciation and obsolescence are not entirely out of the question; because of rapid growth, it is not essential to have a stock figure at the beginning of the period to be covered in order to develop a "perpetual inventory" type of estimate of the gross or net capital stock.

4.7 Government Regulation

Of major importance is the fact that, in many Asiatic countries, government's role in regulating the private sector, participating in production and investment directly, directing economic relations with other countries, and generally influencing the course of the economy, is greater in many respects than in the industrialized countries of the West. More direct participation, subsidies, taxes, rationing and other controls, tend to influence the relative market prices used in measuring and combining the diverse outputs and inputs that enter the calculation of productivity change. These relative prices therefore reflect marginal productivities less adequately than would relative prices set in a free market. As a result the measurements derived report less accurately than they otherwise would, the changes in productivity that we seek to measure. This, you will recognize, involves the differences between social and private costs or benefits. These tend to be wider apart in the Asiatic countries, on the average, than in economies in which the free market is less restricted and less influenced by the activities of government. To try to "correct" the available relative prices, however, would involve the calculation of "shadow prices," the term used to denote the prices that would prevail in the absence of the distortions resulting from the role of government. To determine shadow prices encounters theoretical, statistical, and even political problems of a most difficult and controversial nature. About all we can do, at this stage of our effort to measure productivity, is to note the fact that for this reason also, our productivity measurements must be viewed as no more than approximations.

You will understand that much of what I have said about the "distortions" in the price system caused by government can also be said about those caused by imperfections of competition that arise without the help or even despite the efforts of government. To the extent that these imperfections are materially greater in the Asiatic countries than elsewhere, the reservations surrounding the productivity measurements must also be greater.

5.1 Toward Uniformity of Measurements

The fact of rather wide variation among Asiatic countries in the quantity and quality of the statistical data needed for productivity measurement — reported by the APO member countries in their responses to the APO's questionnaire on data availability — deserves a word. It is this variation that underlies the request of of the Governing Body for a set of uniform measurements. Output per man-hour may be a better measure of labour productivity than output per worker, and it may therefore be desirable to compare productivity growth in different countries by referring to their measures of output per man-hour. But if only output per worker is available for one of the countries, and it is known that hours changed appreciably in that country, its output per worker would be a seriously biased measure of its output per worker-hour. It would then be better to limit the comparison of productivity growth in that country with those in other countries to output per worker. For countries that do have measures of output per worker-hour, the comparison can of course be made of these.

Countries vary also in the classification and detail of their data. To overcome this problem requires imposing a degree of uniformity on the industrial classification of each country. A country may have to limit its measurement to rather gross categories because of lack of data. For comparison with countries that supply a more detailed industrial set of indexes, comparison with the less favoured country can be made only through a consolidation of the detailed sub-classes into the grosser classes available for the other. To meet this requirement, a uniform industrial classification is necessary, and the Tentative Methodology has, as you know, suggested uses of the UN ISIC, with which you are all familiar. It should be understood that even a uniform industrial classification does not guarantee perfect comparability, since the comparability of products, materials, and processes that constitute the basis of the classification will still vary from one country to another because of differences in tastes, resource availability, and economic organization.

5.2 Coverage Problem

Even when the data on output and employment (and also capital assets, materials consumed, and other resources) come from the same source, such as a census of manufactures, they are not entirely comparable. The problem arises in explicit form when the data on output of a firm or industry refer to the quantities of goods produced, and the list of these goods falls short of the full range of goods produced, as they usually do. Data will be lacking on the output of small-volume products, products largely produced in other industries ("secondary products"), repair parts and services, and "in-house" construction. Only for the primary products, and then only for the more important products, will data even be requested in the survey schedule and thus be reported. An index number made up of these will not quite accurately reflect or "cover" the entire output.

The extent of the bias resulting will depend on the degree of coverage, and on the relative difference between the changes in the covered output and in the uncovered output. If the uncovered products are new and have been growing rapidly at the expense of the covered products, for example, the bias will not be negligible; the comparability of the output and input will not be as full as it may seem to be on its face. One solution, favoured in calculating indexes of output in the U.S. and elsewhere, is to make use of a "coverage adjustment." This usually assumes, on the basis of various reasonable criteria, that the price trends of the covered and uncovered products move on the average more closely together than do their respective output trends. Whether the assumption is justified in any particular case is always a question; but I would judge that it is acceptable in those cases in which the coverage ratio is high.

Often, the index of physical output is derived not directly from physical volume data, as just described, but rather from value data deflated by an index of the prices of the kinds of goods produced by the firm or industry. Seldom, however, does the price index fully cover all the products involved. In this case, then, the coverage adjustment is implicit. It rests on essentially the same assumption as does the coverage adjustment in the preceding case, and the same question arises.

Much the same may be said of groups of industries for which productivity indexes are calculated, when indexes for some of the industries in the group are lacking. In this case also, a coverage adjustment should be and usually is made, if the assumption involved appears justified.

When the assumption does not appear to be justified, it is generally better to limit the output and productivity calculation to those firms or industries for which the required data are available, and avoid claiming full coverage. This, in fact, is what is done in the U.S. and some other countries when productivity estimates are restricted to the private domestic business sector, on the ground that output (or sometimes even employment) data for the other sectors are insufficient and no satisfactory coverage adjustment can be made. These other sectors include general government, owner-occupied housing, and the foreign sector.

A similar problem arises when the value added in manufacturing, as reported in the usual census, is taken to represent the gross national product originating in the industry. But in this case, the census value added is grosser than the GNP originating. Census value added is simply gross value of products less cost of materials, fuel and supplies; other purchases from industries -- intermediate products, particularly of the service industries and government (paid for in the form of taxes) -- are not deducted. These other intermediate products are relatively more important, and have been growing more rapidly, than most statisticians realize. In fact, these changes in inter-industry relations are characteristic of a dynamic or developing economy, as study of input-output tables has made clear. Little can be done about this problem; it is simply another reason why productivity indexes must be viewed as approximations even in the circumstances prevailing in an economy, such as the U.S., otherwise richly supplied with statistical data.

6.1 An Alternative to the Double-Deflation Index of Productivity

The double-deflation measure of net output was devised in order to provide a set of industry and sectoral indexes of production that were fully consistent with, and in the same form as, the measure of national output, GNP. The double-deflation measure for an individual industry is, however, highly sensitive to inaccuracies and gaps in the data. It involves the difference between two estimates, the real gross output of the industry and its real purchases from other industries -- "intermediate products." Both of these are subject to error, and the difference between them is subject to the combined errors.

There is, however, an alternative to real net output (as calculated by the double-deflation method) per unit of total input -- the index of total factor productivity. This alternative is less sensitive to error, and in some ways is superior to the former for studying changes within individual industries (or firms). It is the productivity index described in my article on "Productivity" in the *International Encyclopedia of the Social Sciences* as the index of "output per unit of labour, capital, and material input." In this index the gross real output of an industry is compared not only with the services of the labour and tangible capital employed by the industry, but also with these plus materials, components, fuel, supplies, and other commodities and services purchased from other industries – to the extent that information for each of the latter is available. In other words, instead of subtracting these purchases from the numerator of the productivity ratio, they are added to the denominator.

The resulting productivity measure is, then, also an index of total factor productivity, but it is not what is conventionally meant by that term. The national measure of total factor productivity is of course the conventional ratio of net output (real GNP) to labour and capital combined, thus excluding intermediate products from both numerator and denominator. It can be shown, however, that this national measure of total factor productivity is a weighted average of the alternative indexes of total factor productivity measured gross in both numerator and denominator of intermediate products. The weights are of a different sort, naturally, as required by the difference in form of the national and the industry indexes. When the industry indexes are of the form, "net output per unit of labour and capital input," the weight for an industry is the ratio of its net output to GNP; when the industry indexes are of the form, "gross output per unit of labour, capital and material input," the weight for an industry is the ratio of its gross output to GNP. The sum of the latter weights, it may be noted, will be greater than one. (This weight scheme was proposed originally by Domar in 1961; subsequent analyses by others have confirmed the validity of Domar's suggestion.)

The alternative measure of total factor productivity has the advantage of explicitly showing materials, fuel, etc., as inputs that may be substituted for labour and capital, and vice versa. Since the dramatic rise in the relative price of petroleum in 1973 and the subsequent rises in the prices of fertilizer and other intermediate and final products using petroleum, this implicit expression is an especially desirable feature in the analysis and understanding of productivity change.

11

I have been following the convention of using the term, "total factor productivity." I should therefore note that in the U.S. we are beginning to shift to another term, "multi-factor productivity." The reason lies in the somewhat misleading word "total". Even in the narrow sense of "factor", which is generally confined to the basic or primary factors, labour and capital (including land), the capital generally available for statistical purposes does not cover the intangible capital invested in research and development. This is why I have found it desirable to speak of tangible capital, rather than simply of capital, at least at the outset of a discussion, and why "total factor input" incorrectly describes what is only "labour and tangible capital input".

7.1 Distribution of the Gains from Higher Labour Productivity

One of the subjects proposed for inclusion in each of the country papers prepared for this Symposium is the correlation between change in labour productivity and change in other economic variables, such as wages, prices, employment, and profits. It will be interesting to us, in our review of the papers, to see how these correlations compare with one another and with those found to characterize the interrelations between labour productivity and other economic variables in the developed countries. Study of the nature and degree of these correlations, and of the economic behaviour they reflect, is of great value in understanding the dynamics of economic development and its implications for policy.

As a preface to our review of these sections of the country papers, therefore, it would be useful to recall what some of the correlations have been in the United States, and how they have been interpreted there. I shall draw on the many studies of the subject made at the National Bureau of Economic Research and other research institutions in the U.S., and on a monograph I presented in June of last year to the Joint Economic Committee.

I begin with some introductory remarks on the distribution of the gains from higher labour productivity, before considering the relation between labour productivity and wages.

The dominant factor in the 85 percent increase in average real income per capita in the U.S. since World War II was productivity growth. This does not necessarily mean that the increase was widely distributed among the people. That depends on what happened to the distribution of families by size of income during the same period — a question that has disturbed people as much in the developing countries as in those already at advanced stages of development. The crucial additional fact — in the U.S., at least — is that the size distribution of income changed but little over the post-war period; if anything, it became somewhat less, rather than more, widely dispersed. Combining the two facts, we may conclude that on the average the real incomes of American families at *all* levels of income also rose by something like 85 percent. We may say, therefore, that in this general rise in income, the dominant factor was also growth in productivity.

We can, I think, take this conclusion to apply to all or most countries. Even in those countries in which the distribution of income may have worsened somewhat, as some people fear has been the case, the change in the distribution would be of minor importance compared with the upward shift in the whole distribution — essentially the point made by the Italian economist, Pareto, many years ago.

The distribution of income may also be expressed in terms of the conventional categories of income going to labour and to capital. But in these terms, the gains from productivity growth reached workers in the form of higher real wages and better "fringe benefits" (such as payment for vacations, sick leave, and medical bills), to which may be added something for net improvements in working conditions. The gains from productivity growth reached investors and savers in the form of a more or less sustained rate of return on their capital — a rate that would otherwise have been pushed down as capital became relatively more plentiful in relation to the number of people in the labour force, and therefore cheaper. The gains from productivity reached the public at large, including those in the lower-income groups possessing neither capital nor able to perform remunerative labour, as higher tax revenues from increased real national income enabled government to provide more and better public services and to alleviate the lot of the poor.

7.2 Labour Productivity and Real Wages

We are now ready to take a closer look at the relation between labour income and labour productivity.

A person who reads about large-scale wage negotiations might suppose that the major market forces which affect real wages are labour unions, which try to raise wages; business people, who try to keep wages down; and government, which sometimes seems to be trying to do both. Although all market forces operate through people — workers, employers, government officials — it would be wrong to think of them as influencing earnings only when they are involved in activities that get into the news.

In the long run, workers influence the real wages and salaries they receive, mainly by devoting time and effort and money to improving the quality of the labour services they can offer and by moving from jobs that pay less to those that pay more. Labour unions are important in labour-management relations, it is true. They influence the conditions of work, the production process, and, undoubtedly, the money wages (and even the real wages) which their own membership receives. There may also be some "spill-over" effects of wage increases on the wages of non-union workers. But unions have only a modest (if any) effect on the *general* level of real wages. In part, this is because, in the U.S., less than a fourth of the labour force is unionized. In part, it is because the power of a union – even the strongest – is limited by competition between its members and workers in other industries or other places (sometimes other countries) and by competition between members and machines or other labour substitutes. When wages are pushed up too rapidly, work tends to be shifted to workers elsewhere or to substitutes that would otherwise be too expensive.

In the long run, business people influence the wages and salaries they pay by activities aimed at making profits for themselves. They develop new products, try new materials, improve methods of production, open new markets, invest in more and better capital equipment. They seek the labour needed to operate their equipment and to use the new methods and materials. They may often go to considerable expense to enable their help to work with the new machinery, methods, and materials by training the workers on the job. And they try to combine their labour, capital, and technology in the most efficient manner possible to produce the old and new products that offer the best prospects of profits. Business people in an industry may get together to fight a large wage increase; but it is just as true that they are almost always competing for labour with one another, with other industries, and sometimes with other countries.

In the long run, government's influence on the real wages and salaries received by workers through-out the country occur less by intervention in the wage-determination process than by other activities. Real wages are pulled up when government devotes its energies to strengthening law and order, improv-ing public services, removing physical and other obstacles to trade and the movement of people, capital, and enterprise, educating the young and informing the old, stabilizing the economy, and supporting the research, dissemination of information, and other activities that can yield rich returns to society at large.

In short, the average national real wage and salary rate is pushed up mainly by improvement in the quality of labour, by investment in tangible capital, and by increased efficiency in the use of labour and capital. An increase in any of these will exert an upward pressure on average wages and salaries by making labour more valuable in production. For in the long run, and in the U.S. at least, there is enough competition to ensure labour a wage or salary commensurate with its value in production.

7.3 Trends in Real Earnings

The index of national labour productivity – output per hour – reflects all three of the influences named, appropriately combined. We may expect, therefore, that the trend in the national real earnings rate will move closely with the trend in the national labour productivity index. The historical facts support this expectation.

However, the degree of similarity is somewhat less when shorter periods are examined; and when year-to-year changes are compared, there is still less similarity. Sometimes changes in real earnings from one year to the next are substantially greater than the corresponding changes in output per hour, and sometimes they are substantially less. Occasionally, even, the two move in opposite directions. This is because the major factors underlying the long-term trend in real hourly earnings do not exert their effects without delay, interference, or interruption. Other factors, which wash out in the long run, also play their part and are important in the short run.

To illustrate, consider the effect of inflation. Changes in the general level of prices are in effect put aside when money earnings are deflated and we concentrate on *real* earnings. This procedure is sufficient to exclude the effects of changes in price level from the long-term trend of real earnings. But it cannot exclude all the effects of price level changes from the shorter-term changes in real earnings. Delays are frequent in the response of money wages to changes in the cost of living; and delays may be even longer in the response of salary rates to changes in the cost of living. A speeding-up of price inflation, for example, will tend to be followed by a speeding-up of the rate of increase in wages and salaries. But for a time there may be a *decline* in the rate of growth of *real* wages and salaries. Indeed, when the price level accelerates very sharply, real salaries and even real wage rates may actually fall for a while, not simply rise less rapidly than before. When there is a slowing-down of price inflation, these lags will tend to work in the other direction.

The parallel trends between productivity and real wages, to which I have been referring, are characteristic of the *general* level of real wages and the trend in *national* productivity. It is important to understand that this close matching of trends is not characteristic of the trend of wages in an individual industry and the trend in the industry's own productivity. The explanation for the difference can be found in the way an economy operates. Suppose wage and salary rates in any of the industries in which labour productivity had risen very rapidly, were pushed up by their rapid increases in labour productivity. Suppose, also, that wage and salary rates in industries in which labour productivity had risen very slowly were held down by their slow increases in labour productivity. What would result? Disparities in wages and salaries between these two groups of industries would become enormous — indeed, untenable. Even the most severe obstacles to competition, obstacles not only between workers, but also between workers and substitutes for workers in the form of machines and materials, could not preserve such disparities. In fact, large disparities could not arise in the first place, except in the most exceptional circumstances, or last very long when they did appear.

The historical information on trends in individual industries in the U.S. (and other countries) supports this reasoning also. The long-term rise in real hourly earnings in an industry has been closely related to the rise in national output per hour but not to the rise in that industry's own output per hour. In fact, the relationship between the long-term change in an industry's hourly earnings and the long-term change in its own output per hour is small and not significant. This means that trends in the real wages of individual industries, as well as the trend of the national average real wage, were dominated by the economy-wide factors summarized by the trend in *national* output per hour. Hourly earnings in individual industries moved up more or less together — something to be expected in an economy in which workers and employers respond to wage differentials.

However, this is not to say that we should find *closely* parallel changes among the average rates of wages paid by different industries, and it would be surprising if we did. In the American economy, as in other economies, economic advance has brought not only greater efficiency, improved quality of labour, and more tangible capital per worker — the factors that push up real wages in every country — but also other changes. These have occurred in the type of labour used by an industry in the relative scarcity of the skills it employs, in the incentives the industry offers workers to accept technological and other changes, in the values placed on the various non-pecuniary advantages and disadvantages of working in it, and in other determinants of demand and supply. So continuous has the flow of these changes been that adjustment to them has never been completed. Therefore, also to be expected are exceptions to the rule that wages in different industries move together, paralleling national output per hour, and these exceptions appear in the record.

What I have just said about the U.S. will hardly apply exactly to any other country. Mention has already been made of some of the institutional and other differences between countries like the U.S. and the Asiatic countries. We may expect that these will influence the relation between labour productivity and real wages, and in each of the member countries it will differ from the relation I have described. But I would be greatly surprised if the two failed to bear a considerable resemblance to one another.

7.4 Labour Productivity and Relative Price Changes

Essentially the same can be expected of the relation between labour productivity and relative price changes in individual industries, to which I now turn.

In the U.S. all industries, with few, if any, exceptions, have experienced long-term rises in output per hour. But the rate of increase has varied greatly. If industries whose productivity rises over the long-run more rapidly than the average have not pushed up their wages more rapidly than the average, to whom has the benefit of their higher productivity growth gone? A similar question may be raised about industries whose productivity rise has been less than average, but whose wages have generally tended to keep up with the general wage level. Who has had to pay for the higher wages?

The main part of the answer to both questions is that firms with above average productivity growth have, as a rule, voluntarily or under the pressure of competition reduced their prices; or, during inflation, raised them less than prices on the average. Examples are easy to find, and I am sure each of you can think of some in your own country.

There is more to the story, however, in your country as in mine. Consumers tend to buy more of the now cheaper, and less of the now more expensive, goods and services. And when the more expensive goods and services — health services are an example in the U.S. — are wanted despite their higher relative prices because cheaper substitutes were not available, consumers can generally afford them because their incomes were rising with the increase in national productivity. The higher costs thus tend to be offset. On net balance, the consumer price index has risen less than the money incomes of consumers.

To avoid confusion, it must be kept in mind that the relationship between change in the general price level and change in national or overall productivity is *not* being described. The determinants of the general price level lie primarily in the monetary and fiscal realm. They are not the only factors, however, since the price level depends also on the supply of goods and services that is being "chased" by the money, and on the amount of cash people want to hold. Productivity does help determine the supply of goods and services, as was noted earlier, and this can be a significant factor in accounting for the behaviour of the general price level in the short run. But productivity is usually only a minor element in the determination of the general price level in the long-term.

I have already suggested why changes in the relative productivity levels of industries would be associated with changes (in the opposite direction) in relative price levels, but it is worthwhile to specify the reasons.

Given time for the necessary adjustments, competition makes for equality of price and cost per unit (including a normal profit), therefore of relative price and relative cost per unit, and therefore also of changes in these. A major determinant of cost per unit is productivity – output per hour. When productivity rises, less labour is needed to produce a unit of output, and costs tend to fall. While all, or virtually all, industries experienced a rise in productivity in the U.S., the rise was large in some industries and small in others. In those industries in which the rise was large, costs per unit tended to fall more than in the industries in which the rise in efficiency was modest. Under the pressure of competition, relative prices adjusted themselves accordingly.

Although we should expect, and we find, changes in productivity and price to be related, we should not expect, and we do not find, the relationship to be at all perfect. Labour productivity is a major determinant of price, but it is not the only determinant. The relative price of an industry may therefore change more or less than appears to be warranted by its relative productivity change, even given time for adjustment. How much more or less will depend on the importance and behaviour of the determinants other than productivity. Sometimes they are so powerful as to cause relative price and productivity to move in the same rather than in opposite directions.

Among the factors that influence the relative prices of an industry's products, but are not covered by the measure of labour productivity, are changes in the efficiency with which materials, fuel, and services purchased from other industries are put to use. When fuel, for example, is especially important to an industry, as it is to electric power stations, and economies in the utilization of fuel have been very great, the costs and therefore the relative prices of the industry will tend to fall more than would be suggested by the change in its use of labour alone. The result will be the same if an industry has learned to get much more out of its raw materials by using better extractive processes and by turning wastes into useful by-products, as has the cottonseed products industry, or if it has learned to make a more satisfactory product with a thinner coating of protective material, as has the tinplate industry.

The relation between price and output per hour will be altered also in industries that have increased the quantities of capital goods, materials, fuel, and the like, per unit of product, purchased in order to economize on their own labour. The prices that an industry has to pay for these non-labour inputs are also involved. When these prices rise more rapidly than the prices paid by other industries – all other changes being equal – we may expect the relative selling prices of the industry to rise more rapidly than would be indicated solely by the change in the industry's own relative productivity. The electric power industry, greatly affected by the surge in petroleum prices since 1973, again provides the example.

The prices of different raw materials, fuel, and equipment do not move closely together, for the industries producing them do not experience similar rates of productivity increase. Even wage rates (which move much more closely together in different industries than do other input prices) do not exactly parallel one another. In effect, then, the factory price of a refrigerator will reflect changes in the efficiency of *every* industry that is directly or indirectly involved in the production of refrigerators – not only refrigerator manufacturing, but also trucking, power, and the industries which produce electric motors and compressors, cartons, steel sheet, paints, and so on. Looking in the other direction, the productivity of the paint manufacturing industry, and the price of paint, will influence the price of all products in which paint is used – which means virtually every product. But the influence of the price of paint will be greater in some cases than in others. The relation between any particular industry's relative price and relative productivity is thus bound to be loose.

When an industry is not fully competitive, that, too, may influence the relation between the price of the products and its productivity. The adjustment of prices to changes in productivity will be impeded. But this is largely a short-run factor, usually overcome in time. In the long run, competition is felt in most industries.

When the period of time is short, however, imperfections of competition and other factors make for more and bigger differences between changes in relative price and in relative productivity than when the period is long. Lags become important. Less time is available for adjustments of prices to costs as conditions alter. Even with allowance for anticipations, the correlation between price and productivity is weaker.

The immediate impact of increased demand, for example, is largely on price and profits. Prices go up and so do profits. Until new plants are constructed by companies already in the industry, or by outsiders attracted by the high profits, prices will be "out of line" with costs and with productivity. Decreases in demand work in the other direction. The initial impact is on relative prices and profits, and prices will remain out of line with costs and productivity until capacity has been retired.

There are also temporary rises and falls in demand during expansions and contractions of the business-cycle kind. These cyclical changes in demand, and the other developments that take place during business cycles, will make the short-term relation between prices and productivity somewhat different from the long-term relation. The difference will be greater in the "cyclically sensitive" industries than in those with stabler demand.

8.1 Labour Productivity and Employment

My third example of a relationship between labour productivity and an important economic variable concerns employment.

One of the most significant sources of resistance to productivity improvement is the widespread association of the concept with the loss of jobs and unemployment. The question of labour displacement has troubled people since the early days of the machine age. There is no doubt that automation, mechanization, or any advance which makes for higher labour productivity can wipe out jobs. The immediate effect of increases in output per hour is to reduce employment per unit of output. If output is unchanged and hours of work remain the same, this reduction in employment per unit makes for a reduction in the industry's aggregate employment. However, if output is increased, employment can remain the same or be expanded.

Important indirect effects of productivity increases can result in such output increases. A rise in an industry's productivity also presses down on the price of the industry's product. If productivity rises rapidly, reduction in production costs and in selling prices will follow. With demand responding to the reduction in price, output will rise and thus partially or wholly offset the effect of higher output per hour on employment. If demand is sufficiently responsive to the decline in price, the resulting rise in output could even exceed the rise in output per hour. The number of hours worked by all persons in the industry would then go up, not down.

The historical record of the U.S. shows that this is not infrequent. In the long run, industries whose productivity has risen more rapidly than in the whole economy have often raised their employment by a larger percentage than industry generally, and not by a smaller percentage, as might be supposed. Correspondingly, industries whose productivity has seriously lagged have often raised their employment less than industry generally or have actually cut employment. On the other hand, in some industries, relatively rapid increases in productivity have been accompanied by relative or even absolute declines in employment.

Another important fact stands out in the historical records of the U.S. While output per hour rose more rapidly after than before World War II, the rate of unemployment of the labour force as a whole averaged less after than before the war. It is also noteworthy, in this connection, that Japan and many European countries have had substantially lower rates of unemployment but faster rates of productivity increase than has the United States.

The course of employment in an industry also reflects what has been happening to productivity in the country at large. The increase in national productivity and the higher income it has brought have tended to raise the demand of workers in individual industries with increasing productivity. This often offsets the direct adverse effects of the industries' own productivity changes on employment.

The effects of increased income were especially great on the output and employment of industries which produce the goods and services that people buy more freely as they become more affluent and are able to pay higher prices. Increased national productivity helped sustain and often raise employment in these lower-productivity industries. Many of the health service industries, as already mentioned, provide examples of rising prices accompanied by rising rather than falling demand.

Further, unemployment is not necessarily created by declining employment in an industry. When the pace of decline is slow enough, normal attrition by retirement can contribute to avoiding displacement. In addition, although technological change may destroy jobs, it also creates new jobs. Workers are often attracted to these by better pay, and go off to them voluntarily even before their old jobs have become obsolete. In an expanding economy, such shifts can be made with a minimum of lost time.

8.2 Personal Adjustment

Yet it is a fact that technological and other changes within an industry can create serious problems of personal adjustment. Not everybody whose job has become obsolete is ready for retirement, or can move off to a new job elsewhere at the same rate of pay and fringe benefits. The introduction of a computer, for example, may create new jobs for programmers, but displace those whose skills or specialities have become obsolete. Thus, the effects of technological change on particular groups of workers can be serious, even if total employment in an industry is little changed.

The effects of technological change, and also of increases in scale of enterprises as old methods of doing business become obsolete, have posed similar problems for owners of small businesses. The declines of self-employment, it was noted earlier, helped raise productivity by improving the allocation of resources. By the same token, this meant a difficult period of adjustment for many small farmers, owners of what are called "mom-and-pop" stores in the U.S., and operators of handicraft establishments.

The problems of adjustment depend, however, not only on the rate of technological development but also on the capacity of the country to adjust. There is evidence that this capacity has grown on net balance in my country and I expect also in others. A higher level of education, better transportation and communications, a greater reserve in the form of savings — all identified among the sources of higher productivity — also help to ease the problem of adjustment.

In addition, improvement has occurred in aids to adjustment, including unemployment insurance, employment services, retraining programmes, public service employment, and pension vesting. There has also been improvement in private arrangements through collective bargaining. Programmes have been adopted for manpower planning for attrition, for example. Rather than responding to adjustment problems by impeding technological development or the other factors which make for higher productivity, surely arrangements of this sort are to be preferred. Society as a whole benefits from increased productivity; it should help to shoulder the problems of adjusting to the changes that bring increased productivity.

9.1 Proximate Sources of Growth in Labour Productivity

In the discussion to this point, reference has already been made to the tendency for capital in the aggregate and capital per worker to rise, and the contribution of capital to economic growth and growth of labour productivity — directly and in the technology embodied — to be substantial. Growth of capital is part of the process of economic development. It should be clearly visible in every country undergoing such development.

Countries will differ in the level and speed at which the trends involving capital take place. It is precisely this quantitative information that is needed to measure past development and plan for further development. The present edition of the "Tentative Methodology" is confined to labour productivity, however. But we may surely expect that later editions will include a section on the measurement of tangible capital, thus making possible an analysis of the ratio of capital to labour and of capital to output (capital productivity), in the aggregate and in individual industries or sectors. This, in turn, will smooth the way to the estimation of total factor productivity, as was suggested by the Expert Consultant panel in 1972.

Some of the country papers we shall be discussing may already include some material on tangible capital (in addition to the land used in agriculture, which was requested). In time, all will be able to do so as progress is made in developing the required basic data, and all will be able to provide information on capital's role in productivity growth. As already mentioned in the Expert Consultants' memorandum, the task of developing the basic data on capital is not as difficult as it may seem. Indeed, for several Asiatic countries, including Japan, Korea, India, and the Phillippines, if not also for others, there is already such information, at least on a fragmentary basis; and for some, indexes of total productivity are also available.

What I would like to note now is the kind of information we may eventually expect, as we look ahead, as the APO's five-year plan continues to unroll and as the capital data become available. Here again, I shall refer to U.S. estimates and discussions of the factors determining labour productivity. You will recognize that the estimates of the sources of growth of labour productivity are closely related to the sources of growth of national output, as these have been calculated by Edward Denison.

9.2 Three Main Sources

Recall that labour productivity is measured by the average volume of goods and services produced in an hour or day or week of work by an employed person. This person is not working alone. He or she is working with the aid of the capital, technology, business direction and organization, and others of the advantages with which labour is supplied in the modern world. We may say, then, that the factors that directly or immediately impinge on labour productivity — the "proximate" sources of labour productivity growth — fall into the three main groups listed earlier. One is increase in tangible capital per worker. Another is improvement in the quality of labour. A third is increase in the efficiency with which capital and labour are put to use in production.

Back of, or underlying, these proximate factors are the factors that account for the saving and investment which increase tangible capital, the education and training which improve the quality of labour, and the technological and other advances which raise output per unit of labour and capital. Following the discussion of the proximate factors, these basic sources will be considered.

9.3 Tangible Capital

It is natural for people who are concerned about productivity to be concerned about capital, and tangible capital is the first to come to mind. As I have already mentioned, no record, statistical or otherwise, of any country fails to show an upward trend in productivity that is not accompanied by an upward trend in tangible capital per worker. This is by no means a coincidence. There are good economic reasons why the two would move up together. Increase in productivity and the income it brings generate capital formation. And capital formation helps to increase productivity. Tools, machines, rolling stock, buildings of all sorts, improved farm and timber lands, roads and dams, stocks of materials and of other goods have even been called *the* "means of production." Whatever the merit of this designation, the more of these means supplied each worker, the higher tends to be the product obtained from an hour of work.

9.4 Quality of Labour

But tangible capital is not the only "means of production." The improvements in the quality of labour, the second group of productivity growth factors, also represent a form of investment, not in tangible goods but in human beings, made through education, on-the-job training, and in the provision of better health facilities. This type of investment is not usually recognized as capital formation, and the families and governments which make expenditures for these purposes have objectives other than enlarging the productive and earning capacity of labour. But they have that purpose also, and whatever the purpose, the expenditures have that effect, on the whole. In this way "human capital," as economists term it, is built up. In all countries growth in this stock of human capital has been a source, and often a major source, of the rise in output per hour of work.

Changes in the quality of labour occur also because of shifts in the age-sex composition of the labour force. The economic quality or capacity of labour is measured by its market value, which differs, on the average, according to age and sex. The market-value measure of quality is imperfect, it is true, to the extent that there is discrimination, but it is not an unreasonable if rough approximation. The shifts in the age-sex composition may have a negative as well as positive effect on productivity growth, depending on the direction and degree of change in the composition of the population, and in the labour-force participation rates and employment rates of the various age sex groups. Over the postwar period in the U.S. the effect of these changes appears to have been, in fact, negative, on net balance.

9.5 Total Factor Productivity

The third group of factors, which contribute to the rise in the efficient use of labour time combined with the services of tangible and human capital (adjusted for quality), is measured by the "total (or multi-) factor productivity" to which reference has been made. Included in the group is a heterogeneous variety of items.

Most prominent are advances in technology. A separate factor is the speedier diffusion of advances in technology within and between countries, as transportation, communication, and education improve. Another is the finer division of labour and greater degree of specialization of machines made possible by the general increase in the size of business establishments, industries, and countries, as well as by improvements in transportation and communication and reductions in the obstacles to trade.

Government economic policy is also a factor affecting efficiency. Government policy influences the factors already mentioned, as indicated by the references to education and the diffusion of advances in technology. There are also direct effects on efficiency. And whether direct or indirect, the effects of government policies on efficiency, and thus on productivity growth, can be negative as well as positive. Protectionist policies, inept tax codes, and regulatory "interference" can impede efforts to increase or even to maintain efficiency.

Also to be counted as a source of productivity growth is the improved efficiency associated with reduction in the length of the work-day and work-week. So, too, is the better allocation of resources reflecting, for example, a shift from farm and nonfarm self-employment to more productive activity elsewhere, as measured by market values. There are also the trends of labour-management relations, and of labour and management attitudes towards discipline and competition, along with a host of still other proximate sources of positive or negative productivity growth.

Beyond these, there are such short-run factors as changes in the weather, strikes, or lockouts, and the various developments associated with business cycles. But these play a stronger role in influencing the year-to-year changes in productivity than its long-term trend.

9.6 Quantifying the Sources

Difficult problems of concept and measurement accompany efforts to quantify the various proximate sources of productivity growth. Everyone here will have much to learn and to do when, in his future work, he reaches the stage of making such estimates. For example, economists in the United States have not yet come to complete agreement even on the measurement of tangible capital that is most relevant to determining its effect on productivity growth. Available estimates must therefore be considered only as suggestive of the relative magnitudes of the several different sources. But even suggestions are worthwhile, when they are based on careful analysis.

Most complete and up to date, to cite the U.S. figures, are the estimates of tangible business capital prepared by the Department of Commerce, using the so-called "perpetual inventory" method. We find that over the 1948-73 period as a whole, according to these estimates, tangible capital rose at a rate of about 2.9 percent per year after deducting depreciation reserves on fixed assets, 3.0 percent before such deduction. A portion of the resulting increase in the stock of tangible capital was used to outfit, so to speak, the growing labour force employed by business enterprises – a labour force growing at the rate of 1.1 percent per annum, in terms of number of persons employed, 0.7 percent in terms of hours. Tangible capital per hour available for raising productivity, then, rose at a rate of 2.2 to 2.3 percent.

However, it should not be presumed that the percentage increase in productivity would equal, or even come near to equalling, the percentage increase in tangible capital per hour. The resulting increase in output per hour depends on what each additional unit of tangible capital adds to output, given the other factors of production (including intangible capital), as well as on the increase in the number of units of capital. On the assumption that tangible capital is compensated in accordance with what it adds to output – an assumption reasonable in the circumstances, that is, under competition and with regard to long-term changes – the marginal product of tangible capital may be inferred from its rate of compensation as recorded in the income statistics compiled by the Department of Commerce. According to these figures, during the postwar period, the net income received for the use of tangible capital net of depreciation and obsolescence approximated 20 percent of the national income. Each 1 percent increase in tangible capital per hour may then be expected to raise output per hour by two-tenths of 1 percent. The contribution to productivity growth of the increase in tangible capital, so measured, is 2.3 multiplied by 0.2, or a bit under 0.5 percentage points. This is about a sixth or seventh of the 3.0 percent per year increase in labour productivity over the period under consideration. The rest, 2.5 of the 3.0 percent rate of increase in productivity, is attributed to other sources.

The identification and weighing of the other sources depends on the availability of data and the willingness of the estimator to use his judgment when the evidence is less than adequate. Although necessarily rough, private estimates made by E.F. Denison are more detailed than most, and deserve the attention they have attracted everywhere. With some adaptation for the present purpose, the published estimates covering the period 1948-69, are summarized in the accompanying Table 1.1.

Improvement in the quality of labour brought about through formal education is one source for which an estimate has been made. Another, negative in sign, resulted from a shift in the age-sex mix of the labour force towards less qualified workers. Together, these changes in the quality of labour yielded a net contribution to growth of productivity of about 0.4 percentage points. Economies resulting from increase in the scale of operations, an entirely different type of factor, provide another 0.5 points. Offsets to reduction in hours per person at work, resulting first from the improved efficiency associated with the reduction, and second from shifts of workers out of self-employment and its attendant long hours, contributed almost 0.2 percentage points. Better resource allocation, reflecting the shift of employment from farm and nonfarm self-employment to more productive activity elsewhere (as measured by market values), contributed another 0.4 percentage points. Working in the other direction was a net decline in the intensity of demand, resulting in differences in the extent to which full capacity was reached in 1948 and 1969; this tended to reduce productivity growth by 0.2 percentage points.

19

The total of these contributions so far is 1.8. The remaining 1.4 percentage points are accounted for by Denison under the heading of advances in technology and other sources "not elsewhere classified," with technology presumably the major component of this residual.

Table 1.1 Sources of Labour Productivity Growth in the United States, 1948-69,
Nonresidential Business Sector

	Contribution to Rate of Growth of Output per Hour, Percentage Points (per annum)
Output per hour of all persons	3.15
Tangible capital per hour	
Inventories	0.11
Structures and equipment (net of depreciation and obsolescence)	0.37
Land	-0.02
Labour quality	
Education	0.50
Age-sex composition	-0.12
Output per unit of labour and capital	
Advances in knowledge, and not elsewhere classified	1.44
Improved resource allocation	
Farm	0.29
Nonfarm self-employment	0.08
Economies of scale	0.51
Offsets to reduction in hours	0.16
Irregular factors	-0.18

Source: Adapted from estimates of Edward F. Denison.

Education and technology could, of course, be classified as intangible capital. Combined with tangible capital, then, it would appear that the bulk of the sources of productivity growth consist of capital. It is tangible capital held by business firms, but also skills and other intangible capital held by workers and management; and in the case of technology, largely by the economy as a whole. The remaining sources distinguished by Denison, apart from capital, may then be said to be the factors accounting for the efficiency with which tangible and intangible capital and labour time are utilized.

Questions arise, of course, about the accuracy of the data and of the assumptions, as I have stressed. Some sources of productivity growth have been omitted or, more accurately, lumped together in the "not elsewhere classified" category. One of these is the health of the labour force, which has presumably improved, but no measure is available. There are also questions about inter-relationships among the various sources and the extent to which their separate contributions can be determined. To some degree, the several types of labour and capital input are substitutes for one another. Thus, for example, were the rates of increase in other inputs to remain constant, doubling the rate of increase in capital would not double capital's contribution because of diminishing returns as the proportion of capital to the other inputs increased.

Also, to some extent, inputs complement one another. Technological change is, in some degree, embodied in tangible capital in order to be put to use in production. On this reasoning, the contribution of technology depends in part on the rate of increase in capital as well as on its own rate of increase. On the other hand, the contribution of tangible capital, in the form of analysis represented by the table, is being credited with some of the contribution of technology (and other factors) that reduces the real cost of capital goods. However, in either case, the question is largely one of how to classify some of the contributions to productivity growth between types of capital – technology, an intangible form, or plant and equipment, a tangible form. But the question also has important implications for policy to raise productivity.

10.1 Basic Sources of Growth in Labour Productivity

The proximate sources of productivity growth are proximate only because they are rooted in the more fundamental sources that account for them. To understand why productivity in the U.S. economy has tended to rise persistently over the years, and in the long run in virtually all sectors of the economy, it is worthwhile to identify these factors and to appreciate the process by which they raise productivity, even though quantitative measurements of them are not yet possible. Public and private policies related to productivity will be better if they are based on what is known about these forces and this process.

Consider, then, the key question of the increase in output per worker-hour, so widespread in the United States.

10.2 Incentives for Striving

A basic reason can be found in the incentives which impel people everywhere in the economy to strive constantly to advance themselves and their enterprises. To raise their standard of living, they tax themselves for their own and their families' education and training. They save to increase the tangible capital of their own businesses or professions or their investment in businesses in which they can acquire shares. They devise new techniques, and short-cuts in old methods. They improve old products and invent new products. They seek better sources of supply of old materials and develop new materials. Improved technology affords not only opportunities to increase income; it also serves to satisfy each person's instinct of workmanship.

Some of the forces making for a general increase in tangible and intangible capital per worker and efficiency operate through the markets for labour and capital. Thus, when savings make tangible capital plentiful in relation to labour, and the services of labour become more expensive than the services of tangible capital, managers in all industries – and also in governmental enterprises and bureaus – find it profitable or economical to increase the volume of tangible capital per worker. When education levels rise as the result of higher private expenditures on education because of higher incomes and expanded government support, the relative prices of high-quality labour tend to fall and industries everywhere find it profitable to seek ways to put the improved labour to use.

10.3 Spread of Knowledge

Another widespread source of growth is diffusion of new products by the market system. When technological developments are potentially versatile enough to be put to use in different industries, sooner or later the profit motive and competitive pressures see to it that they are used in different industries. In all these industries, technology, wherever it may originate, helps to raise efficiency in the use of labour and capital. Because many technological developments – the steam engine two centuries ago, the computer in our own time – must be embodied in equipment or other tangible capital and operated by trained people, these developments also add inducements to increase capital per worker and employ better-educated workers or train them on the job.

Other knowledge – of innovations in production layout, or materials, or marketing methods, or business organization – which initially appears to be of use only in a few industries may sooner or later be adapted to the peculiar conditions of other industries. This is the history of the principle of interchangeable parts, scientific management, and plastics. Further, the results of Research and Development (R & D), whether done privately or by government, are disseminated widely by an active diffusion industry made up of firms and consultants whose business it is to convey and adapt new knowledge, as well as by various governmental agencies.

The forces that make for an increase in labour productivity operate broadly across the entire economy. They may affect different industries at different times and in different degrees. The revolutionary changes in this or that industry will stand out and become well-known. But in every industry a host of small technological innovations, which are often unnoticed by outsiders, crop up almost continuously over the full range of economic activity and exert their cumulative effects.

In short, the high productivity of the American economy is the end result of a great many different activities involving decisions by millions of scientists, engineers, and technicians in laboratories and industry; educators in schools, universities, and training centers; managers and owners of production facilities; workers and their families and unions; and government officials. Increase of the country's output per hour over the long run is the result of the energy, ingenuity, and skill with which all people, individually and as a Nation, manage their resources of production. This is surely the situation also in the Asiatic countries, as well as in countries on other continents.

11.1 Concluding Remarks

Many conceptual, statistical and theoretic-economics problems arise in measuring and analyzing productivity levels and changes, and in applying the results to the formulation and criticism of economic policy. I could go on to discuss more adequately those problems I have described or at least noted earlier. And I could add to that list. The panel of experts on U.S. productivity statistics — set up under the auspices of the National Research Council at the request of the National Center for Productivity and Quality of Working Life — struggled with the difficult problems of how to deal with the changing quality of output, for example. And there were others — the choice among hours paid for, hours in the work-place, and hours actually worked (the "coffee-break" question) in measuring labour input; the measure-ment of gross and net investment in intangible capital; the meaning and measurement of depreciation and obsolescence of tangible capital; and the form of the functional relation between output and the several inputs (the "shape" of production function). But I have said enough to provide perspective for our proceedings here.

I hope the pains I have taken to impress on you the fact that the subject of productivity measure-ment is large does not serve to intimidate you. Remember: Even the primitive data we now have, and the rough measurements we can make at this stage of our effort, can be put to use immediately. We need not wait until every puzzle that arises in productivity measurement has been unraveled, before we can receive a return on our investment. But there are such puzzles, they are not trivial, and eventually they must be faced.